David Ragan

a native of Jackson, Tennessee, and for several years a resident of Hollywood, began writing about screen personalities for national periodicals while still in his teens. Working exclusively in the show-business field, he started his career in magazine publishing as managing editor of *Tele-Views*, a Los Angeles–based television monthly. Later in New York, he was editorial director of entertainment magazines both at Macfadden and Warner Communications, where he also created and served as publisher of *Movie Digest* and *Words and Music*. In addition to editing and writing for magazines, he is the author of numerous books about film personnel. Among them are *Who's Who in Hollywood 1900–1976*, a critically acclaimed one-volume encyclopedia on motion picture actors and actresses, and a recent biography of actor Mel Gibson. He lives in New York City with his wife, Claire, and children, David Nathaniel, Sarah, and Jennifer.

DAVID RAGAN

Movie Stars of the 30s

A Complete Reference Guide for the Film Historian or Trivia Buff

A SPECTRUM BOOK

Prentice-Hall, Inc., Englewood Cliffs, New Jersey 07632

Library of Congress Cataloging in Publication Data

Ragan, David.
  Movie stars of the '30s.

  "A Spectrum Book."
  Includes index.
  1. Moving-picture actors and actresses—
Biography—Dictionaries.   I. Title.
PN1998.A2R29 1985   791.43'028'0922 [B]   85-529
ISBN 0-13-604901-X
ISBN 0-13-604893-5 (pbk.)

This book is available at a special discount when ordered in
bulk quantities. Contact Prentice-Hall, Inc., General
Publishing Division, Special Sales, Englewood Cliffs, N.J. 07632.

10 9 8 7 6 5 4 3 2 1

ISBN 0-13-604901-X

ISBN 0-13-604893-5 {PBK.}

Editorial/production supervision
and book design by Eric Newman
Cover design by Hal Siegel
Cover illustration by Debi Hoeffner
Manufacturing buyer: Carol Bystrom

Prentice-Hall International (UK) Limited, *London*
Prentice-Hall of Australia Pty. Limited, *Sydney*
Prentice-Hall Canada Inc., *Toronto*
Prentice-Hall Hispanoamericana, S.A., *Mexico*
Prentice-Hall of India Private Limited, *New Delhi*
Prentice-Hall of Japan, Inc., *Tokyo*
Prentice-Hall of Southeast Asia Pte. Ltd., *Singapore*
Whitehall Books Limited, *Wellington, New Zealand*
Editora Prentice-Hall do Brasil Ltda., *Rio de Janeiro*

This is for Garret McClung,
friend and giver.

PREFACE

Most stars' careers do not, of course, begin and end in a particular decade.

Lionel Barrymore, for example, worked continuously in movies from 1909 to 1953, the year before his death. Yet he appears in this volume for two reasons: The 1930s was the decade in which he was most active (47 films), and he won his Academy Award in a picture, A *Free Soul*, released in 1931. John Barrymore is listed here also because he was in more movies in the 1930s than in any other period. And, lest the non-appearance of Ethel Barrymore be questioned, it should be remembered that she was in only one feature in the 1930s, *Rasputin and the Empress*. Most fans are likely to recall her work in the 1940s, when she was in a dozen films, including *None But the Lonely Heart*, for which she received the Best Supporting Actress Oscar. Thus she will be found in the volume covering that decade. Conversely, Wendy Hiller, an Academy Award winner (Best Supporting Actress) for her performance in 1958's *Separate Tables*, and who did other admirable work before and after that, does appear here. It was in the 1930s that she came to prominence on the screen. And, though she starred in only two films in the decade, it was in one of them, *Pygmalion*, as Eliza Doolittle, that she gave a portrayal still cited by many as her best.

Players appearing in *Movie Stars of the '30s*, then, or other volumes in the series, have been selected by one rule of thumb: They are strongly identified with the decade, either by having first achieved fame or having enjoyed many of their most memorable screen moments in it.

MOVIE STARS
OF THE '30s

Don Ameche

(b. Domenico Felix Amici, May 31, 1908, Kenosha, Wis.) 20th
Century–Fox star, with a razzle-dazzle smile, musketeer mustache, and
velvet-smooth voice, whose charm erupted like a geyser of sincerity and
friendliness; maybe it wasn't enough to win Alice Faye from Tyrone
Power, but it was quite sufficient to make him, at one time, the highest-
paid Hollywood actor ($7500 a week), and win him millions of fans; the
second of eight children of an Italian-born saloon keeper, he gave up
prelaw studies at the University of Wisconsin for the stage after starring in a
drama club production of *The Devil's Disciple*; toured in vaudeville with
Texas ("Hello, Sucker") Guinan and, between bit roles behind the footlights, worked in a mattress factory; first won fame on radio in Chicago,
starring in *The Empire Builders*, *The First Nighter*, etc.; failed one screen
test, clicked in his second, Darryl F. Zanuck choosing to star him in '36 in
a dual role in *Sins of Man*, as the sons of Jean Hersholt; remained a major
star at 20th, in roles alternately dramatic (*The Story of Alexander Graham
Bell*), comedic (*Heaven Can Wait*), and musical (*Down Argentine Way*),
through 1944's *A Wing and a Prayer*; freelanced thereafter; married his one
wife, childhood sweetheart Honore Prendergast, when 24; four sons (Don-

nie, Ronnie, Tommie, Lonnie) and two adopted daughters (Bonnie and Connie); a horse lover, he was once (no more) one of the turf world's legendary bettors, reportedly dropping "close to a million" at the tracks; as screen career fizzled in the '50s, he triumphed on Broadway in musicals *(Silk Stockings)* and comedies *(Holiday for Lovers)*; made a major movie comeback in '83, as a character actor, in *Trading Places*.

MOVIE HIGHLIGHTS: *Ramona, Love Is News, Happy Landing, In Old Chicago, Alexander's Ragtime Band, Hollywood Cavalcade, Four Sons, Lillian Russell, Moon Over Miami, That Night in Rio, Guest Wife, Happy Land, Something to Shout About, Sleep My Love.*

Annabella

(b. Suzanne Georgette Charpentier, July 14, 1909, Verenne-Saint Hilaire, France) Ash-blonde gamine whose Hollywood career suffered because in '39 she "dared" to marry Tyrone Power, then the screen's reigning young prince; his army of femme fans could not forgive that she was not a ranking beauty ("What could he see in *her*?"), was five years older, the mother of a young daughter, and only recently divorced from French idol Jean Murat *(Carnival in Flanders)*; she and Power met and fell in love a year earlier while starring in 20th Century–Fox's *Suez*; screen name derived from the Poe poem "Annabelle Lee"; as a teenager, this daughter of a journalist played bits in French films *(Napoleon, La Bacarolle d'Amour)*; was soon "discovered" by great comedy director Rene Clair, who promoted her to leads in *Le Million* and *Un Soir de Raffle*, which were such hits that she was quickly acclaimed "Continental Film Star Number 1"; also starred on Berlin and Vienna stages; summoned to Hollywood, she first acted in French versions of American movies (the custom then was to film the same picture on the same sets in another language with a different cast); mastering English and settling in London, while also returning to France for movies, she headlined in three British films; one, *Wings of the Morning*, in the still-new Technicolor process, was so outstanding that 20th Century–Fox lured her back to Hollywood; took time out in the '40s to conquer Broadway in a comedy *(Jacobowsky and the Colonel)* and a Sartre drama *(No Exit)*; left Hollywood after *13 Rue Madeleine* with Cagney, divorced Tyrone Power the following year ('48) and never remarried, made one more French film, *Dernier Amour*, and was no longer seen on the screen.

MOVIE HIGHLIGHTS: *La Bataille, Maison de la Fleche, Under the Red Robe, Dinner at the Ritz, The Baroness and the Butler, Hotel du Nord, Sacrifice d'Honneur, Bridal Suite, Tonight We Raid Calais, Bomber's Moon.*

Richard Arlen

(b. Cornelius Van Mattimore, Sept. 1, 1900, Charlottesville, Va.; d. March 28, 1976) His all-male heartiness and humor, coupled with a rugged build and handsome leathery face, made femme fans' hearts beat faster for decades; men also liked him because he was a two-fisted man of action; after years of minor roles in silents, *Wings* ('27), that epochal film about aerial combat in WW I, made him a star; landed the part by a fluke; was required in his test to weep on cue; unable to do so even with a raw onion at hand, he made an obscene gesture while the camera still rolled; intrigued by this spontaneous macho reaction, the director impulsively asked, "Are you a flyer?"; the two years he'd spent as a volunteer in the British Royal Air Force carried the day for him; *Wings* also provided him with a new wife; divorced from non-pro Ruth Austin (one daughter: Rosemarie), he promptly fell in love with brunette Jobyna Ralston, the movie's second female lead; their marriage, lasting from '27 to '45, when they divorced, produced a son, Richard Ralston; was wed from '46 on to Margaret Kinsella; starred (mostly at Paramount) in 48 pictures in the '30s and almost as many in the '40s (notably an action-packed series of Pine-Thomas thrillers like *Power Dive* that were Saturday afternoon staples); suddenly there was a lull—the actor became totally deaf; working with Grable in *When My Baby Smiles at Me*, he had to memorize everyone's lines and study lip reading to finish the film; treatment at Johns Hopkins eventually restored his hearing; final movie: *Buckskin* ('68); a wealthy man, he spent his retirement years on campus tours lecturing on pornography, obscenity, and narcotics—against, naturally.

MOVIE HIGHLIGHTS: *The Conquering Horde, Tiger Shark, Come On, Marines, Island of Lost Souls, Hell and High Water, Artists and Models, Torpedo Boat, Minesweeper, Alaska Highway, Aerial Gunner, Blood on Sun, Silver City, Warlock, The Best Man.*

Jean Arthur

(b. Gladys Georgianna Greene, Oct. 17, 1905, New York, N.Y.) Frank Capra's great comedies would not have been the same without this blonde, quirky-voiced charmer; reigned for ten years as Queen of Columbia—unhappily; was as publicity-shy as Garbo; in 72 films but never ceased doubting her talent; says director Capra of his "favorite actress": "Never have I seen a performer plagued with such a chronic case of stage jitters . . . When the cameras stopped she'd run to her dressing room, lock herself in—and cry . . . Those weren't butterflies in her stomach. They were wasps. But push that neurotic girl forcibly, but gently, in front of the cameras . . . and that whining mop would magically blossom into a warm, lovely, poised and confident actress"; fought, in and out of court, with gruff studio topper Harry Cohn; completing her contract in '44, she ran through studio streets shouting, "I'm free! I'm free!"; her next-to-last Columbia comedy, *The More the Merrier*, rated her a Best Actress Oscar nomination; made two more pictures, at Paramount, *A Foreign Affair* and *Shane*, before leaving the screen; was first a photographers' model; played small parts in many silents (starting in '23 in John Gilbert's *Cameo Kirby*) before achieving stardom in 1928's *Warming Up*; at 61, artfully made up and donning a blond wig (covering snow-white hair), attempted a comeback on TV, doing 13 episodes of "The Jean Arthur Show", a sitcom; next, for four years at Vassar and one at the North Carolina School of the Arts, taught drama; divorced since '49 from second husband Frank Ross, she lives alone in a fine weathered house in Carmel—behind a high redwood fence.

MOVIE HIGHLIGHTS: *The Canary Murder Case, Halfway to Heaven, The Whole Town's Talking, Diamond Jim, Mr. Deeds Goes to Town, You Can't Take It With You, Only Angels Have Wings, Mr. Smith Goes to Washington, Too Many Husbands, Arizona, The Devil and Miss Jones, The Talk of the Town, A Lady Takes a Chance, The Impatient Years.*

Fred Astaire

(b. Frederick Austerlitz Jr., May 10, 1899, Omaha, Neb.) The screen's nonpareil male dancer, elegant in or out of tux; debuted in vaudeville at 10 with 12-year-old sister Adele as his partner; 1917 marked their first time on Broadway in the musical comedy *Over the Top*, starring comedian Ed

Wynn; headlined with his sister in other stage hits: *The Passing Show of 1918, Lady Be Good, Funny Face, The Band Wagon*, etc.; became the toast of two continents, as often their shows also played in London; in '31, after their screen debut in a Vitaphone short, Adele married Lord Charles Cavendish and retired; a solo success on stage in *The Gay Divorce*, Astaire was tested for Hollywood by Producer David O. Selznick (The verdict: "I am still a little uncertain about the man, but I feel, in spite of his enormous ears and bad chin line, that his charm is so tremendous that it comes through even in this wretched test"); debuted, as himself, in a '33 Crawford pic, *Dancing Lady*; hit his stride when next paired with Ginger Rogers in *Flying Down to Rio*; this superbly matched team made 11 films together (*Roberta, Top Hat, Swing Time*, etc.), and between 1935–37, was among the Box-Office Top 10; later partners: Eleanor Powell, Paulette Goddard, Rita Hayworth, Marjorie Reynolds, Joan Leslie, Lucille Bremer, Judy Garland, Vera-Ellen, Jane Powell, Cyd Charisse, Leslie Caron, Audrey Hepburn, Ann Miller; was wed to Phyllis Baker Potter from July '33 until her death in '54; two children: Fred Jr. and Ava; made his dramatic debut in *On the Beach* ('57); won 9 Emmy Awards in his first TV special, "An Evening with Fred Astaire" ('58); in '80, at 80, this longtime owner of race horses wed jockey Robyn Smith, 36.

MOVIE HIGHLIGHTS: *Broadway Melody of 1940, Holiday Inn, You Were Never Lovelier, Ziegfeld Follies, Blue Skies, Easter Parade, The Barkleys of Broadway, Three Little Words, Royal Wedding, The Band Wagon, Funny Face, Silk Stockings.*

Mary Astor

(b. Lucile Vasconcella Langhanke, May 3, 1906, Quincy, Ill.) The daughter of a German immigrant, she was one star who had more in her kit bag than classic beauty and a gift for subtly dynamic histrionics; since '59 she has published seven books: five novels (*The Incredible Charlie Carewe*, etc.) and two best-selling autobiographies, *Mary Astor, My Story* and *A Life on Film*; following *Hush . . . Hush, Sweet Charlotte* ('64), after 44 years before the cameras, she voluntarily wrote *finis* to her cinematic life; she had her Oscar (Best Support, *The Great Lie*); she'd had enough of being "rediscovered" every few years; and she'd had enough of headlines— widowhood (first husband, director Kenneth Hawks, died in a plane crash in '30, two years after they wed), marriage and divorce (three), child custody battles (second husband Franklyn Thorpe initiated those—Astor won), speculation as to what was or was not in her famous "Purple Diary" (anyone recalling what newspapers of the '30s printed of its alleged contents might keep in mind that the star maintains to this day that the "lurid lines" were quoted from a forgery), and gossip about her "drinking problem" (it didn't impair her work, she insists, and movie colleagues support her in this); perhaps she'd also "had it" with Hollywood's lack of generosity; in '56, when she hadn't worked for three years, she was offered one week's work in a long-forgotten pic, *A Kiss Before Dying*—$300; she took it, saying, "The three hundred dollars looked wonderful"; the mother of two, Marilyn Thorpe and Anthony del Campo, and a five-time great-grandmother now, she has lived for years at the Motion Picture Country Home.

MOVIE HIGHLIGHTS: *White Shoulders, Red Dust, Page Miss Glory, Dodsworth, The Prisoner of Zenda, The Hurricane, Midnight, The Maltese Falcon, Across the Pacific, The Palm Beach Story, Meet Me in St. Louis, Claudia and David, Little Women, Any Number Can Play, Return to Peyton Place.*

Gene Autry

(b. Orvon Gene Autry, Sept. 29, 1907, Tioga, Texas) The movies' first "Singing Cowboy"; starred in more than 90 tune-filled shoot-'em-ups for Republic and, later, Columbia; always rode high as a Top Money-Making Western Star; in '36, first year of the poll, ranked third; between '37 and '42 was first; three years out for war duty as a flight officer in the U.S. Air Force; between '46 and '54, the final year of the poll and his last on the big screen, placed second behind Roy Rogers; was on TV through '60; grew up on a ranch in Ravia, Okla., the son of a livestock trader; "took to singing to keep myself awake" when a telegrapher on the Frisco R.R.; at 21 did a radio show in Tulsa (as "Oklahoma's Yodelin' Cowboy") and began making records, which led to a show in Chicago (there met comedian Smiley Burnette, who was his movie sidekick for decades), then to a better radio program in Hollywood; clicked in movies at 27 when he sang a couple of songs in a Ken Maynard Western, *In Old Santa Fe*; first played the lead, for an independent company, in a 13-chapter serial, *Phantom Empire*;

6

Republic began starring him in '35 in *Tumblin' Tumbleweeds*; always played a character named Gene Autry; sold more than 30 million records, composing many songs he sang ("That Silver Haired Daddy of Mine," "Back in the Saddle Again," "Be Honest With Me," and 200 more); Champion, the famous chestnut stallion that shared billing with him and died many years ago, was chosen (and bought for $1,000) because he was an exact duplicate of the first horse Autry rode in movies; that one had been in Tom Mix Westerns as Tony Jr., but his registered name was Lindy; the star's estimated worth: $200 million.

MOVIE HIGHLIGHTS: *Red River Valley, The Singing Cowboy, Springtime in the Rockies, The Man from Music Mountain, Mexicali Rose, South of the Border, Carolina Moon, Melody Ranch, Under Fiesta Stars, The Bells of Capistrano, Twilight on the Rio Grande, Gene Autry and the Mounties.*

Lew Ayres

(b. Frederick Lewis Ayres, Dec. 28, 1908, Minneapolis, Minn.) Noted for an acting style reflecting gentleness and modest charm, he will be forever associated with the role of Dr. Kildare; played the part, between '38 and '42, 9 times (*Young Dr. Kildare, Calling Dr. Kildare*, etc., and finally, *Dr. Kildare's Victory*); his favorite role, though, remains that of Hepburn's alcoholic playboy brother in *Holiday*; began, at 17, as a banjo player in the orchestra of Henry (Hank) Halstead; discovered by a talent scout in the lobby of Hollywood's Roosevelt Hotel, he signed a Pathé contract and, at 21, made his debut in a bit in *The Sophomore*; Garbo picked him that same year as her leading man in *The Kiss*; next came contracts at Universal (the classic *All Quiet on the Western Front* was his first there), Fox (where his best was *State Fair* with Janet Gaynor), and Republic (there, temporarily giving up acting, he directed James Dunn in *Hearts in Bondage*); then it was on to greater glory at Metro, starting with *Rich Man, Poor Girl* in '38; deeply religious, he reaped unpleasant headlines in WW II by declaring himself a conscientious objector; won public favor again by serving with honor in combat areas as a medical corpsman and assistant chaplain; explanation for his decision was given to war correspondent Will Oursler, who encountered him in the Dutch New Guinea jungles: "To me war was the greatest sin. I couldn't bring myself to kill other men"; divorced from

Lola Lane and Ginger Rogers, he's been married since '64 to English-born Diana Hall; became the father of a son, Justin, at 60.

MOVIE HIGHLIGHTS: *Spirit of Notre Dame, Broadway Serenade, These Glamour Girls, Maisie Was a Lady, The Dark Mirror, The Unfaithful, Johnny Belinda* (nominated for Best Actor Oscar), *Donovan's Brain, Advise and Consent, Damien—Omen II.*

Wendy Barrie

(b. Wendy Jenkins, April 18, 1912, Hong Kong; d. Feb. 2, 1978) Effervescent beauty with red-gold hair, pencil-slim and brightly charming, whose specialty was playing society girls and, occasionally, titled ladies; the daughter of a British barrister who practiced in China, she attended the finest schools in Switzerland and England; parents named her after the child in James M. Barrie's *Peter Pan*; took the author's surname at the start of her career; worked first in a beauty parlor, then as a secretary; crashed movies in London at 19; made seven minor British films before producer Sir Alexander Korda signed her to play Jane Seymour, young wife of the king who died in childbirth, in *The Private Life of Henry VIII* in '33; this poignant portrayal resulted in a Paramount contract; between '35 and '43 in Hollywood, was in 39 movies, many of them B's; best outings were in *Dead End* ('37), as a millionaire's mistress living in a swank apartment next door to East River slums, and *The Hound of the Baskervilles* ('39); was three times—always as a different character—George Sanders' leading lady in "The Saint" series; for years was one of Hollywood's most popular bachelor girls, pursued by Cary Grant among many others; close association with mobster Bugsy Siegel brought her movie career to a screeching halt; moving to New York, she starred on Broadway opposite Gregory Peck in *The Morning Star*, then enjoyed a lengthy career on radio ("Wendy Barrie's Celebrity Parade," syndicated coast to coast on 360 stations); did Revlon commercials on TV's "The $64,000 Question" and, breezily and brainily, headlined various local interview shows; appeared last on screen as herself, a talk-show hostess, in Jack Lemmon's *It Should Happen to You.*

MOVIE HIGHLIGHTS: *Big Broadcast of 1936, Love on a Bet, Millions in the Air, Wings Over Honolulu, I Am the Law, The Saint Strikes Back, Five Came Back, Daytime Wife, Women in War, The Gay Falcon, Forever and a Day.*

John Barrymore

(b. John Barrymore, Feb. 15, 1882, Philadelphia, Pa.; d. May 29, 1942) The Great Profile—flamboyant, alcoholic, and, more than a half-century later, still acclaimed as the American stage's greatest Hamlet; of illustrious theatrical parents, Maurice Barrymore and Georgie Drew, he was the father of actress Diana (by poet Michael Strange) and actor John Drew Barrymore (by screen star Dolores Costello), and the grandfather of moppet Drew Barrymore; had no offspring by last wife Elaine Barrie; in the teens, while one of Broadway's brightest lights, starred in New York–made silents: *An American Citizen* (debut in '13), *Are You a Mason?*, *Red Widow*, etc.; when 42, he accepted a Warner Bros. contract at $75,000 per film (preferring play and the pursuit of beautiful women to toiling on stage, he said, "In Hollywood I can loaf and earn ten times more than I do on the stage"); became the studio's great matinee idol in such silents as *Beau Brummel*, *Don Juan*, *The Sea Beast*, *Beloved Rogue*; his first classical role in films— and the first time his golden voice was heard by movie fans—was a *Richard III* cameo in *The Show of Shows*, a '29 all-talkie extravaganza; his star soared even higher in talking pictures until his predilection for wine, women, and wild times took its toll and he began playing ravaged, hammy caricatures of himself; the subject of many books, he was best served by Gene Fowler in *Good Night, Sweet Prince*; was portrayed by Errol Flynn in *Too Much, Too Soon*, based on Diana Barrymore's autobiography, and Jack Cassidy in *W.C. Fields and Me*.

MOVIE HIGHLIGHTS: *Moby Dick, Svengali, A Bill of Divorcement, Rasputin and the Empress* (only film co-starring John, Lionel, and Ethel Barrymore), *Grand Hotel, Dinner at 8, Counsellor-at-Law, Romeo and Juliet, Marie Antoinette, Midnight, The Great Man Votes*.

Lionel Barrymore

(b. Lionel Barrymore, April 28, 1878, Philadelphia, Pa.; d. Nov. 15, 1954) Winner of the Best Actor Oscar for 1931's *A Free Soul* (his only nomination), he made his stage debut with his parents as a crying child of 5; educated in New York, he traveled all over the world in stage productions; a man of many talents—actor, musician, composer—he studied art in Paris intending to become a painter; worked as an illustrator in Manhattan for a year then yielded to brother John's persuasion and returned to the

9

boards, scoring a sensation in *The Copperhead*, repeating the role in a silent movie; later starred on stage with John in *The Claw*; following his first movie in '09, D.W. Griffith's *Friends*, appeared in more than 80 silents: *The New York Hat, Peter Ibbetson, The Iron Man, Sadie Thompson*, etc.; directed films between acting stints: *The Rogue Song, Ten Cents a Dance, Madame X* starring Ruth Chatterton; divorced from actress Doris Rankin, he was married to actress Irene Fenwick, once brother John's mistress, from '23 until she died in '36; the rumor was that she married him to punish him for breaking up her affair with John; director George Cukor once noted that "Irene treated Lionel with cruelty, almost sadistically, [but] Lionel worshiped her, then her memory, until the day he died"; did wheelchair roles when crippled by arthritis; of MGM boss Louis B. Mayer, he once told reporter James Bacon: "L.B. gets me $400 worth of cocaine a day to ease my pain. I don't know where he gets it. And I don't care. But I bless him every time it puts me to sleep."

MOVIE HIGHLIGHTS: *Mata Hari, Grand Hotel, Reunion in Vienna, David Copperfield, Camille, Captains Courageous, Test Pilot, You Can't Take It with You*, the "Kildare" and "Dr. Gillespie" series, *It's a Wonderful Life, Key Largo*.

Freddie Bartholomew

(b. Frederick Llewellyn, March 28, 1924, London, England) MGM's great boy star of the era, with black curls, perfect manners, and British accent; American kids thought him a prig but their moms found him adorable; born in the industrial end of London, the son of a minor government employee who lost a leg in World War I and could not provide for two older daughters and the boy; paternal grandparents in Warminster agreed to take him; his father's spinster sister, "Aunt Cissy," who also lived there and recognized his potential as an actor, gave him elocution lessons; made his debut in small roles in British pix *(Fascination, Toyland)* at 6; when 10, Hollywood signed him (at $175 per week) to star in *David Copperfield*; his parents promptly came to America to petition the courts for his custody and a share of his earnings; "Aunt Cissy" won custody but his salary was split up—10% to his parents, 5% to his sisters, 10% (plus living expenses) to "Aunt Cissy," with the remainder put in trust for him, but the court battles continued; has said, "I guess I grew up in court. It was hard sometimes but we muddled through. Actually, the year 1937 was the happiest of my professional life. I made *Captains Courageous* with Spencer Tracy. We took a year to film, went on location to Florida and Catalina, and it was fun"; became an American citizen at 18 and served in the Air Force; was briefly married at 22 to Maely Danielle, 8 years his senior, by whom he has a daughter; since '53 has been married to Aileen Paul; they have a son and daughter.

MOVIE HIGHLIGHTS: *Anna Karenina, Lloyds of London, Little Lord Fauntleroy, Kidnapped, Lord Jeff, Spirit of Culver, Tom Brown's Schooldays, Swiss Family Robinson, A Yank at Eton, St. Benny the Dip* (in '51, his last).

Warner Baxter

(b. Warner Baxter, March 29, 1889, Columbus, Ohio; d. May 7, 1951) Stalwart, handsome lead, with pencil moustache, whose zesty performance as the Cisco Kid in 1929's *In Old Arizona* rated him a Best Actor Oscar; played the character again in *The Cisco Kid* ('31) and *Return of the Cisco Kid* ('39); may be best known now for his "Crime Doctor" role in a 10-film series in the '40s (*Crime Doctor's Strangest Case, Crime Doctor's Warning*, etc.); briefly on the stage, he was a partner in a garage in Oklahoma before going to Hollywood in the teens; appeared in many silents: *The Traitor, Sheltered Daughter, Alimony, The Golden Bed, Ramona, Craig's Wife*, etc.; at 20 was married for seven months to nonpro Viola Caldwell; from '17 until his death was married to actress Winifred Bryson, his leading lady in *The Awful Truth* ('24); was one of the highest paid stars of the '30s and, being particularly adept at sophisticated comedies, was eagerly sought by femme stars such as Myrna Loy (*To Mary—With Love*) and Loretta Young (*Wife, Doctor and Nurse*); was never an "easy" person, guarding his privacy as zealously as Garbo, and his romantic screen persona, it was generally agreed, was a mask for a stubborn and often quarrelsome personality; following *Adam Had Four Sons*, with Ingrid Bergman, suffered a nervous breakdown and was off screen for three years; recovered via a long South Seas yachting cruise in search of buried pirate treasure—never found.

MOVIE HIGHLIGHTS: *Doctor's Wives, Daddy Long Legs, Man About Town, 42nd Street, Stand Up and Cheer, Broadway Bill, King of Burlesque, Prisoner of Shark Island, Road to Glory, Vogues of 1938, I'll Give a Million, Wife, Husband and Friend, Barricade, Kidnapped, Lady in the Dark, The Razor's Edge, Smoky, Prison Warden.*

Wallace Beery

(b. Wallace Beery, April 1, 1885, Kansas City, Mo.; d. April 15, 1949) Metro's lovable big lug, slow talking, often in need of a shave; younger brother of Noah Beery Sr., uncle of Noah Jr.; won the Best Actor Oscar in *The Champ*; nominated in the same category in *The Big House*; first job: engine wiper in a railroad round house; next joined Ringling Bros. Circus as an elephant handler; later was a chorus boy in Broadway musical comedies; turning actor, he replaced Raymond Hitchcock as the star of *The Yankee Tourist*, then toured the country in many plays; began his movie career at Essanay in Chicago in 1914, starring in the "Sweedie" comedies, playing, in drag, a dumb Swedish maid; there he met Gloria Swanson, then a bit player, who became his wife (and she had some wicked things to say about him in her autobiography, *Swanson on Swanson*, published in '80); in Hollywood was first a comedian in Mack Sennett's Keystone Comedies; in '17, in *Behind the Door*, he played the first of many villainous roles before conceiving the idea of combining menace with humor, the type of characterization that sped him to stardom; among his silents: *The Four Horsemen, The Three Musketeers, The Sea Hawk,* and *Old Ironsides*; signing an MGM contract in 1930, he quickly became one of the greatest box office attractions of all; was never better than when teamed with combative comedienne Marie Dressler in *Min and Bill* and *Tugboat Annie*, or with juvenile star Mickey Rooney in *Slave Ship* and *Stablemates*.

MOVIE HIGHLIGHTS: *Grand Hotel, Dinner at 8, The Bowery, Treasure Island, Viva Villa!, The Mighty Barnum, Ah, Wilderness, Old Hutch, China Seas* (in which adopted daughter Carol Ann played a bit), *Good Old Soak, Bad Man of Brimstone, Thunder Afloat, Stand Up and Fight, Salute to the Marines,* and, in 1949, *Big Jack,* his last.

Constance Bennett

(b. Constance Campbell Bennett, Oct. 22, 1905, New York, N.Y.; d. July 24, 1965) Blonde and worldly-wise daughter of stage-screen idol Richard Bennett, sister of Joan, who was the ultimate in chic; seemed undressed without diamond bracelets on both wrists; began playing leads in silents when in her teens; reviewing one of her early films, 1922's *What's Wrong with Women?*, *Photoplay's* critic raved, "Miss Bennett is a film find," then added of the picture, "Not for the children!"; same warning was appropriate for many of her movies; possessed a lively and malicious wit that flowed most delightfully in high comedy; ruffled the feathers of many with her ruthless efficiency and flair for getting her own way; was peculiarly adept at antagonizing the press; many reporters agreed with the one who found her "a very superior sort of person, with a rich amused voice, who is at once sophisticated and attractive, but keeps the common herd in place"; "I was a stormy child," she confessed, and some argued that she remained one; in her heyday was famous as Hollywood's best-dressed and highest-paid ($30,000 per week at one time) actress; also had a considerable reputation as a high stakes poker player, sitting in with—and usually winning over—moguls such as Zanuck; eloped with playboy Chester Moorhead at 16 (marriage annulled); also wed and divorced wealthy Philip Plant (one son: Peter), the Marquis de la Falaise de la Coudraye (he later insisted it was no marriage as he wasn't properly divorced from Swanson), Gilbert Roland (two daughters: Lorinda, Gyl); final husband: U.S. Air Force General John Coulter; self-appraisal as an actress: "I was no Sarah Bernhardt."

MOVIE HIGHLIGHTS: *Rich People, Three Faces East, Lady With a Past, What Price Hollywood?, Our Betters, The Affairs of Cellini, Topper, Merrily We Live, Topper Takes a Trip, Tailspin, Two-Faced Woman, Paris Underground, Centennial Summer, The Unsuspected, Madame X.*

Joan Bennett

(b. Joan Geraldine Bennett, Feb. 27, 1910, Palisades, N.J.) Unlike sister Constance, this veteran of more than 70 films was one of Hollywood's most popular citizens; was educated at posh schools in Connecticut and France; made her acting debut with her father at 18 in the Broadway production of *Jarnegan*, and entered movies—first in small roles—the next year; hit her sultry-voiced stride, opposite Ronald Colman, in a '29 talkie, *Bulldog Drummond*; stayed at the top for nearly three decades by cleverly shifting her style to suit whatever was then popular with the public: musicals *(Puttin' on the Ritz)*, sentimental dramas *(Little Women)*, madcap comedies *(Twin Beds)*, Westerns *(The Texans)*, spy stories *(I Married a Nazi)*, psychological dramas *(The Woman in the Window)*; was a blonde her first decade in movies; donning a dark-haired wig for *Trade Winds* ('39), she liked the effect; dyeing, she has remained a brunette, though the change did make her look startlingly like new sensation Hedy Lamarr (then the bride of Bennett's ex, writer Gene Markey); career took a nosedive in the '50s through no fault of hers; her then husband, producer Walter Wanger, served time in a prison farm after being convicted of assault with a deadly weapon in the shooting of Jennings Lang, an agent Wanger thought was threatening his marriage; denying there were grounds for this belief, she remained Wanger's wife until they divorced in '62, ending a 22-year marriage; next starred on stage and in a TV soap, "Dark Shadows"; in '70 published *The Bennett Playbill* (written with Lois Kibbee), a book about the five generations of her famous theatrical family; married again and living in Scarsdale, N.Y., she has four daughters and nine grandchildren.

MOVIE HIGHLIGHTS: *Disraeli, Mississippi, Private Worlds, Vogues of 1938, Artists and Models, The Man in the Iron Mask, Man Hunt, Margin for Error, Scarlet Street, The Macomber Affair, Woman on the Beach, Father of the Bride, We're No Angels.*

Charles Bickford

(b. Charles Bickford, Jan. 1, 1891, Cambridge, Mass.; d. Nov. 9, 1967) Redheaded and a two-fisted rebel, he once said of his birth, "It's appropriate that I should have come in on the wings of a blizzard—I've been blowing up a storm ever since"; "pure devil" is how he described himself as a youth; few actors ever raised the blood pressure of producers and directors higher than he, a battler for quality; his combative nature was shaped by early rugged experiences—in logging camps and hobo jungles, as a wheat harvester, brewery truck driver, carnival barker, and even as a sparring partner of world's heavyweight champ James J. Corbett; was as big character-wise as physically; when Louis B. Mayer once viciously maligned him, he's the man who told the most powerful of Hollywood chieftains to go f— himself; blackballed in movies for a while, he worked on the docks; his hard-nosed personal and professional integrity paid off; garnered three Oscar nominations as Best Support—in *The Song of Bernadette*, *The Farmer's Daughter*, *Johnny Belinda*; started acting in a burlesque show, graduating to stock companies where he spent 12 years training as an actor; was on Broadway for three seasons before Cecil B. DeMille starred him in *Dynamite* ('29); 90 more pix followed, including his last, *A Big Hand for the Little Lady* ('66); segued effortlessly from leads to character star parts; became a millionaire via investments; was a genuine man of mystery whose oldest friends, even, did not know him fully; in his autobiography, *Bulls, Balls, Bicycles & Actors* ('65) there is no mention of his one wife, Beatrice Loring, whom he married in '19, or their children, Doris and Rex; asked about the omission, he said only, reluctantly, that his life had been "touched with tragedy."

MOVIE HIGHLIGHTS: *Anna Christie, East of Borneo, Little Miss Marker, The Plainsman, High, Wide and Handsome, Stand Up and Fight, Of Mice and Men, Reap the Wild Wind, Mr. Lucky, Duel in the Sun, Brute Force, Woman on the Beach, A Star Is Born, The Big Country.*

Joan Blondell

(b. Rose Blondell, Aug. 30, 1906, New York, N.Y.; d. Dec. 25, 1979) Laughing and cracking wise, singing and dancing, rattling off dialogue a mile-a-minute, and batting those long-lashed baby blues, she was surely the most lovable leading lady ever seen on the Warner lot; and she was a survivor; returning to the studio in '72 to star in a TV series, "Banyon," she found that of the famous WB "stock company" that made movie history on the premises—Bogart, Cagney, Flynn, Davis et al.—she was the only one there; traveled the world over as a youngster trouping (from age 3) alongside her vaudeville parents; a brace of Broadway hits, *Maggie the Magnificent* and *Penny Arcade*, catapulted her and her co-star in both, James Cagney, to Hollywood and international stardom; their joint movie debut in 1930's *Sinner's Holiday* was followed by more Cagney–Blondell successes (*Public Enemy, The Crowd Roars, Footlight Parade*, etc.); was less lucky in her marriages—three divorces: cinematographer George Barnes (1932–35; son: Norman, who was adopted by her next), Dick Powell (1936–45; daughter: Ellen), impresario Mike Todd (1947–50; starred for him on Broadway in

15

The Naked Genius); said of her husbands: "Barnes provided my first real home, Powell was my security man, and Todd was my passion—but I loved them all"; acted opposite Dick Powell in many, including, just before they parted, *I Want a Divorce*; published a novel in '72, *Center Door Fancy*, that contained a few shockers and read like a thinly-veiled autobiography; won two Emmys on TV for "Here Come the Brides" and a Best Supporting Oscar nomination for *The Blue Veil*; favorite role: fun-loving Aunt Cissy in *A Tree Grows in Brooklyn*.

MOVIE HIGHLIGHTS: *Three on a Match, Gold Diggers of 1933, Dames, Stand-In, The King and the Chorus Girl, The Perfect Specimen, East Side of Heaven, Good Girls Go to Paris, Model Wife, Cry Havoc, Nightmare Alley, Desk Set, The Cincinnati Kid, Support Your Local Gun-fighter.*

John Boles

(b. John Love Boles Jr., Oct. 27, 1895, Greenville, Texas; d. Feb. 27, 1969) Dark and sleekly handsome, with a cleft chin, trim moustache, and perfect features, he was the Arrow Collar–ad man come to life—the ideal romantic lead for the '30s; ever and obviously a blueblood, he was typecast first as a musical comedy star (lifting his splendid baritone in *Rio Rita, The Desert Song*, etc.) before emerging as a dramatic lead in melodramas like *Seed*; also danced and starred in comedies, adventure flicks, and tearjerkers, and while critics rarely raved about him, many considered him Hollywood's most versatile actor at the time; Gloria Swanson discovered him singing and dancing on Broadway in *Kitty's Kisses*, found him a "refined Southern gentleman with a beautiful accent," signed him to a personal contract and introduced him to the screen in '27 in her *Loves of Sunya*; chose him again as her co-star seven years later in *Music in the Air*; though a pacifist, he had enlisted in General Pershing's A.E.F. the day after World War I was declared, becoming later a counterespionage agent in Belgium; was also a moralist; thoroughly disapproved of the parts in *Back Street* and *Only Yesterday* that brought his greatest screen success—each being the role of a husband in love with another woman; played them with such dexterity that fans liked the man when a cool analysis would reveal him as no better than a philanderer; was wed from '17 on to college sweetheart Marcelite Dobbs, by whom he had two sons; a canny investor, he became extremely rich; in age, even when his hair was Redi Whip-white, remained a supremely handsome man.

MOVIE HIGHLIGHTS: *Shepherd of the Hills, Fazil, Captain of the Guard, Beloved, Stand Up and Cheer, White Parade, Age of Innocence, Curly Top, Orchids to You, The Littlest Rebel, Craig's Wife, Between Us Girls, Romance in the Dark, Thousands Cheer, Babes in Bagdad* (in '52, his first in nine years, and his swan song).

Beulah Bondi

(b. Beulah Bondy, May 3, 1892, Chicago, Ill.; d. Jan. 11, 1981) Superlative character actress who, for 32 years in 65 movies, had a corner on playing elderly women—grandmothers, spinsters, schoolmarms, women of warm hearts, and, sometimes, icy; in the superb *Make Way for Tomorrow*, done when she was 45, was seen as a white-haired matriarch in her 70s; makeup job had her so old that even when she was actually past 80, retaining her dark hair and avid fascination with life, she did not look so ancient; growing up in Valparaiso, Ind., she got her B.A. at a Catholic college in Montreal and returned to win her Master's in oratory at the University of Valparaiso, then directed school dramatics in the town for several years; called herself one of the "fortunates" for knowing quite early what her goal in life was; once said, "Ideals were set and wishes made—but training and work were intensive, which resulted in opportunities presenting themselves at seemingly the right moment. Wishes—with work—*do* come true!"; became a professional actress at 27, devoting the next 12 years to stock and the New York stage; made her Broadway debut in *One of the Family*, playing a 70-year-old when 33; first movie: *Street Scene* ('31); acted with all the top stars and recalled each association as "one of happy memories"; was twice nominated for Best Support Oscars, in *The Gorgeous Hussy* and *Of Human Hearts*; always denied having had a favorite role: "It has always been the one I was playing at the moment that I liked best"; never married, she quit movies at 71 and traveled "around the world twice and made many return trips to Europe"; guest-starred on TV in a special episode of "The Waltons" in '74 and won an Emmy.

MOVIE HIGHLIGHTS: *Arrowsmith, Rain, The Good Fairy, Trail of the Lonesome Pine, Maid of Salem, On Borrowed Time, Mr. Smith Goes to*

Washington, Our Town, Watch on the Rhine, The Southerner, It's a Wonderful Life, The Snake Pit, A Summer Place.

William Boyd

(b. William Lawrence Boyd, June 5, 1895, Hendrysburg, Ohio; d. Sept. 12, 1972) Prematurely silver-haired, he became at 40 the screen's well-loved "Hopalong Cassidy"; had been in movies, first as an extra then as a romantic lead in dozens of silents and talkies, since he was 23; among the silents putting him in the league of idols like Wallace Reid: *New Loves for Old, The Volga Boatman, Two Arabian Knights*; the son of a poor farm laborer, he quit school when both his parents died; the blond 13-year-old supported himself as a sawmill worker in Arizona before heading to California, where he packed oranges, sold automobiles, was an oil field driller; as "Hoppy," he was a Western rarity, a middle-aged Galahad and a "good guy" who wore black; this pleasant-tempered character did not smoke, drink, or swear (and captured villains rather than shoot them); the hero role transformed the one-time Hollywood playboy (and wild gambler) into an upstanding ideal for youth; founded a club, Hoppy's Troopers, with thousands of members whose code of conduct preached loyalty, honesty, kindness; when "Hoppy" came along, he was, by misfortune, a screen has-been; career plummeted in '32 when a stage actor with the same name as his was arrested at a drinking and gambling party and, erroneously, this star's photo was printed in papers with the story; couldn't ride a horse when he signed for Westerns; became an expert rider, chasing villains in 66 features aboard trusty white steed Topper; won a legion of new fans and a fortune when the "Hoppy" movies (which he'd wisely bought) went on TV; from June 5, 1937 to the end was wed to blonde actress Grace Bradley; had been divorced from actresses Ruth Miller (their son, his only child, died at nine months), Elinor Fair, Dorothy Sebastian.

MOVIE HIGHLIGHTS: *Yankee Clipper, City Streets, Sky Devils, Bar 20 Rides Again, Hopalong Cassidy Returns, Borderland, Trail Dust, Old Wyoming, Silver on the Sage, Twilight on the Trail.*

Charles Boyer

(b. Charles Boyer, Aug. 28, 1899, Figeac, France; d. Aug. 26, 1978) Suave "Great Lover"—and superb actor—whose smoldering deep-set dark eyes, accent, and classic Gallic features made the screen sizzle; movie image was enhanced by his romantic voice and the repeated use of closeups; was not, physically, all that his compelling face implied, as he was not tall (5'9"), nearly bald (always wore a toupee in movies) and had a paunch; no matter, those love scenes with Lamarr (*Algiers*), Dunne (*Love Affair*), and Darrieux (*Mayerling*) scintillate still; most actresses who shared such interludes would agree with Joan Fontaine (his *Constant Nymph* co-star), who has hailed him as "the perfect gentleman and the best leading man I ever had"; was in French and German films before '31 when he arrived in Hollywood, first acting in French-language versions of movies starring others in English; became a major star in '36 in *Garden of Allah* with Dietrich; was four times Oscar nominated as Best Actor—in *Conquest, Algiers, Gaslight, Fanny*; was married just once, in '34, to British actress Pat Paterson (only child, Michael, 21, committed suicide in '65); returned to France to live in the early '60s, making many European films and commuting to Hollywood for others; his last, France's *Stavisky* ('74), brought glorious reviews and the New York Film Critics Award; in '78 brought his cancer-stricken wife to the U.S. for treatment; two days after her death, he took an overdose of Seconal; were buried together at a Hollywood cemetery, beside their son, on what would have been the star's 79th birthday.

MOVIE HIGHLIGHTS: *Liliom, Red-Haired Woman, Caravan, Private Worlds, Tovarich, All This and Heaven Too, Back Street, Hold Back the Dawn, Flesh and Fantasy, Cluny Brown, Together Again, Earrings of Madame de, The Cobweb, La Parisienne, Is Paris Burning?, Barefoot in the Park.*

Alice Brady

(b. Alice Brady, Nov. 2, 1892, New York, N.Y.; d. Oct. 28, 1939) Character star, the daughter of famed theatrical producer William A. Brady, who played everything from dizzy dames (*My Man Godfrey*, which snagged her a Best Supporting Oscar nomination) to devoted mothers (Tyrone Power's in *In Old Chicago*, which won her an Academy Award in the same category); as early as 1914 she was starring in silents (*As Ye Sow*, *La Boheme*, etc.) and, before Mary Pickford hit her stride, was the highest-paid actress in films; at the same time was one of the brightest lights on the stage; was married but once, in '19, and briefly, to stage actor James L. Crane, by whom she had a son, Donald; movie moguls discovered her a second time as a Broadway character actress, in '33, in the Theatre Guild's production of Eugene O'Neill's *Mourning Becomes Electra*, in which she played the tragic mother of Nazimova (an actress 13 years older than she); began her new screen career in what was possibly the most hilarious role of the season, that of a gushing, tactless society women in *When Ladies Meet*; stole the picture from under the noses of Robert Montgomery and Myrna Loy and repeated the feat in so many subsequent movies that stars, sensibly, began dreading working with her; continually astonished all by alternating daffy roles with performances like the exquisitely poignant one of the hard-worked, ignorant farm woman in *The Harvester*; off screen was decidedly chic though a trifle outré; always wore black—for cause; her weakness was the color red, and everything in her Beverly Hills mansion—walls, furnishings, picture frames, candelabra, chinaware—was red and white.

MOVIE HIGHLIGHTS: *Stage Mother, Should Ladies Behave?, The Gay Divorcee, Gold Diggers of 1935, Metropolitan, Go West Young Man, Three Smart Girls, Merry-Go-Round of 1938, 100 Men and a Girl, Call It a Day, Joy of Living, Mama Steps Out, Mr. Dodd Takes the Air, Young Mr. Lincoln.*

Walter Brennan

(b. Walter Brennan, July 25, 1894, Swampscott, Mass.; d. Sept. 21, 1974) "I never wanted anything out of this business except a good living," he said. "Never wanted to be a star—just wanted to be good at what I was doin' "; what he was doing was playing crotchety, lovable old guys; was so good at it that he became the first to win three Academy Awards (all Supporting)—*Come and Get It* ('36), *Kentucky* ('38), *The Westerner* ('40); also got another nomination in *Sergeant York*; descended from early New England settlers, he left home at 11; got his degree in engineering in '15, worked in smalltime vaudeville, served in France with the 101st Field Artillery during WW I, and was a ditchdigger, bank messenger, and real estate salesman before entering movies as a bit player in '23 in *Lorraine of the Lions*; became the buddy of another extra, Gary Cooper, with whom he later made eight pictures (*Pride of the Yankees*, *Meet John Doe*, etc.); got his teeth knocked out falling off horses as a stuntman in silents, leading to his specializing as a charming old codger in more than 100 films; *The Wedding Night* (with Cooper) rated him a lucrative five-year contract with Goldwyn; professed to never having a hobby "except acting," but friends knew him to be an avid old-coin collector; advised tyro actors: "Go ahead and learn how to act, but don't get caught at it"; appreciative of his fans, he said, "I can't stand performers who snub the people they work for"; was hugely successful as the star of TV's "The Real McCoys" (1957–63; 244 episodes) but less so in later ones: "Tycoon," "The Guns of Will Sonnett," "To Rome with Love"; wealthy, he owned two Oregon ranches, one a 12,000-acre spread; the father of a daughter and two sons, he was married to childhood sweetheart Ruth Wells for 54 years.

MOVIE HIGHLIGHTS: *Seven Keys to Baldpate, Barbara Coast, Fury, Banjo on My Knee, These Three, The Buccaneer, The Story of Vernon and Irene Castle, Northwest Passage, Hangmen Also Die, Home in Indiana, My Darling Clementine, Red River, Task Force, Rio Bravo.*

Helen Broderick

(b. Helen Broderick, Aug. 11, 1891, Philadelphia, Pa.; d. Sept. 25, 1959) No beauty, with a crooked nose and cracked voice, she was a glorious deadpan comedienne; though her theatrical parents (light opera stars) discouraged her entry into show business, she became a chorus girl at 14; before graduating to the Ziegfeld Follies, was teamed in vaudeville with her husband, Lester Crawford ("Crawford & Broderick: Songs, Dances, Funny Sayings"); starred in many Broadway musical comedies (*As Thousands Cheer, The Band Wagon,* etc.); without scriptwriters was the mistress of the quick dry quip; once during rehearsals for a show that was clearly doomed to flop, playwright George S. Kaufman said to her, "Helen, your slip is showing"; her comeback: "George, your show is slipping"; was vigorously opposed to the acting ambitions of her son (only child), Broderick Crawford; argued that it would be better to be a plumber—he worked regularly, but when Broderick persisted, gave him just one piece of advice: "Always be ready"; following that, he went on to win an Academy

Award in *All the King's Men*; idolizing his mother, he still keeps a framed picture of her in his living room, and says, "She was the most beautiful woman God ever put on this earth"; but he still laughs at how, when he was a young bachelor, she scuttled all his girlfriends by doing devastating impressions of them; she was in a few silents (*High Speed, The Mystery Club*, etc.) and one early talkie, *Fifty Million Frenchmen* (based on her stage success); in '35 returned to Hollywood with her great pop eyes and sparkling wit for *Top Hat*, and, appearing in 27 others in the next 11 years, she had moviegoers rolling in the aisles.

MOVIE HIGHLIGHTS: *Love on a Bet, Swing Time, Smartest Girl in Town, Radio City Revels, Life of the Party, Rage of Paris, Stand Up and Fight, Honeymoon in Bali, No, No, Nanette, Virginia, Nice Girl?, Father Takes a Wife, Her Primitive Man, Because of Him.*

Clive Brook

(b. Clifford Brook, June 1, 1887, London, Eng.; d. Nov. 17, 1974) Silk-smooth leading man, long at Paramount, whose great successes were *Cavalcade* and *Shanghai Express*; went to Hollywood in '24, after starring in two British films, for just one picture, *Christine of the Hungry Heart*; stayed for a decade, making 30 other silents and even more talkies; ever typed as the suave, reserved British gentleman, he earned the nickname "Rock of Gibraltar"; the son of an opera singer and a father owning West African mining interests, he began as a newspaper reporter; during WW I, joined the British Artists' Rifles as a private; after harrowing duty in the trenches, he emerged from the war with medals for gallantry and the rank of major; acted in the English provinces in '18 in *Fair and Warmer*, making his London debut, and rapidly rising to stardom, two years later; in '20 was married, lastingly, to English actress Mildred Evelyn, the leading lady in his early stage hit *Over Sunday*; two children, Lyndon, who became a playwright, and Faith, an actress; Hollywood's most glamorous sirens—Marlene Dietrich, Tallulah Bankhead, Miriam Hopkins—clamored for him as their vis-à-vis for his elegance made them shine more brightly still; returned to England to live and work in '34; during WW II, making few movies, he produced and acted in propaganda films, and was active in broadcasting for the British Ministry of Information; quit movies in '45 for the stage; came back once, for a cameo role in John Huston's *The*

List of Adrian Messenger ('63); the year before his death, he told this author: "I have written an autobiography, but publishers are hard to find. I still have hopes!"; they were never fulfilled.

MOVIE HIGHLIGHTS: *Enticement, Seven Sinners, Three Faces East, French Dressing, Hula, Four Feathers, Return of Sherlock Holmes, Slightly Scarlet, Tarnished Lady, The Man from Yesterday, Charming Sinners, Convoy, The Ware Case, On Approval.*

Joe E. Brown

(b. Joseph Evan Brown, July 28, 1892, Holgate, Ohio; d. July 6, 1973) In *Alibi Ike*, playing an inept baseball rookie and missing a pitch by a mile, he grinned and quipped: "I don't bat my best on Wednesdays"; to the minds of movie fans everywhere, the big-mouthed (and big-hearted) comedian delivered his best each time he was up at bat; for more than three side-splitting decades and in 60 films, he had the world howling, from his early comedies in '28 (*Take Me Home*, etc.) right through *Some Like It Hot*; was among the Box Office Top Ten in '32, '35, '36; a warm, lovable man, unlike many comics, he ran away from home at 9 to join the circus and soon was the youngest member of the Five Marvelous Ashtons, an aerial acrobatic team that was a main attraction of Ringling Brothers; went into burlesque in '18 and, in '21, became a Broadway star in *Listen Lester*; prior to his stage career was a professional baseball player with the St. Paul (Minn.) team; fanatical about baseball, he insisted on an unusual clause when signing a long-term contract at Warners—the company had to maintain a complete ball team for him among studio employees; was ecstatic in '55 when son Joe L. Brown became general manager of the Pittsburgh Pirates; married from '15 on to nonpro Kathryn McGraw, he also had two daughters and another son; that son, Capt. Don Evan Brown, was killed in a crash in '42 while ferrying an Army bomber; to assuage his grief, the comedian devoted himself wholeheartedly to entertaining American troops, journeying more than 200,000 air miles to bases all over the globe, often where the action was heaviest; always said his only ambition was "to make people happy," and he did.

MOVIE HIGHLIGHTS: *Molly and Me, Painted Faces, Top Speed, You said a Mouthful, Elmer the Great* (his personal favorite), *Six-Day Bike*

Rider, Circus Clown, Polo Joe, Chatterbox, The Gladiator, $1,000 a Touchdown, Shut My Big Mouth, Joan of the Ozarks, Pin-Up Girl, Show Boat.

Johnny Mack Brown

(b. Johnny Mack Brown, Sept. 1, 1904, Dothan, Ala.; d. Nov. 14, 1974) Few actors ever made such a dramatic switch as this University of Alabama All-American gridiron hero; went from love scenes with Garbo (A Woman of Affairs) to being one of the great cowboy stars; was snapped up for movies (discovered by Erich von Stroheim) after leading his team to Rose Bowl glory in '26 (a feat that, in '57, got him named to the College Football Hall of Fame); rugged, with a handsome face and raven-black hair (perhaps inherited from his great, great grandmother, an Indian princess), he was an ideal tuxedoed playboy in many silents: Our Dancing Daughters, Soft Living, etc.; making his first Westerns, Montana Moon and Billy the Kid, in '30, he alternated between romantic leads and cowboy pictures (including serials such as Fighting with Kit Carson) for years; in '36, he jumped the corral fence for good, starring exclusively then in scores of boots-and-saddles epics; between '40 and '50 was in the Top Ten Western Stars list each year, usually just a notch behind his best movietown buddy, Charles Starrett, and always aboard trusty steed Reno; had his last starring role in '53 in The Marshall's Daughter, but returned a dozen years later for cameo parts in three (Requiem for a Gunfighter, etc.); off screen was the same straight-shooter as the guy in the ten-gallon hat who tirelessly rode at the head of the posse; during WW II, cleaned up $15 million for Uncle Sam on bond tours, and was a Boy Scout leader; married to college sweetheart Cornelia Foster, he was the father of a son and three daughters, collected antiques, and lived in a southern colonial (naturally) mansion in Beverly Hills; in retirement was the genial greeter at the swank Tail o' the Cock restaurant in Hollywood.

MOVIE HIGHLIGHTS: The Fair Co-Ed, Divine Woman, Coquette, The Great Meadow, Belle of the Nineties, Guns in the Dark, Born to the West, Oklahoma Frontier, Law of the Range, Chip of the Flying U, Flashing Guns, Overland Trail, Panhandle, Six-Gun Mesa.

Virginia Bruce

(b. Virginia Briggs, Sept. 29, 1909, Minneapolis, Minn.; d. Feb. 24, 1982) Fragile blonde, with big blue eyes and a milky-white complexion (considered by make-up artists to be Hollywood's loveliest), who was for almost a decade one of Metro's most prized leading ladies; it was not for nothing that in *The Great Ziegfeld*'s most extravagant production number, she was to be found perched, alone, atop that massive sky-high white column encircled by what seemed to be hundreds of beautiful showgirls; in '31 had been a Ziegfeld star herself, enchanting theater-going audiences in *Smiles*; clearly a young woman of quality, she was the daughter of a wealthy insurance broker and an amateur golf champion mother; discovered by Hollywood at 20, she played minor roles in a few films including Chevalier's *The Love Parade* (as a lady-in-waiting) before making her mark on Broadway; signed her MGM contract in '32, starring first in *Sky Bride* and *Winner Take All*; soon co-starred with legendary lover John Gilbert in *Downstairs*, which he also wrote; married him on Aug. 10, 1932, presented him with a daughter, Susan Ann, in '33, divorced him in '34; love life remained traumatic; was married to young director J. Walter Ruben in '37 and, after giving birth to a son, Christopher, was widowed in '41; in '46, married Turkish-born Ali Ipar, 13 years her junior, who later, while visiting his homeland, was imprisoned by the military junta that had taken over the country; starring career continued through the '40s; was in just two in the '50s; returned in '60 for *Strangers When We Meet*, in which she played Kim Novak's mother.

MOVIE HIGHLIGHTS: *The Wet Parade, Jane Eyre, Society Doctor, The Garden Murder Case, Metropolitan, Born to Dance, Wife, Doctor and Nurse, Yellow Jack, There Goes My Heart, Let Freedom Ring, Stronger Than Desire, Hired Wife, The Invisible Woman, Pardon My Sarong, Brazil.*

Billie Burke

(b. Mary William Ethelbert Appleton Burke, Aug. 7, 1885, Washington, D.C.; d. May 14, 1970) A dithery red-haired delight, she was the daughter of Billy Burke, internationally famous P.T. Barnum clown; sent to school in Great Britain, she began appearing on English stages, in comedies and musicals, at 14; made her Broadway debut at 21 in *My Wife* and for years was one of New York's reigning stars; became the wife of producer Florenz Ziegfeld when 29 and remained married to him until his death in '32; theirs was a tempestuous marriage, thanks to his many flings with other actresses; film historian DeWitt Bodeen reports that Ziegfeld once "brought her a $20,000 diamond bracelet as a peace offering, but she flung it across the room, watching carefully to see where it landed and claiming it as soon as she could"; in the movie *The Great Ziegfeld* was portrayed by Myrna Loy; between '16 and '21, while still appearing on stage, she starred in 14 films, beginning with *Peggy* (at $10,000 a week), followed by a 20-chapter serial, *Gloria's Romance*, for which she was paid $300,000; returned to movies as a character star in '32, playing Hepburn's mother in A *Bill of Divorcement*; the following year played her first feather-brained role in *Dinner at 8*, and the die was cast, her dizzy zenith being reached later in *Topper* and *The Wizard of Oz*, as Garland's good witch, Glinda; published her autobiography, *With a Feather on My Nose*, in '49.

MOVIE HIGHLIGHTS: *Only Yesterday, Society Doctor, My American Wife, Navy Blue and Gold, Merrily We Live* (nominated for Best Supporting Actress Oscar), *Young at Heart, Dulcy, The Man Who Came to Dinner, In This Our Life, They All Kissed the Bride, Father of the Bride, Small Town Girl, The Young Philadelphians*.

Burns & Allen

George Burns (b. Nathan Birnbaum, Jan. 20, 1896, New York, N.Y.) and **Gracie Allen** (b. Grace Ethel Cecile Rosalie Allen, July 26, 1902, San Francisco, Calif.; d. Aug. 27, 1964) At 7 on Manhattan's Lower East Side, he began singing on street corners and passing the hat with the Peewee Quartet (neighborhood kids), went on to become a dance teacher and, in vaudeville, a trick roller skater and comedian; she, after a stint in vaudeville, quit to be a secretary; they met in Union City, N.J., in '23 and the historic comedy team— destined for stage, radio, movie and TV fame—was born; he played the comic in just one performance—their first; discovering the audience loved her and she was getting the laughs, he switched the act; forever after he was the bemused, cigar-puffing straight man to her delightfully daffy scatterbrain; teamed up in marriage on Jan. 7, 1926, in Cleveland, Ohio; pattern of their routine, Burns has said, was always "illogical logic"; example: she puts the salt in the pepper shaker, and vice versa; says he, "Gracie, why do you do that?"; says she, "Because people are always getting mixed up, and now when they get mixed up, they're right"; made their radio debut, creating a sensation, for the British Broadcasting Co. while playing the London Palladium in '30; guested on the Rudy Vallee–Guy Lombardo radio program for a season; got their own show in '33 and remained on the air for 21 years; began making movie shorts in '30; did their first feature, *The Big Broadcast*, in '32; were parents of two adopted children: Sandra, Ronnie; their top-rated TV show lasted from '50 to '58, when Gracie retired; she would have been proud to see him, in '75, win the Best Supporting Oscar for *The Sunshine Boys*.

MOVIE HIGHLIGHTS: *International House, College Humor, Six of a Kind, We're Not Dressing, Love in Bloom, The Big Broadcast of 1937, A Damsel in Distress, Many Happy Returns, Here Comes Cookie, College Swing, The Big Broadcast of 1938, Honolulu.*

Spring Byington

(b. Spring Byington, Oct. 17, 1886, Colorado Springs, Colo.; d. Sept. 7, 1971) Blonde and merrily charming, she "mothered" everybody in movies and, as Jean Arthur's mom in *You Can't Take It With You*, was Oscar-nominated as Best Supporting Actress; privately, a divorcee, she was the mother of two daughters and, eventually, the grandmother of three; to TV fans, she will always be the blithe "Lily Ruskin," the central character in the popular, long-running (1954–59) CBS series "December Bride"; her cheerful, optimistic on-screen image, a reflection of her own personality, pleased her (always said, "It's very simple—Lady Macbeth and I aren't friends"); acted on stage, in touring companies, and repertory, for many years before bowing on Broadway in '24 in the George S. Kaufman-Marc Connelly comedy *Beggar on Horseback*; 20 other Broadway plays followed in the next decade: *Tonight at 12, Ladies Don't Lie, Once in a Lifetime*, etc.; called to Hollywood in '34, she debuted in *Little Women* as Marmee, the mother of Katharine Hepburn, Joan Bennett, Frances Dee, and Jean Parker; it was followed by 92 more movies including her own highly popular "Jones Family" series (*Off to the Races, The Jones Family in Hollywood*, etc.); the twinkling, aging darling that audiences came to love first emerged clearly in '41 in the comedy *The Devil and Miss Jones*, when paired with Charles Coburn; following her final movie, *Please Don't Eat the Daisies*, she appeared for two seasons (1961–63) in the TV series "Laramie," playing the surrogate mother of a family of ranchers.

MOVIE HIGHLIGHTS: *Ah, Wilderness, Dodsworth, Theodora Goes Wild, Jezebel, The Blue Bird, Lucky Partners, Meet John Doe, Roxie Hart, Heaven Can Wait, I'll Be Seeing You, The Enchanted Cottage, Dragonwyck, In the Good Old Summer Time.*

Bruce Cabot

(b. Jacques Etienne Pellissier de Bujac, April 20, 1903, Coresheo, N.M.; d. May 3, 1972) Mention of the name of this big (6'2", 190 lb.), two-fisted, good-looking guy prompts most fans to say, "King Kong"; in that most famous of his 186 movies, he was, of course, the courageous guy who rescued Fay Wray from the clutches of the giant, love-smitten ape atop the Empire State Building; was usually, but not always, the hero; one critic noted in '36: "It is always a question when his name appears in a cast whether he is to marry the girl or murder her"; before crashing movies in '33, this well-educated son of a wealthy oil company lawyer-executive worked on ranches and tramp steamers, was a prize fighter, peddled real estate, and managed a nightclub; David O. Selznick met him at a Hollywood party and gave him a screen test, which was "rather awful" but led to his debut, as a villain, in *Roadhouse Murder*; was divorced by all his wives: nonpro Grace Mary Mather Smith (one daughter, Jennifer), actress Adrienne Ames (were married twice—1933–35, 1936–37; legally adopted her daughter, Dorothy Jane, but she regained custody), Franchesca de Scaffa (one son, Bruce Michael Tonnes); between marriages was one of Hollywood's most eligible bachelors, squiring Joan Crawford and other big-name beauties; during WW II was an intelligence and operations officer in the Air Force, serving in the North African and Italian campaigns; a heavy drinking good-time guy, he hobnobbed with Egypt's playboy King Farouk, skylarked with Errol Flynn and his cronies, and was a fixture at the gambling casinos of Europe; he and great pal John Wayne were in 15 pix together, including, in '71, *Big Jake*, Cabot's last.

MOVIE HIGHLIGHTS: *Flying Devils, Ann Vickers, Show Them No*

Mercy, Fury, The Last of the Mohicans, Bad Man of Brimstone, You and Me, Dodge City, Susan and God, The Flame of New Orleans, Salty O'Rourke, The Angel and the Badman, Sorrowful Jones, Best of the Badmen, Hatari!, In Harm's Way, Cat Ballou.

James Cagney

(b. James Francis Cagney Jr., July 17, 1899, New York, N.Y.) "Top of the world, Ma!" he cried in the fadeout of *White Heat*, and that's where, as a star, this feisty, pugnacious little Irisher was throughout his 31-year Hollywood career; majority of his memorable roles came during his (tumultuous) 1930–42 reign as a Warner Bros. contract star; nominated for the Best Actor Oscar in *Angels with Dirty Faces*, he won in the same category in *Yankee Doodle Dandy* (exuberant film biography of song-and-dance man George M. Cohan; the star's favorite movie), and was nominated again later in *Love Me or Leave Me*; was in the Box Office Top Ten each year from '39 to '43; versatility was his gift; starred in movies of every genre— gangster dramas (*The Roaring Twenties*), musicals (*Footlight Parade*), comedies (*Boy Meets Girl*), action epics (*The Crowd Roars*), Westerns (*The Oklahoma Kid*), even Shakespeare (*A Midsummer Night's Dream*); one critic, though, noted: "He never, not even in his most sympathetic roles, lost the mannerisms of the gangster, the staccato delivery, the curling lip, the odd hitch of the trousers with his clenched fists"; always insisted he was just "a journeyman actor," adding, "With me, a career was just the simple matter of putting the groceries on the table"; the son of a saloon keeper, he had the customary odd jobs (bellhop, ticket clerk, waiter) before going into vaudeville—working first in a musical act requiring that he wear female clothing; married his one wife, chorus girl Frances ("Bill") Vernon, in '22; adopted a son, James Jr. (died in '84), and a daughter, Casey; published his autobiography, *Cagney by Cagney*, in '76; made a movie comeback, after a 20-year absence, in 1981's *Ragtime*.

MOVIE HIGHLIGHTS: *Public Enemy, Taxi!, G-Men, Ceiling Zero, Each Dawn I Die, The Fighting 69th, City for Conquest, Strawberry Blonde, 13 Rue Madeleine, What Price Glory, Mr. Roberts, Man of a Thousand Faces, Shake Hands with the Devil, The Gallant Hours, One, Two, Three.*

Eddie Cantor

(b. Edward Israel Iskowitz, Jan. 31, 1892, New York, N.Y.; d. Oct. 10, 1964) Enormously popular comedian, small with great popping orbs (nickname: Banjo Eyes), famous for boundless energy (dancing about a stage, clapping his hands and singing "If You Knew Susie"), blackface routines, Jewish humor, jokes about wife Ida (his childhood sweetheart, they were married from '14 until her death in '62) and their five daughters; growing up singing and clowning on the streets of New York's Lower East Side, he made his music hall debut at 14; vaudeville and burlesque led to stardom on Broadway in the *Follies, Make It Snappy*, the musical *Kid Boots* (became his screen debut vehicle in '26); for 11 years, starting in '31, was one of radio's best-loved stars; on radio introduced his singing protegees Dinah Shore, Deanna Durbin, Bobby Breen; popularity reached such a peak in '37 that the week of Oct. 24–30 was observed nationally as Eddie Cantor Anniversary Week, with Eleanor Roosevelt serving on the honorary committee; famed, too, for his humanitarianism (the March of Dimes was his creation); starred in films through 1952's *The Story of Will Rogers*, about his friend of many years; published two autobiographies: *My Life's In Your Hands* ('28) and *Take My Life* ('57); was portrayed by Keefe Brasselle in 1954's *The Eddie Cantor Story*; starred on TV (1950–54) in *The Colgate Comedy Hour*; was given a special Oscar in '56 for "distinguished service to the film industry"; for his humanitarian endeavors, Pres. Lyndon B. Johnson awarded him the U.S. Service Medal in '64.

MOVIE HIGHLIGHTS: *Special Delivery, Whoopee, Palmy Days, The Kid from Spain, Roman Scandals, Kid Millions, Strike Me Pink, Ali Baba Goes to Town, Forty Little Mothers, Hollywood Canteen, Show Business, Rhapsody in Blue, If You Knew Susie.*

Madeleine Carroll

(b. Marie-Madeleine Bernadette O'Carroll, Feb. 26, 1902, West Bromwich, Staffordshire, England) Sublimely lovely blue-eyed blonde (no matter that she had naturally dark hair) who was at her zenith as the virginal Princess Flavia in Selznick's *The Prisoner of Zenda*; admitting having had a "problem" with her by insisting she wear little make-up in the role, the producer said, "Now and then she would sneak something in when no one was looking"; in Hollywood just two years then, she had not become one of the best-paid stars (over $250,000 a year) by being a shrinking violet; in view of the fame achieved in the U.S., her movie career here was astonishingly brief: 1936–42; returned to England when her sister was killed in the blitz and devoted herself to war efforts, notably with the Red Cross in Italy and France; was accorded France's Legion of Honor and the Medal of Freedom from the U.S.; from '46 to '49 was wed to Henri Lavorel (her third husband), a French officer of the resistance; triumphed on Broadway after the war in *Goodbye My Fancy*; the daughter of an Irish philosophy professor and a French mother, she lived in France from soon after her birth until she was 9, when the family went back to England; studying at the University of Birmingham to be a teacher, she switched ambitions after acting in a school play in her senior year; was a private French tutor prior to a British stage and film (1928–35) career; international fame came in Hitchcock's *The 39 Steps*; divorced first husband Philip Astley, of the King's Guards (1931–39); two later husbands divorced her—Sterling Hayden (1942–46), *Life* publisher Andrew Heiskell (1950–65; their only child, Anne-Madeleine, died in '83).

MOVIE HIGHLIGHTS: *Atlantic, Young Woodley, I Was a Spy, The General Died at Dawn, Lloyds of London, On the Avenue, Blockade, Cafe Society, Honeymoon in Bali, My Son, My Son, Northwest Mounted Police, Virginia, Bahama Passage, My Favorite Blonde, White Cradle Inn* (aka *High Fury*), *An Innocent Affair, The Fan.*

Nancy Carroll

(b. Ann Veronica LaHiff, Nov. 19, 1904, New York, N.Y.; d. Aug. 6, 1965) Once Paramount's box office ace-in-the-hole, she was a delectable redhead with a heart-shaped face and trigger-quick temper—both breathtaking; tantrums eventually played havoc with her career; was one star who could do it all: musicals (sang and danced in several hits with Buddy Rogers—*Close Harmony, Heads Up!*, etc.), sophisticated comedy (*Laughter*), drama (*The Devil's Holiday*, which rated her a Best Actress Oscar nomination); an audience poll in '30 named her as the most popular actress in movies; born to Irish-Catholic parents, she was that "lucky" seventh child of a seventh child; broke into vaudeville, singing and hoofing, in her teens, soon becoming a chorine in musicals; debuted as an actress on

Broadway in *Mayflowers* after marrying playwright Jack *(Tobacco Road)* Kirkland in '24; one child, Patricia Kirkland, who became an actress; went to Hollywood with her husband, starred on stage there in *Chicago*; after a few minor movie parts won the title role in the movie *Abie's Irish Rose* ('28); *The Shopworn Angel*, the following year, made her a major star; divorced Kirkland in '31; one week later was the bride of *Life* editor Bolton Mallory; this volcanic marriage ended in '35; popularity burst like a bubble after one box office disaster, *Night Angel*; later starred in many at other studios but she had reached and slipped from the heights; left the screen in '38 and was a Broadway success in *I Must Love Someone*, penned by ex-husband Kirkland; wed wealthy Dutch auto manufacturer C.H.J. Groen in '55; did radio, stock, TV (guested often on "The Egg and I," playing the mother of the series' star, her own daughter); acted last on Broadway in '64 in *Cindy*, a flop.

MOVIE HIGHLIGHTS: *Dance of Life, Sweetie, Illusion, Stolen Heaven, Broken Lullaby, Undercover Man, Child of Manhattan, I Love That Man, Springtime for Henry, Jealousy, There Goes My Heart, After the Dance, That Certain Age.*

Ruth Chatterton

(b. Ruth Chatterton, Dec. 24, 1893, New York, N.Y.; d. Nov. 24, 1961) Distinguished blonde star whose good fortune was that talkies demanded actresses who could handle dialogue; had been such a success on Broadway that she once turned down $300,000 to make silents; her long career, though, dating from 1909, had faltered by the time she made her first talking picture at 36, *The Doctor's Secret*, and was bound for new glory; had made her screen debut in a silent (her only one), *Sins of the Fathers*, the previous year ('28); most famous roles were in the tearjerkers *Madame X* and *Sarah and Son*, each bringing her Best Actress Oscar nominations, and *Dodsworth*, which should have but inexplicably didn't; fans still speak of her tour de force in *The Right to Love*—played three roles: a young girl, the same character in middle age, then her daughter; had a habit of marrying her leading men; first was Ralph Forbes (1924–32), who acted opposite her on stage in *The Magnolia Lady* and in the movie *Lady of Scandal*; the day after he divorced her, she married George Brent, 10 years younger than she; in their two years together they co-starred in four movies

(The Rich Are Always with Us, The Crash, Lilly Turner, Female); returned to the stage when her screen career fizzled after 10 years and fell in love with Barry Thomson, her leading man in a revival of *Pygmalion*; were wed from '42 until his death in '60; a woman of many interests and talents, she was a stage producer *(The Green Hat)*, director *(Mary Rose)*, a play translator *(La Tendresse)*, a composer, licensed pilot, novelist *(Homeward Borne, The Southern Wild)*; last films, *The Rat* and *A Royal Divorce* (both in '38), were British; continued starring—on Broadway, radio, "live" TV, and in summer stock—to the end.

MOVIE HIGHLIGHTS: *The Dummy, The Laughing Lady, High Road, Charming Sinners, Once a Lady, Anybody's Woman, Tomorrow and Tomorrow, The Unfaithful, The Magnificent Lie, Frisco Jenny, Lady of Secrets, Girls' Dormitory.*

Maurice Chevalier

(b. Maurice Auguste Chevalier, Sept. 12, 1888, Menilmontante, France; d. Jan. 1, 1972) From youth to 80, when he retired, he was show business's incomparable song-and-dance man; with his straw hat, bow tie, and shovel lip, he durably presented the face of the blithe-spirited rogue and lover to the public; was as much of a French institution as the Eiffel Tower; had few intimate friends but those who knew him best professionally found a strange contrast between the debonair boulevardier who radiated the joy of living on stage and the man who, privately, was remote and morose; was interned more than once in mental institutions when overcome by spells of depthless dejection; began entertaining professionally in his teens in dingy Parisian cafes; graduated to the finest music halls, to silent movies, talkies, radio, Hollywood, Broadway, TV; his swan song, when old, was an arduous one-man show—singing "Mimi," "Louise," et al.—which took him to 60 cities all over the world; also said he "preferred a successful career to success with women"; enjoyed little of the latter; at the end of an early 15-year liaison with much-older music hall queen Mistinguette, he attempted suicide; his one marriage (1927–35), to actress Yvonne Vallee, ended in divorce; during WW II his love was Nita Rey, a Jewish woman; attempting to protect her, he entertained Allied troops in Nazi POW camps; later sentenced to death by the Marquis for alleged Nazi collaboration, he was finally vindicated; ironically, in WW I, as a soldier captured

33

by the Germans, he'd been held prisoner for two years; cherishing the memory of his mother, he had a stone bust of her in the garden of his magnificent estate outside Paris and, daily, stopped before it to pray.

MOVIE HIGHLIGHTS: *The Love Parade, The Smiling Lieutenant, One Hour With You, Love Me Tonight, The Merry Widow, The Beloved Vagabond, Man About Town, Love in the Afternoon, Can-Can, Gigi, Fanny, In Search of the Castaways, Monkeys Go Home.*

Claudette Colbert

(b. Claudette Lily Chauchoin, Sept. 13, 1903, Paris, France) Sophisticated and lovely, with a face and form that have defied time, she sparkled—whether in clothes elegant *(Midnight)* or plain *(Maid of Salem)*, in drama *(Imitation of Life)* or madcap comedy *(It Happened One Night)*; won an Oscar for that one; was nominated later in *Private Worlds* and *Since You Went Away*; starred in 62 between 1927's *For the Love of Mike* and 1961's *Parrish*; lived in Paris until she was 9, when her banker father took his family to New York; paid for her dramatic training at the Art Students' League by working in a dress shop; made her Broadway debut in '23; had leads in many *(Ghost Train*, etc.); played opposite Norman Foster in 1927's *The Barker*, married him in '28, co-starred with him in the movie *Young Man of Manhattan* ('30), divorced him in '35; was married from '35 until his death in '68 to Dr. Joel Pressman; her first six movies were made in New York; one of them, *The Big Pond*, she and co-star Maurice Chevalier did twice, filming simultaneously English and French versions; another one with him, *The Smiling Lieutenant*, launched her as the screen's most durably enchanting comedienne; was one of Hollywood's best-dressed and best-paid (she only did *It Happened One Night* after demanding $50,000—a fortune in '34—for four weeks' work); her movies retain their crisp chic by having been filmed in black-and-white; *Drums Along the Mohawk* ('39) was her first in color; didn't make another until *Royal Affairs in Versailles* in '57; borrowed her professional name from Louis XIV's chief minister.

MOVIE HIGHLIGHTS: *Manslaughter, The Sign of the Cross, Secrets of a Secretary, The Phantom President, Cleopatra, The Gilded Lily, She Mar-*

ried Her Boss, Tovarich, I Met Him in Paris, Bluebeard's Eighth Wife, Arise My Love, Boom Town, Skylark, Remember the Day, The Palm Beach Story, Practically Yours, Guest Wife, Tomorrow Is Forever, Without Reservations, The Egg and I, Sleep My Love, Three Came Home.

Ronald Colman

(b. Ronald Charles Colman, Feb. 9, 1891, Richmond, Surrey, England; d. May 19, 1958) A great star in silents (starting in Hollywood in '23), this most handsome man, blessed with boundless charm, became an even greater one in talkies—thanks to that magnificent voice; his first sound films, *Bulldog Drummond* and *Condemned*, brought him (combined) an Oscar nomination; was nominated again in *Random Harvest* before winning an Oscar in 1947's *A Double Life*; forever a monastic mystery man, he did not relish the notoriety that accompanies stardom; in '75, his daughter (only child), Juliet Benita Colman, published a biography of him, accurately subtitled "A Very Private Person"; "Fame," he told friends at the height of his popularity, "has robbed me of my freedom and shut me up in prison, and because the prison walls are gilded, and the key that locks me in is gold, does not make it any more tolerable"; the one compensation, he noted, was "my work—I love the work, itself"; for most of his early years in Hollywood was regarded as an eligible, albeit elusive, bachelor; actually, back in England, he had a wife, stage actress Thelma Raye, an "arbitrary, domineering" woman; she shared the flat of this struggling actor while still wed to a wealthy Australian, who sued for divorce, naming Colman as corespondent; in '20, before sailing for America, she demanded marriage; after tolerating her shrewish ways for four years, he left her; she got a $25,000 settlement and $1,500 a month from '24 to '34, when she divorced him; continued to make his life hell for years via threats to write a tell-all book; from '38 on, enjoyed a most happy marriage to English actress Benita Hume (his co-star on radio and TV in "Halls of Ivy").

MOVIE HIGHLIGHTS: *The White Sister, Romola, Tarnish, Dark Angel, Beau Geste, Stella Dallas* (silents), *Raffles, Arrowsmith, Cynara, Clive of India, A Tale of Two Cities, Lost Horizon, The Prisoner of Zenda, If I Were King, The Light That Failed, The Talk of the Town, Kismet, The Late George Apley.*

Gary Cooper

(b. Frank James Cooper, May 7, 1901, Helena, Mont.; d. May 13, 1961) Long, lean, leathery, laconic, he was the heterosexual male at its ultimate—sensitive yet strong—and born to be a hero; "Every line in his face spelled honesty," said director Frank Capra. "So innate was his integrity that he could be cast in phony parts, but never look phony himself"; life was a study in contrasts; a deep-dyed Westerner, the son of a rancher-judge, he received his early education at an elitist school in Dunstable, Bedfordshire, England; first an extra in mob scenes in silents (after a failed career as a newspaper cartoonist), he quickly became a multimillionaire; genuinely shy, he was early on the randiest bachelor in Hollywood and, reportedly, the one who never failed to score—rumors of his physical attributes and "phenomenal" staying power helped in this area; preferring cowboy roles, he was, on the Beverly Hills beat, the supreme sophisticate, hobnobbing with royalty and the screen's creme de la creme; after consorting with wild-living sexpots like Lupe Velez, was married from '33 on to Park Avenue socialite Veronica Balfe (a young post-debutante briefly on screen as Sandra Shaw); one child: Maria (married to pianist Byron Janis); his marriage was threatened (but endured) 16 years later when he fell in love with Patricia Neal, his young leading lady in *The Fountainhead*; years after the end of their lengthy affair (a great secret then), the actress told a *New York Times* reporter: "He was the most gorgeously attractive man—bright, too, although some people didn't think so"; won two Oscars *(Sergeant York, High Noon)*; nominated also for *Mr. Deeds Goes to Town*, *Pride of the Yankees, For Whom the Bell Tolls.*

MOVIE HIGHLIGHTS: *Lilac Time, The Shopworn Angel, The Virginian, A Farewell to Arms, Design for Living, The General Died at Dawn, The Plainsman, Beau Geste, The Westerner, Ball of Fire, The Story of Dr. Wassell, Saratoga Trunk, Unconquered.*

Jackie Cooper

(b. John Cooper Jr. (?), Sept. 15, 1922, Los Angeles, Calif.) Blond and natural-acting, with a petulant lower lip, a slow smile, and a youthful aggressiveness that charmed millions, he was, pre–Mickey Rooney, MGM's great boy star; copped a Best Actor Oscar nomination at 9 in

Skippy; as the script required, he shed buckets of tears on camera after the director (his uncle), Norman Taurog, threatened to have his dog shot; hence the title of the star's '81 autobiography, *Please Don't Shoot My Dog*; the book contained a number of shockers, including an account of his teenage seduction by the considerably older Joan Crawford; his manager-mother was the late Mabel Leonard, who had been on the musical stage, but his father, whom he has said he never knew, is a mystery figure; some sources in the '30s cited his name as Charles J. Bigelow; began movie work at 3 "working as an extra with my grandmother at Columbia"; graduated quickly from "Our Gang" and Lloyd Hamilton comedies to solo stardom; made an easy transition to teenage roles *(That Certain Age, Seventeen)*; left Hollywood during WW II for service in the Navy (is now a Captain in the USNR) but the welcome mat was not out when he returned; taking John Garfield's advice he reestablished himself as a star on Broadway in comedies *(Remains to Be Seen, King of Hearts)*; TV glory followed in "The People's Choice" and "Hennessey"; still an actor *(Superman, etc.)*, he has been a successful Hollywood producer and director (a "M*A*S*H" episode won him an Emmy); marital record: two failures—to June Horne (son: John) and actress Hildy Parks—and one success, since '54, to Barbara Kraus (kids: Russell, Julie, Christina).

MOVIE HIGHLIGHTS: *The Champ, Sooky, When a Feller Needs a Friend, The Bowery, Treasure Island, Peck's Bad Boy, Dinky, The Devil Is a Sissy, White Banners, What a Life!, The Return of Frank James, Ziegfeld Girl, Syncopation, Kilroy Was Here, The Joker Is Wild, Superman II.*

Ricardo Cortez

(b. Jack Kranze, Sept. 19, 1899, Vienna, Austria; d. April 28, 1977) Paramount took this darkly handsome Jewish boy from Brooklyn (grew up there after age 3), the son of Austrian and Hungarian emigrants, and, because he looked the part (resembled Valentino), turned him into a Latin lover; screen name came from a box of Tampa-made cigars; as a youth was a runner on Wall Street where, after movie fame, he was a successful broker; began in bits in New York-made movies such as a 1920 Vitagraph two-reeler, *Thimble, Thimble*; first Hollywood job was that of bodyguard to a heavy-drinking top star, his duty being to get him to the studio sober enough to work; being tall, suave, sleek, and a superb ballroom dancer, stardom on his own was inevitable; among the silents making him a "name": *Sixty Cents an Hour, Feet of Clay, Argentine Love, The Spaniard*; by '26 was important enough to be billed above Swedish import Greta Garbo in her first American film, *The Torrent*; career skyrocketed in the '30s when he made screen love to all the great femme stars, from Colbert to Dolores Del Rio, Kay Francis, Bette Davis, and Irene Dunne; off screen, was initially less fortunate in his love life; was married from '26 until her death in '31 to beautiful, doomed actress Alma Rubens—spent a mint trying to save her from morphine addiction; he and N.Y. socialite Christine Lee parted soon after they wed in '34 but only divorced in '50; was then married, happily, to much-younger Margarette Belle; was the director of several: Preston Foster's *Chasing Danger*, etc.; was there ahead of Bogart as Sam Spade in *The Maltese Falcon* ('31) and of TV's Raymond Burr as Perry Mason (*The Case of the Black Cat*, '36).

MOVIE HIGHLIGHTS: *Thirteen Women, Symphony of Six Million, The House on 56th Street, Wonder Bar, The White Cockatoo, A Lost Lady, Mandalay, Hat, Coat and Glove, Midnight Mary, Torch Singer, West of Shanghai, White Shoulders, The Man with Two Faces, Murder Over New York, The Locket.*

Larry "Buster" Crabbe

(b. Clarence Linden Crabbe, Feb. 7, 1908, Oakland, Calif.; d. April 23, 1983) With his Herculean physique and the visage of the fabled Paris, he was not only an Olympic swimming champ (400-meter gold medalist in '32) but a screen star holding other records; was the only actor to portray Tarzan (*Tarzan the Fearless*, '33), Flash Gordon (in the '36, '38 and '40 serials), Billy the Kid (in 1941–42 Westerns), and Buck Rogers (the '39 serial); grew up on a pineapple plantation (father was its overseer) in Hawaii where he perfected his swim skills, was such a natural athlete that he was a 16-letter man in high school and, while at the University of Hawaii, won Hawaii's light-heavyweight boxing championship; was briefly a stunt double for Joel McCrea before playing leads in movies——94 in all, counting his many chapter-plays, the last of which was 1952's *King of the Congo*; learned to act by studying the more experienced actors in his movies; long starring career—mostly in B's, Westerns, serials—faded in the '50s; found new fame on TV; starred in two different "Captain Gallant" series for

NBC, first in '55 and again in '62, when his then 10-year-old son, "Cuffy" (Cullen), portrayed his adopted son; married from '33 on to Adah Virginia Held, he had two daughters: Caren (deceased) and Susan; with a later career as a Wall Street broker, and being active in various business enterprises (notably a swimming pool construction company), he returned to do several Westerns in the 60's—usually playing a heavy; for the record: his hair, naturally straight and dark blond, was blondined and given a permanent for his famous Flash Gordon serials.

MOVIE HIGHLIGHTS: *Sweetheart of Sigma Chi, Wanderer of the Wasteland, Rose Bowl, Nevada, Sophie Lang Goes West, Million Dollar Legs, Colorado Sunset, A Sailor's Lady, Jungle Siren, Queen of Broadway, Swamp Fire, Prairie Badmen.*

Joan Crawford

(b. Lucille LeSeuer, March 23, 1904, San Antonio, Tex.; d. May 10, 1977) The quintessential movie star; lived the part on camera and off, and her life was fan mag fodder for five decades; glamour, artistry (finally), temperament—she had it all; said accurately of self: "I have an incredible drive that neither time nor pain can dim"; pals called her The Empress, detractors used less kind labels; came to movies after dancing in Broadway revues and appearing in a porno flick or two (forever denied this but *Oui* magazine, in '84, published photographic proof, the fact then being reported by newscaster Diane Sawyer on *CBS Morning News*); film debut: *Pretty Ladies* ('25); was 18 years under contract at MGM; in the Box Office Top Ten 1932–36; pegged as "box office poison" in '37, she soon made exhibitors eat their words; a towering presence on screen, she was shorter, at 5'4", than many fans guessed; was bitterly jealous of rival Norma Shearer, wed to Metro production genius Irving Thalberg and getting first crack at roles; married and divorced actors Douglas Fairbanks Jr. (1929–33), Franchot Tone (1935–39), Philip Terry (1942–46); was last married to—and made a widow by—Pepsi-Cola exec Alfred Steele (1955–59); made no secret, though, that the "great love" of her life was Gable, with whom she had a torrid affair in the '30s; adopted four children: Christina, Christopher, Cynthia, Cathy; won the Best Actress Oscar in *Mildred Pierce* ('45); published her autobiography, *A Portrait of Joan* (with Jane Kesner Ardmore), in '62; daughter Christina's shocking best seller about the star, *Mommie Dearest*, was filmed ('81) with Faye Dunaway as Crawford.

MOVIE HIGHLIGHTS: *Our Dancing Daughters, Grand Hotel, Chained, The Gorgeous Hussy, The Women, Susan and God, A Woman's Face, Humoresque, Possessed, Harriet Craig, Sudden Fear, Queen Bee, Autumn Leaves, Female on the Beach, Whatever Happened to Baby Jane?*

Bing Crosby

(b. Harry Lillis Crosby, May 2, 1903, Tacoma, Wash.; d. Oct. 14, 1977) Inimitable fun-loving star and golfer whose crooning voice and relaxed humor captivated millions around the world for half a century; got the nickname "Bing" at 7 because he was mad about a newspaper comic strip, *The Bingville Bugle*; came by his musical talents naturally—father Harry (of Danish descent) played mandolin, mother Kate (Irish; maiden name Harrigan) sang in the church choir, and a maternal uncle, George, a baritone, had helped make famous the song "Harrigan, That's Me"; left Gonzaga College (was in the glee club; studied law), went to Hollywood and, in '26, formed The Rhythm Boys with Harry Barris and Al Rinker (Mildred Bailey's brother); trio toured with Paul Whiteman's band then was on the radio while also singing with Gus Arnheim's band at Hollywood's Cocoanut Grove; went solo first in eight musical shorts in which he sang "The Blue of the Night" (always his theme), "Just One More Chance," and others becoming Crosby standards; his starring feature debut, *The Big Broadcast of 1932*, launched the phenomenal career that brought him a Best Actor Oscar *(Going My Way)* and two other nominations *(The Bells of St. Mary's, The Country Girl)*; was a Paramount luminary for 25 years; was among the Box Office Top Ten in '34, '37, '40, and each year from '43 through '54 (1944–48 was number 1); between '40 and '62 was in seven "Road" romps with Bob Hope *(The Road to Singapore* to *The Road to Hong Kong)*; was twice married to actresses—Dixie Lee (from '30 until her death in '52; four sons) and Kathryn Grant (after '57; two sons, one daughter [Mary Crosby, whose character was finally revealed to have shot J.R. in "Dallas" in 1980]); records sold in the hundreds of millions— "Silent Night" always being the leader.

MOVIE HIGHLIGHTS: *College Humor, We're Not Dressing, Mississippi, Rhythm on the Range, Pennies from Heaven, Waikiki Wedding, Sing You Sinners, Birth of the Blues, Holiday Inn, Dixie, Blue Skies, The Emperor Waltz, Riding High, White Christmas, Anything Goes, High Society, Man on Fire.*

Robert Cummings

(b. Charles Clarence Robert Orville Cummings, June 9, 1910, Joplin, Mo.) Light-hearted star who managed to play youthful roles for decades, perhaps because of his long dedication to natural foods and vitamins that he consumed by the bushel; has had a phethora of names; called "Charlie" in school, he only discovered at 20 that he had four given names—and why; physician-father Charles Clarence delivered him, filled in the birth certificate, named him Robert (for a favorite uncle), Orville (for friend Orville Wright); insisting that he be named after his father, his minister mom inserted the others; spent one year each at three universities including Carnegie Tech (engineering); studied at the American Academy of Dramatic Arts in '31 ("They paid *me* to go there—$14 a week—as they had many female students and needed more actors"), went to London, acquired a British accent (English actors being in demand then), returned as "Blade Stanhope-Conway" and landed a role on Broadway in *The Roof*; popped up as "Brice Hutchens" in the *Ziegfeld Follies of 1934*; switched to "Robert Cummings" and a Southern drawl to win his first movie role in 1935's *So Red the Rose*; is a believer in "mind dynamics" ("If I have a problem, I get expert counsel then ask the opinion of a good psychic"); since '46 has made most life-career decisions via astrology; one astrologer urged him to do a TV series—made him rich; another named all his children: Robert Richard, Sharon Patricia, Laurel Ann, Mary Melinda, Anthony Bob; they're by Mary Elliott (1945–69); was earlier divorced by high school sweetheart Edna Emma Myers and Vivian Janis; at 60 married Regina Fong, 32, with two astrologers and a numerologist—working independently—picking the same date and time: March 27, 1971—between 11:34 and 11:44 A.M.

MOVIE HIGHLIGHTS: *Souls at Sea, Wells Fargo, Three Smart Girls Grow Up, Spring Parade, The Devil and Miss Jones, Saboteur, Kings Row, Princess O'Rourke, You Came Along, The Bride Wore Boots, Sleep My Love, Paid in Full, Dial M for Murder, Lucky Me, How to Be Very, Very Popular.*

Jane Darwell

(b. Pattie Woodard, Oct. 15, 1879, Palmyra, Mo.; d. Aug. 13, 1967) Plump character actress whose presence in a movie—and she was omnipresent—reassured fans that, however poor the picture, they wouldn't be bored, at least while she was around; occasionally played gossipy old women ("Dolly Merriweather" in GWTW) or vindictive ones (the monstrous cowtown woman in *The Ox-Bow Incident*); most often, though, was the warmhearted nurse or housekeeper, the wise granny, or indomitable mother ("Ma Joad," the Okie countrywoman in *The Grapes of Wrath*, won her a Best Supporting Oscar and provided her with a stirring speech, in closeup, at the fadeout: "They can't keep us down—we're the people"); actually, she had no children, was never married, and came from a monied family; a direct descendant of Andrew Jackson, she was educated at exclusive girls' schools in Louisville, Chicago, and Boston, where she studied voice and piano; had further training in dramatics in various European capitals before winning a part in a play, *Stubbornness of Geraldine*, while visiting in Chicago at the turn of the century; acted in a few silent movies *(Rose of the Rancho)* as early as '14 but the early emphasis was on the legitimate stage—a three-year tour in London, Paris, and Berlin, plus lengthy stock stints in San Francisco and Seattle; made her Broadway debut in '20 in *Merchants of Venus*; went to Hollywood in '30 to play Jackie Coogan's "Aunt Polly" in *Tom Sawyer*; was under contract for a decade at 20th Century–Fox and was the favorite character actress of director John Ford, for whom she acted in many *(Three Godfathers, My Darling Clementine, Wagonmaster,* etc.); was in more than 200 films.

MOVIE HIGHLIGHTS: *Huckleberry Finn, Back Street, Only Yesterday, The Scarlet Empress, Bright Eyes, Curly Top, Captain January, The Country Doctor, Wife, Doctor and Nurse, Jesse James, The Rains Came, All That Money Can Buy, Tender Comrade, Fourteen Hours, Mary Poppins.*

Bette Davis

(b. Ruth Elizabeth Davis, April 5, 1908, Lowell, Mass.) If this magnificent star had not existed, the brothers Warner might well have had to shut down the factory; she gave them a run for the money—both temperamentally (battled continually with tough Jack Warner—in the courts once; lost) and at the box office; after finally winning her fight for quality scripts ('36 was the year), she gave the studio one blockbuster after another; did all right for herself too; commanded a towering salary ($5,000-plus per week), won two

Oscars (*Dangerous* and *Jezebel*) and four other nominations in WB movies (*Dark Victory, The Letter, Now Voyager, Mr. Skeffington*); garnered additional nominations for Goldwyn's *The Little Foxes* (made on loan–out), 20th Century–Fox's *All About Eve* and *The Star*, and, later, *What Ever Happened to Baby Jane?*, an independent merely released by Warners; the role of doomed Judith Traherne in *Dark Victory* remains her personal favorite, though many objective critics plump for Margo Channing in *All About Eve* as her definitive characterization; won the latter role by default— Claudette Colbert, already contracted for it, suffered a back injury and withdrew at the last minute; stage-trained, she broke into movies in *Bad Sister* in '31; made her first impact on audiences in '32 in George Arliss' *The Man Who Played God*, but it was the Cockney waitress-bitch Mildred in *Of Human Bondage* (on loan-out to RKO in '34) that made her a bona fide star; divorced from bandleader Harmon O. Nelson (1932–38), was widowed by businessman Arthur Farnsworth in '43 (m. in '40), divorced artist William Grant Sherry (1945–49; child: Barbara), Gary Merrill (1950–60; two adopted children: Margo, Michael); published her autobiography, *The Lonely Life*, in '62.

MOVIE HIGHLIGHTS: *Bordertown, The Petrified Forest, The Sisters, The Private Lives of Elizabeth and Essex, The Old Maid, Juarez, All This and Heaven Too, The Great Lie, The Man Who Came to Dinner, Old Acquaintance, The Corn Is Green, A Stolen Life, June Bride, Payment on Demand, The Catered Affair.*

Joan Davis

(b. Madonna Josephine Davis, June 29, 1907, St. Paul, Minn.; d. May 23, 1961) Rowdy, raucous, falling-down comedienne, and ever the crowd's pet; off the screen, with auburn hair and green eyes, she was a far more attractive woman than on; knew this and it pained her; "I don't get it," she would sigh in that memorable nasal whine. "Unless my mirror lies to me, I'm not bad looking. But let me get one look at that face on the screen and I'm sick for a week"; unlike many comics, though, she was not a moody soul, being privately as humorous (with wit, not pratfalls) as she was professionally; was also a practicing, devoutly religious Catholic; aspired to serious drama as a child but audience response to her in amateur theatricals convinced her comedy was her forte; friends called her "Happy Hooligan"; entire life, from teen years on, was spent as an entertainer—in vaudeville with Si Wills (her only husband, from '31 until they divorced in '47), with her eye-batting, heel-sliding, singing her stuttering song; on radio, the screen and TV ("I Married Joan," co-starring Jim Backus, was one of NBC's major 1952–55 hits, in which her real-life daughter, Beverly Wills, appeared as her much-younger college-student sister); after she made her screen debut in '34 in a short, *Way Up Thar*, and clowning for Paramount in *Millions in the Air* ('35), 20th Century–Fox had her under exclusive contract from '37 to '42; for her antics in *Sally, Irene and Mary* and *My Lucky Star*, the New York Film Critics honored her as Best Comedienne of the Year in '38; last movie was *Harem Girl* ('52); daughter Beverly (only child) followed in her footsteps and won praise in a very "Joan Davis" role in *Some Like It Hot*, but two years after her mother's death, when only 31, perished in a fire at her home.

MOVIE HIGHLIGHTS: *Wake Up and Live, You Can't Have Everything, Thin Ice, On the Avenue, Tailspin, Daytime Wife, Sun Valley Serenade, Yokel Boy, Show Business, She Wrote the Book, If You Knew Susie, Kansas City Kitty, Love That Brute, The Groom Wore Spurs.*

Frances Dee

(b. Frances Dee, Nov. 26, 1907, Los Angeles, Calif.) "He's not my type," said the ethereal brunette, resolutely refusing for three years to let friends introduce an actor they all liked; they finally met when Paramount loaned her to RKO to co-star with him in *The Silver Cord* and, four months after saying "Hello," she and Joel McCrea said "I do," on Oct. 20, 1933; all these years (plus three sons and several grandchildren) later, they're still happily wed, living wealthily (and long retired from acting) in a Spanish hacienda on a mammoth (four square miles) ranch in Simi Valley, far north of Hollywood; sons Jody, David, and Peter all became ranchers—Jody being the only one to give acting a fleeting try; after attending the University of Chicago, she studied at the Pasadena Playhouse and, in '29, worked as an extra in *Manslaughter* and *Words and Music*; spotting her on a set, a director tested her and persuaded the studio to sign her; was promptly cast as Chevalier's leading lady in *Playboy of Paris* in '30; her haunting, bittersweet smile and exquisite features captivated fans; critic James Agee once said she was "one of the very few women in movies who really had a face"; roles showing this to perfection: the rich beauty in *An American Tragedy* (same part Elizabeth Taylor played in *A Place in the Sun*) and Colman's love in *If I Were King*; often cast in virtuous roles, she was versatile enough to play, in movies like *Blood Money*, seemingly admirable young women who, secretly, were evil; busiest year: 1933—13 movies (*Little Women*, *Of Human Bondage*, etc.); later never did more than two a year, and usually one; co-starred with McCrea in *One Man's Journey*, *Wells Fargo*, *Four Faces West*; quit after 1954's *Gypsy Colt*.

MOVIE HIGHLIGHTS: *June Moon*, *Sky Bride*, *College Humor*, *Finishing School*, *Becky Sharp*, *Souls at Sea*, *Half Angel*, *So Ends Our Night*, *I Walked with a Zombie*, *Happy Land*, *Private Affairs of Bel Ami*, *Payment on Demand*, *Because of You*, *Mr. Scoutmaster*.

Olivia de Havilland

(b. Olivia de Havilland, July 1, 1916, Tokyo, Japan) Errol Flynn adored this brown-eyed, strong-willed beauty, on screen and off, but his advances were welcomed only when cameras turned; that was often: *Captain Blood*, *Dodge City*, *They Died With Their Boots On*, etc.; the daughter of an English mother and father (a patent attorney), she was discovered at 19 when playing Hermia in Max Reinhardt's Hollywood Bowl production of *A Midsummer Night's Dream*; did the same role--Dick Powell (as Lysander) delivering her first screen kiss—in the movie version; was actually her screen debut but the public saw her in two others (*Alibi Ike*, *The Irish in Us*) before its release; suspensions often ensued as she battled for good roles at Warners; when her seven-year contract ended, the studio insisted she still owed them six months; became a movietown heroine by taking WB to court, at great expense, and winning; the ruling that no contract could extend beyond its specified time is known as "The de Havilland Law"; winning Best Actress Oscars for *To Each His Own* and *The Heiress*, she was also nominated for *Hold Back the Dawn* (sister Joan Fontaine beat her out then in *Suspicion*) and *The Snake Pit*; was nominated as Best Support for her glowing performance as Melanie in *GWTW*; once avidly pursued by Howard Hughes and other eligible bachelors, she married novelist Marcus Goodrich in '46 (son: Benjamin), divorced him in '52; in '55 wed *Paris Match* editor Pierre Galante (daughter: Gisele), from whom she's long been separated; penned a mirthful memoir, *Every Frenchman Has One*, in '62.

MOVIE HIGHLIGHTS: *Anthony Adverse, The Adventures of Robin Hood, Wings of the Navy, The Private Lives of Elizabeth and Essex, Santa Fe Trail, The Strawberry Blonde, In This Our Life, The Male Animal, Princess O'Rourke, Devotion, The Dark Mirror, Lady in a Cage, Light in the Piazza, Airport '77.*

Dolores Del Rio

(b. Lolita Dolores Ansunsolo de Martinez, Aug. 3, 1905, Durango, Tex.; d. April 11, 1983) Throughout her years in Hollywood, from her '25 debut to *Journey Into Fear* ('42), producers regarded her mainly as an exquisite *objet d'art*, all in shades of copper, gold, and black; perhaps seeing her this way too, second husband Cedric Gibbons (MGM's great art director) designed and built for her a beach mansion all in white, the better to show off her dark beauty; also showered her with jewels and such exotic gifts as a costly bird from Asia able to talk in Spanish, French, and English; leaving Hollywood, she proved her mettle, becoming Mexico's foremost actress on stage (in *Camille*, etc.) and in films (was honored with four Arieles, Mexico's Oscar equivalent, for her performances in *Maria Candelaria*, etc.); the convent-educated daughter of a bank president, she married wealthy, aristocratic Jaime del Rio at 16; entertained by the young couple in Mexico City, movie director Edwin Carewe, himself a newlywed, swept her off to Hollywood, directed her in several films (*Joanna*, her first, the great hit *Ramona*, etc.), and—their marriages notwithstanding—vowed to make her his wife; Jaime del Rio conveniently died in '28 but Carewe's hoped-for wedding never took place; while wed to Cedric Gibbons (1930–41), the star moved among Hollywood's elite (the Goldwyns, the Thalbergs, etc.); a sizzling romance with Orson Welles followed their divorce; married to American millionaire Lewis Riley from '55 on, she lived and reigned like a queen in Mexico City, remaining forever incomparably lovely; beauty secret: "Take care of your inner, spiritual beauty—that will reflect in your face"; also did not smoke or drink, and slept 16 hours a day.

MOVIE HIGHLIGHTS: *What Price Glory, Resurrection, The Loves of Carmen, The Dove* (all silents), *Bird of Paradise, Wonder Bar, Madame du Barry, Flying Down to Rio, In Caliente, Lancer Spy, The Fugitive, Flor Silvestre, La Otra, Flaming Star, Cheyenne Autumn.*

Marlene Dietrich

(b. Maria Magdalene von Losch, Dec. 27, 1901, Berlin, Germany) Fans found her an intriguing mystery for there were, always, two of her; first there was the creation (mainly of love-enslaved director Josef von Sternberg)—Paramount's shimmering blonde (forever backlighted) goddess, the femme fatale with the other-worldly eyebrows, eyes, and cheekbones, and ever-present cigarette, who posed statuelike and undulated in sinuous slow motion; off screen there was the Earth Mother who, while shocking the nation by sporting masculine attire, nourished ailing colleagues with chicken soup of her own making, had an army of loyal friends (men *and* women), boasted proudly of her daughter Maria (stars hid their children then) and, later, her grandsons, and had one husband, Rudolf Sieber (married in '24), whom she never divorced; there were other loves in her life—France's great Jean Gabin, primarily, and also John Wayne—but she and Sieber, having an "understanding," remained devoted friends until his death; seven years (1931–37) the queen of the Paramount lot, she was then labeled, by U.S. exhibitors, "box office poison"; made them look foolish two years later by discarding her stereotyped persona and bursting boisterously forth as Western saloon hostess Frenchy in *Destry Rides Again*, which gave her a whole new career; proudly Germanic but vehemently anti-Nazi, she became an American citizen in '38; during WW II made a prodigious contribution to the Allied efforts: sold war bonds on nationwide tours and entertained troops (singing, joking, playing the musical saw) throughout the European Theater, often as near the front as a civilian was permitted; Congress awarded her a well-deserved Medal of Honor and France made her a Chevaliere of the Legion.

MOVIE HIGHLIGHTS: *The Blue Angel, Morocco, Shanghai Express, Blonde Venus, Desire, Angel, Knight Without Armor, Seven Sinners, The Flame of New Orleans, Manpower, The Spoilers, Pittsburgh, Kismet, Golden Earrings, A Foreign Affair, Rancho Notorious, Witness for the Prosecution, Touch of Evil, Judgment at Nuremberg.*

Richard Dix

(b. Ernest Carlton Brimmer, Aug. 8, 1893, St. Paul, Minn.; d. Sept. 20, 1949) A thorough man's man—and a good man in fight (in countless

Grade A Westerns) and frolic (Hollywood's number 1 playboy till he married for the first time at 40)—his staying power as a star was remarkable; was on screen in leads in 97 movies from 1921's *Not Guilty* to 1947's *The 13th Hour*; after *Cimarron* ('31) rated him an Oscar nomination, his fame, fortune, and personal wealth were second to none in the movie capital—in the depths of the Depression his annual salary was upwards of $250,000; while enjoying luxurious living, he invested and saved much of it—left a $3 million estate; was proud of the fact that his Brimmer ancestors came to America aboard the *Mayflower*; slated to be a surgeon, he got the acting bug doing plays at the University of Minnesota, where he was also a football hero; went on the stage in his teens, gained stock experience in Pennsylvania and Canada, and made his Broadway debut at 21 in a minor role in *The Hawk*; footlight fame followed quickly, as did movie stardom; putting him over the top was the fifth film he made in his first year, *The Sin Flood* ("an exquisite bloom in a desert of mediocrity," said one critic); projected in it the stalwart masculine personality that male and female fans found appealing for decades; his first wife (1931–33), by whom he had a daughter, Martha, was one-time shop girl Winifred Coe; an adopted child, she met the star because her foster brother's wife's sister was married to Dix's brother; was wed from '34 on to his former secretary, Virginia Webster; had twin sons, Robert (once briefly an actor) and Richard (now deceased), and adopted a daughter, Sara Sue.

MOVIE HIGHLIGHTS: *The Glorious Fool, Call of the Canyon, The Christian, The Ten Commandments, Moran of the Marines* (silents), *Seven Keys to Baldpate, Donovan's Kid, The Lost Squadron, Stingaree, The Devil's Squadron, Blind Alibi, Man of Conquest, Cherokee Strip, American Empire, Mark of the Whistler* (and four others in the Columbia series).

Robert Donat

(b. Robert Donat, March 18, 1905, Withington, Manchester, England; d. June 9, 1958) Modest, handsome star who, in *Goodbye, Mr. Chips*, beat out Gable (in *GWTW*) for the Best Actor Oscar; severe asthma attacks hampered his career—oxygen tanks were always at hand when he performed; starred in only 19 films in 25 years on screen; blessed with an exquisite speaking voice, this son of a shipping clerk made his professional stage debut in Birmingham at 16, playing Lucius in *Julius Caesar*; always alternated between stage and screen; made his London stage debut in '31 in *Knave and Queen*; first came to the attention of American movie audiences as Thomas Culpepper, Charles Laughton's love rival in *The Private Life of Henry VIII*; his next, *The Count of Monte Cristo*, in '34, was the only film he ever made in Hollywood; as he was tall (6'), dashing, and an expert fencer, Warners sought to star him in both *Captain Blood* and *The Adventures of Robin Hood* but, disliking Hollywood and its climate that aggravated his asthma, he declined—to Flynn's advantage; often performed at the Old Vic, where his greatest success was as Becket in T. S. Eliot's *Murder in the Cathedral*; had two failed marriages—to actress Ella Voysey (1929–48), mother of his three children, then to actress Renee Asherson, who co-starred with him in two pictures; made his final film, *The Inn of the Sixth Happiness*, playing an ancient Chinese mandarin, knowing he was dying; his last scene was a death scene; to Ingrid Bergman (as a missionary), he said: "Stay here for a time. It will comfort me as I leave to know it. We shall never see each other again, I think. Farewell."

MOVIE HIGHLIGHTS: *Men of Tomorrow, That Night in London, The 39 Steps, The Ghost Goes West, Knight Without Armour, The Citadel* (Oscar nominated), *Young Mr. Pitt, The Winslow Boy, The Magic Box, Lease of Life, The Cure for Love*.

Brian Donlevy

(b. Brian Waldo Donlevy, Feb. 9, 1899, Portadown, County Armagh, Ireland; d. April 5, 1972) Chesty, ham-fisted, and (on film) brawling for a fight, he played the blackest-hearted villains in the '30s—classic example: sadistic Sergeant Markov in *Beau Geste*—before becoming, in the '40s, a big-hearted hero (*The Great McGinty* softened him up for that); brought to America at 2, he grew up in Wisconsin and, at 17, ran away to join General Pershing's Mexican expedition against Pancho Villa; after a dozen years of playing comedy drunks on Broadway and minor parts in two '29 movies (*Mother's Day* and *Gentlemen of the Press*), he was launched in Hollywood in 1935's *Barbary Coast*—playing gangster Edward G. Robinson's chief henchman, a killer named Knuckles; was strange casting for a poetry-writing onetime aviator ace in the legendary Lafayette Escadrille—and even stranger for a guy whose handsome "all-American" face made him New York's best-known male model in the '20s, posing mostly for

Arrow shirt-collar ads and the illustrated covers of *The Saturday Evening Post*; for *Barbary Coast*, the costume department outfitted him in the black shirt Gable wore in *Call of the Wild*; confident that it would bring him luck, the superstitious neophyte stole it and wore it for years; winning a 20th Century–Fox contract, he played heroes in a few B's but was relentlessly cast in A's as a heavy; privately was an easygoing, quiet-spoken "softie"; divorced from his first wife in his 20s, he was then wed (1936–47) to singer Marjorie Lane, who dubbed the movie songs of Harlow and Eleanor Powell (one child: Judith), and finally, in '66, to Lillian Lugosi, Bela's widow; earned millions—left an estate of $8,000.

MOVIE HIGHLIGHTS: *Midnight Taxi, 36 Hours to Kill, In Old Chicago, Human Cargo, Jesse James, Destry Rides Again, Union Pacific, Allegheny Uprising, I Wanted Wings, Billy the Kid, The Great Man's Lady, Wake Island, The Glass Key, The Miracle of Morgan's Creek, Two Years Before the Mast, An American Romance, Command Decision, Never So Few.*

Melvyn Douglas

(b. Melvyn Edouard Hesselberg, April 5, 1901, Macon, Ga.; d. Aug. 3, 1981) Segued from sophisticated leading men roles ("He knows just how to be exquisitely insolent," said one critic) to a splendid second career as a character actor, winning two Best Supporting Actor Oscars—for *Hud* and *Being There*; was nominated as Best Actor in *I Never Sang for My Father*; also won a Broadway Tony for *The Best Man*; son of a Russian-born, internationally known concert pianist-composer, Edouard Hesselberg; his father hoped he'd be a musician, his Kentucky-born mother wanted him to study law, he wanted to be a poet—they compromised; following service as a medical corpsman in WW I, he acted in repertory in the Midwest while supporting himself as a gas meter reader; was briefly wed to Rosalind Hitower, by whom he had a son, Gregory; met his second wife, Helen Gahagan, when they co-starred on Broadway in *Tonight or Never*, which, in '31, marked his screen debut—but with Gloria Swanson opposite; that same year, he and Gahagan married (on his birthday) and were together until her death in '80; both were active in politics long before she was elected (in '44 and '46) a U.S. Congresswoman from California; their children: Peter and Mary; was appointed a California State Commissioner of Relief in '39; his early anti-Nazi league activities caused Berlin to ban MGM movies; did three years of WW II military duty as an army officer in the China–Burma–India theater.

MOVIE HIGHLIGHTS: *As You Desire Me, Counsellor-at-Law, Theodora Goes Wild, I Met Him in Paris, Angel, The Shining Hour, Ninotchka, Too Many Husbands, We Were Dancing, Mr. Blandings Builds His Dream House, Sea of Grass, Inherit the Wind, The Best Man, The Americanization of Emily, The Candidate, One is a Lonely Number, The Seduction of Joe Tynan.*

Marie Dressler

(b. Leila Koerber, Nov. 9, 1869, Cobourg, Ont., Canada; d. July 28, 1934) In 1933, when Hollywood put its highest premium on golden youth, this well-wrinkled, 5'8", 60-ish woman—with the mouth of a whale, the jowl of an elephant, and the heft of a hippo—was #1 at the box office and the best-loved woman on the screen; but no silk-shawled sugar of a grandmother she, being loud, rowdy, filled with life and the love of life; her triumphant second crack at fame was fairytale stuff; had been a hugely popular comic in vaudeville and silent movies (*Tillie's Punctured Romance*, '14); in 1916, after 33 years as a trouper, she was dropped from a Broadway show during rehearsals because, the producers said, the public wanted new faces; a rocky decade followed until finally, on her uppers, she was checking Want Ads for a housekeeper's job; a scriptwriter pal, Frances Marion, penned a riotous comedy for her, *The Callahans and the Murphys*, and persuaded Metro to sign her (at $1500 a week) and pair her with Polly Moran; she was off to the races—again; was so cherished by the public that one year ('30) she headlined in no fewer than ten features, including the immortal *Anna Christie* (as barfly Marthy, stealing all her scenes with Garbo) and *Min and Bill*, which won her a Best Actress Oscar; got another nomination in *Emma* two years later; never married; loved and lived for 20 years with attorney Jim Dalton, her manager, but they could not marry for he had a wife who denied him a divorce—and claimed him for burial when he died; made six movies after learning in '31 that she was terminally ill with cancer.

MOVIE HIGHLIGHTS: *The Patsy, Vagabond Lover, Caught Short, Let*

Us Be Gay, Chasing Rainbows, One Romantic Night, Call of the Flesh, Politics, Reducing, Prosperity, Derelict, The Late Christopher Bean, Dinner at 8.

Ellen Drew

(b. Terry Ray, Nov. 23, 1915, Kansas City, Mo.) With that enchanting smile, it mattered little if she could act—and she could, in comedy *(Christmas in July)* and costume drama *(If I Were King)*; full-lipped, with expressive hazel eyes and a mirthful personality, she possessed a particularly special charm and early gave exciting promise of becoming a glamorous comedienne in the Colbert vein; growing up in Chicago as the daughter of a barber, she went to Hollywood in her late teens, after winning a beauty contest, hopeful of becoming an actress—and worked as a carhop at a drive-in; under her real name, she finally landed bit parts in two dozen 1936–38 films: *Rose Bowl, The Buccaneer*, etc., including Bing Crosby's *Rhythm on the Range*; character actor William Demarest, then an agent, discovered her and got her a contract at Paramount, where her first major role was that of Crosby's leading lady in *Sing You Sinners*; at Paramount through '44, she was later under contract at both RKO and Columbia, starring in 41 movies before leaving the screen after 1951's *Man in the Saddle*; her only film comeback was a supporting role in Dane Clark's *Outlaw's Son* in '57 but, between '52 and '61, she was the guest star in many TV series ("Schlitz Playhouse," "Ford Theatre," etc.); married first (1935–40) to Hollywood make-up man Fred Wallace (child: David), she was later wed ('41) to scriptwriter Sy Bartlett; filing for divorce in '46, they reconciled, then eventually divorced in '50; that stormy union was followed by another (1951–66), to millionaire William T. Walker (their battles sometimes made headlines); in '71 became the wife of wealthy James Edward Herbert, former Motorola executive, and retired to Palm Desert, Calif.

MOVIE HIGHLIGHTS: *The Lady's From Kentucky, Geronimo, French Without Tears, Buck Benny Rides Again, The Mad Doctor, Reaching for the Sun, Our Wife, The Remarkable Andrew, My Favorite Spy, Dark Mountain, Isle of the Dead, The Swordsman, Johnny O'Clock, Stars in My Crown.*

James Dunn

(b. James Howard Dunn, Nov. 2, 1901, New York, N.Y.; d. Sept. 1, 1967) The most charming of Irishmen, he deservedly won a Best Supporting Oscar playing just that—lovable, hard-drinking Johnny Nolan in *A Tree Grows in Brooklyn* ('45), when Hollywood said he was "washed up"; simultaneously with his Academy Award, he won another "second chance" that brought even more lasting happiness; on March 7, 1945, he married singer Edna Rush, a beautiful brunette with whom he fell in love when they first met in '26, backstage at a theater in, appropriately, Brooklyn; as he was then only an extra in movies made in New York, they agreed to "wait"; years passed—she married someone else and he went through two divorces, from Edna D'Olier and movie actress Frances Gifford ("Subconsciously, I was always comparing every other woman to Edna"); in '41, when his screen career was on the skids, he went to Broadway and starred for 87 SRO weeks in the musical *Panama Hattie* (that triumph still cutting no ice in Hollywood), met his first love again and, to his pleasure, discovered she was again free; the son of a stockbroker who "either had a million or nothing," he grew up in New Rochelle, N.Y., next door to the vaudeville-famous Eddie Foy family—the Foy kids being his best friends—which inspired him to go on the stage; was a hoofer on Broadway before his debut movie, *Bad Girl* ('31), in which he played the lead, made him an overnight sensation; after five years of major stardom came scores of leads in B's before the Oscar put him back on top; headlined last on TV in a 1954–56 sitcom, "It's a Great Life," which he claimed it always was for him.

MOVIE HIGHLIGHTS: *Dance Team, Sob Sister, Walking Down Broadway, Jimmy and Sally, A Sailor's Luck, Bad Boy, Baby Take a Bow, Bright Eyes, Stand Up and Cheer, She Learned About Sailors, George White's Scandals of 1935, The Darling Young Man, Hearts in Bondage, Shadows Over Shanghai, The Living Ghost, Government Girl, Killer McCoy.*

Irene Dunne

(b. Irene Marie Dunne, Dec. 20, 1901, Louisville, Ky.) Beautiful—in face, figure, style, talent, and life; and when, with an amused, mischievous twinkle in her eye, she put tongue in cheek, her leading man was about to be rocked to his socks or reeled in; starred for 22 years, in 40 pictures, from *Leatherstocking* ('30) to *It Grows on Trees* ('52); ran the gamut: musicals *(Show Boat)*, sentimental dramas *(Magnificent Obsession)*, comedies stylish *(My Favorite Wife)* or screwball *(Theodora Goes Wild)*; even played elderly Queen Victoria, splendidly, in *The Mudlark*; was Oscar-nominated as Best Actress for *Cimarron*, *The Awful Truth*, *Theodora Goes Wild*, *Love Affair*, *I Remember Mama*; the latter two films remain her favorites; favorite leading men: Charles Boyer and Cary Grant; Catholic and convent-educated at St. Louis' Loretta Academy, she later graduated from Chicago Musical College; dreamed of singing soprano at the Met; this ambition thwarted as she failed the audition, she turned to the musical stage, first singing in the chorus of *Irene* ('20) on Broadway and, finally, starring as Magnolia in the Chicago company of *Show Boat* ('29); with her second movie role, Sabra in *Cimarron*, aging from 17 to 80, she became a front-rank star; sang first on the screen in *Stingaree*, a big-budget Western with Richard Dix; commanded a huge salary: $400,000 annually at her peak; led an exemplary private life; was married to her one husband, Dr. Francis D. Griffin, a noted dentist, from '28 until his death in '65; adopted a daughter, Mary Frances; investing her earnings wisely in shopping centers and other real estate, the doctor made her a very wealthy woman; many of her best films were remade, and there are copyright entanglements, so TV viewers have rarely, if ever, had the privilege of seeing her in *Roberta*, *Love Affair*, *Anna and the King of Siam*, etc.

MOVIE HIGHLIGHTS: *Thirteen Women, The Silver Cord, The Age of Innocence, Sweet Adeline, High, Wide and Handsome, Joy of Living, Penny Serenade, A Guy Named Joe, Together Again, The White Cliffs of Dover, Life With Father, Never a Dull Moment.*

Jimmy Durante

(b. James Francis Durante, Feb. 10, 1893, New York, N.Y.; d. Jan. 29, 1980) Great nose, great heart, great fun; *Schnozzola*, his nickname, was the title of his biography; "There's a million good-lookin' guys but I'm a novelty," he gleefully insisted; a true clown, he eschewed vulgarity and insult humor, poking fun only at himself and drawing upon boundless energy and his inexhaustible good will; sporting a battered fedora and doing that inimitable penguin strut, he merrily made his way through a million deliveries of "Inka Dinka Doo," and fans never wearied of it; was a star in every medium: movies, clubs, vaudeville, records, theater, radio, and television; the Bowery-born son of Italian immigrant parents, he earned a fortune but gave much of it away to good causes; helped out as a kid in the family barbershop, peddled newspapers, even gave photoengraving a try before breaking into showbiz at 17 as a $25-a-week piano player, sometimes accompanying singing waiter Eddie Cantor; soon was a member of the nightclub comedy team of (Lou) Clayton, (Eddie) Jackson, and Durante, which debuted on Broadway in Ziegfeld's *Show Girl* ('28), then in the movie *Roadhouse Nights* ('29); went solo in '30; was wed to singer Jeanne Olsen from '16 until her death in '43, then, from '60 on, to Marge Little, with whom he adopted a daughter, CeCe Alicia, in '61; "Goodnight, Mrs. Calabash, wherever you are" was his famous sign-off, but fans never learned who she was, or even if she was real; always said, "I like to make people laugh. Dey like me. What more could I want?"

MOVIE HIGHLIGHTS: *Cuban Love Song, Blondie of the Follies, Hollywood Party, Sally, Irene and Mary, The Man Who Came to Dinner, Two Girls and a Sailor, Ziegfeld Follies, Two Sisters from Boston, On an Island with You, The Yellow Cab Man, Jumbo, It's a Mad, Mad, Mad, Mad World.*

Deanna Durbin

(b. Edna Mae Durbin, Dec. 4, 1921, Winnipeg, Canada) As a teenager, dark-haired and golden-voiced, with a refreshingly aggressive personality, she was such a huge and instantaneous favorite with fans that, singlehandedly and quite literally, she saved Universal Pictures from bankruptcy; a pair of '37 films, *One Hundred Men and a Girl* and *Three Smart Girls*, rating her a special Oscar, started the popularity avalanche; perhaps the only person in the world who did not appreciate her singing was irascible W. C. Fields, who lived next door in Westwood and loathed hearing her rehearse; no one admired her more than British Prime Minister Winston Churchill, who often had her pictures screened privately; was first on screen at 15 in a musical short, *Every Sunday*, with another hopeful, Judy Garland, the one MGM opted to put under contract with, as it turned out, first glorious, then disastrous consequences (nervous breakdowns, suicide attempts, etc.); equally famous at her own studio, this star, having wise parents and career advisors, and being a cheerfully staunch soul herself, suffered no such personal misfortunes; before voluntarily retiring from the screen at 27, she sailed smoothly through 21 hits; in '48 was America's highest-paid woman, earning $323,000; fans applauded her "storybook" wedding at 19 to handsome young studio exec Vaughn Paul (but they divorced two years later), and were appalled when, at 23, she became the fourth wife of producer Felix Jackson, 43; had a daughter, Jessica, before divorcing in '48; in '50, married (lastingly) a still older director, Charles David, settled in France, had a son, Peter, and—still slender, lovely, and French-speaking— lives in stylish, guarded seclusion; laughingly, she refers to the girl she was as "a fairytale character."

MOVIE HIGHLIGHTS: *Mad About Music, That Certain Age, It's a Date, Spring Parade, Nice Girl?, It Started With Eve, His Butler's Sister, Hers to Hold, Christmas Holiday, Lady on a Train, Because of Him, Something in the Wind, Up in Central Park, For the Love of Mary.*

Ann Dvorak

(b. Ann McKim, Aug. 2, 1912, New York, N.Y.; d. Dec. 10, 1979) Star reminiscent of Crawford, dark-haired, with a ferociously kinetic acting style, who might have given Bette Davis a run for the money at Warners; she didn't because she possessed a temperament that matched (at least) her talent and studio boss Jack Warner, finally fed up, gave her the gate; the daughter of Shakespearean actor Edward McKim, she took her screen name from Bohemian ancestors of her mother's; made her movie debut as a child actress in 1920's *The Five Dollar Plate* and did many small roles in silents while attending Hollywood High; landing a job as assistant dance director at MGM, she hoofed in the chorus of 1929's *Hollywood Revue* and soon became the protegee of Joan Crawford; another actress friend, Karen Morley, introduced her to Howard Hughes, who gave her leads in two '32 films, *Sky Devils* and the classic *Scarface*, her work so impressing Warners that the studio bought her contract from him; WB cast her in sudsy dramas, mostly B's, and frequently as a wayward woman; married British actor-director Leslie Fenton in '32; was with him in England throughout WW II; a member of the Women's Land Army she was an ambulance driver during the blitz while he commanded MTB boats until, severely wounded in the raid at St. Nazaire, he was assigned to the Ministry of Information; starred in a few morale-boosting films while in England (*Squadron Leader X, Escape to Danger,* etc.); divorced in '45, soon after her return to Hollywood, she was later (1947–50) married to Russian-born dancer Igor Dega, whom she met when he was hired as her dancing partner in *The Bachelor's Daughters*; career continued through '51; married Nicholas Wade, president of a chemical company, retired to Hawaii.

MOVIE HIGHLIGHTS: *Three on a Match, Love Is a Racket, The Crowd Roars, Midnight Alibi, Side Streets, G-Men, Dr. Socrates, Midnight Court, Merrily We Live, Stronger Than Desire, Flame of the Barbary Coast, Abilene Town, The Long Night, Out of the Blue, The Affairs of Bel Ami, Walls of Jericho, Our Very Own, A Life of Her Own.*

Nelson Eddy

(b. Nelson Eddy, June 29, 1901, Providence, R.I.; d. March 6, 1967) Blond baritone, a descendant of Pres. Martin Van Buren, became a movie heartthrob in his 30s; son of an inventor; first job: telephone operator at the Mott Iron Works in his home town; after working in the art department of the *Philadelphia Press,* was for five years a reporter and copy reader on that city's *Evening Ledger* and *Bulletin;* next wrote advertising copy for a big agency but was fired because, also studying opera, he paid too much attention to music; first sang in public as a boy soprano at Grace and All Saints' Churches in Providence; learned operatic arias, at the start, from phonograph records; after grammar school was night-school educated; made his stage debut in '22 in a society show, *The Marriage Tax;* in '33, at a Los Angeles auditorium, was a last-minute substitute for a scheduled opera star who had fallen critically ill; an unknown, he was obliged to give 14 encores; within the week MGM signed him for movies; sang his first song for the screen, "That's the Rhythm of the Day," in Crawford's *Dancing Lady;* teamed for the first time in 1935's *Naughty Marietta,* he and Jeanette MacDonald were an overnight sensation, with fans demanding to see them together again in a long string of operettas; moviegoers were less enthralled when he later sang with other sopranos—Rise Stevens in *The Chocolate Soldier,* Ilona Massey in *Balalaika,* and Susanna Foster in *The Phantom of the Opera;* on Jan. 19, 1939, for the first and only time, he was married—to Ann Franklin, former wife of director Sidney Franklin.

MOVIE HIGHLIGHTS: *Broadway to Hollywood, Rose Marie, Rosalie, Girl of the Golden West, Sweethearts, New Moon, Bittersweet, I Married an Angel, Knickerbocker Holiday, Make Mine Music, Northwest Outpost.*

Sally Eilers

(b. Dorothea Sally Eilers, Dec. 11, 1908, New York, N.Y.; d. Jan. 5, 1978) Her performance as the appealing young tenement bride in *Bad Girl* ('31) made this blonde an instant star after four years of playing ingenues in Mack Sennett comedies *(The Goodbye Kiss)* and heroines in Westerns *(Roaring Ranch)* starring Hoot Gibson; was married to the cowboy star 1930–33; Sennett discovered her in a studio commissary while lunching with a young friend, an actress named Jane Peters (later to be famous as Carole Lombard), who was in her graduating class at Hollywood's Fairfax High; had begun playing extras in silents while still in school (and a brunette) with the aid of star Marian Nixon; reciprocated the favor later—when Nixon's career was faltering, Eilers managed to get her a new contract at Fox; known always to be frank, honest, and ambitious, Eilers was adored by the Hollywood press; "My life is about as private as an exhibit at the World's Fair," she laughed, "but I like the limelight—I'm a girl who yearned to be an actress and got her wish"; second husband, for a decade, was producer Harry Joe Brown; child: Harry Jr.; career as an in-demand star lasted through 1939's *Full Confession*; appeared in just four during the '40s *(Strange Illusion, Coroner Creek, etc.)*, then retired after 1950's *Stage to Tucson*; was divorced twice more—from Navy Capt. Howard Barney and director John Hollingsworth Morse; age altered her looks (drastically) but not her wacky sense of humor; when old pal Gloria Swanson toured in her last play, Eilers was unrecognized by her when visiting backstage to have her program autographed; to Swanson, she said, "Oh, just sign it to Mrs. Hoot Gibson from Mrs. Wallace Beery"—dropping the names of both their first spouses.

MOVIE HIGHLIGHTS: *Let Us Be Gay, Dance Team, Hat Check Girl, State Fair, Walls of Gold, Bad Boy, Sailor's Luck, She Made Her Bed, Carnival, Strike Me Pink, Florida Special, Alias Mary Dow, Without Orders, Condemned Women, Tarnished Angels, They Made Her a Spy.*

James Ellison

(b. James Ellison Smith, May 4, 1910, Valier, Mont.) Handsome, big and brawny guy (6'3", 185 lbs.) who was a great favorite with the Saturday afternoon brigade as the ever-smiling, two-fisted hero of countless B pictures (*Annapolis Salute, Army Surgeon*), serials (*The Desert Hawk*), and Westerns (*Call of the Prairie*, etc.); born on a ranch (though he went to high school in Hollywood), it is only natural that he was so at ease in chaps and spurs; in his early movie years, he was eight times the young saddlemate, Johnny Nelson, of Bill "Hopalong Cassidy" Boyd (*Bar 20 Rides Again, Hopalong Cassidy Returns*, etc.); prior to that, he had studied nights at the Pasadena Playhouse, winning a screen test, while working days as a film developer in the laboratory at Warner Bros.; was the first to see his initial test—printed it himself "and it was awful; I knew I was doomed to remain in the lab"; more training resulted in a new test and a false start in pictures—a few minor parts while under contract at Metro (*Reckless, The Winning Ticket*, etc.), before his option was dropped; a childhood ambition had been to be a National Park Ranger, which was his renewed intention when rediscovered for the Cassidy shoot-'em-ups; De Mille's *The Plainsman*, the actor's first big-budget Western, put him on the map; the famous director stunned Hollywood, after testing Fred MacMurray and Randolph Scott, by casting the neophyte as young Buffalo Bill; despite good notices, major fame never came his way, but other movies did—dozens—right through '52; from '33 until her death in '70 was wed to Gertrude Durkin (one son and a daughter, now deceased); later married onetime ballerina Shelly Keats.

MOVIE HIGHLIGHTS: *Vivacious Lady, Mother Carey's Chickens, Hotel for Women, Fifth Avenue Girl, Anne of Windy Poplars, You Can't Fool Your Wife, Charley's Aunt, I Walked with a Zombie, The Gang's All Here, Trocadero, The Undying Monster, Calendar Girl, The Hammond Mystery, I Killed Geronimo.*

Stuart Erwin

(b. Stuart Erwin, Feb. 14, 1902, Squaw Valley, Calif.; d. Dec. 21, 1967) His friendly, folksy, hometown face was one that, for decades, movie audiences were always pleased to see, from 1928's *Mother Knows Best* right through 1964's *The Misadventures of Merlin Jones*; quintessential Erwin roles were those of the Yankee milkman, Howie Newsome, in *Our Town*, Judy Garland's football-playing hayseed brother in *Pigskin Parade* (rated him a Best Supporting Oscar nomination), and the lead as the movie-mad bumpkin in *Make Me a Star* (the talkie remake of *Merton of the Movies*); after graduating from the University of California at Berkeley, he studied at the Egan Dramatic School in Hollywood, making his professional debut there in '24 in *White Collars*; for the next four years, before crashing movies, he was a stage manager and actor in Los Angeles stock companies; surprised more than a few in '31 by wooing and winning the lovely June Collyer, who had played romantic leads opposite Gary Cooper and Richard Dix, and was among the most sought-after beauties in Hollywood; had two children: Stuart Jr., who became a producer, and Judy; in the '50s (1950–55), he and his wife joined professional forces to star in an ABC-TV sitcom, "The Stu Erwin Show" (first known as "Life with the Erwins," and later "The Trouble with Father") which, said a critic, was "perhaps the leading bumbling-father series" of the time; they also played together in summer theaters; on his own, between movies, the actor starred on Broadway in *Mr. Sycamore* and *Great to be Alive*, and on a later TV series, "The Greatest Show on Earth"; his motion pictures finally totaled more than 125.

MOVIE HIGHLIGHTS: *Sweetie, Young Eagles, Love Among the Millionaires, Going Hollywood, Hold Your Man, Joe Palooka, Viva Villa!, Chained, Three Men on a Horse, All American Chump, Slim, Checkers, Mr. Boggs Steps Out, Small Town Boy, Three Blind Mice, Hollywood Cavalcade, He Hired the Boss, Father Is a Bachelor.*

Madge Evans

(b. Margherita Evans, July 1, 1909, New York, N.Y.; d. April 26, 1981) Born gorgeous and heavenly blonde, she first won notice by posing in the nude—she was the famous "Fairy Soap" baby in magazine ads; further modeling resulted, first, in bits in early silents and then to her becoming, at six, a child star in movies, playing Pauline Frederick's daughter in *Zaza*; this was followed by juvenile leads in 27 more silents (*Seven Sisters, Little Duchess, Sudden Riches*, etc.) before she turned 15; that year, she starred on Broadway in *Daisy Mayme*, remaining on the stage until she was 22;

returned to movies then as a leading lady, via the backdoor; helping out an actor making his screen test in New York, she was offered an MGM contract, while he was rejected; new career began with the romantic lead opposite Ramon Novarro in *Son of India*; charm, talent, and a most distinctive face made her immediately popular; one year, '33, she played leads in 10 movies, including the classic *Dinner at Eight*; at Metro for seven years, she starred in 37 films, a number of them being made on loan-out, such as *Mayor of Hell* with Cagney at Warners, *Stand Up and Cheer* with Shirley Temple at Fox, and *Men Without Names* with Fred MacMurray at Paramount; following her MGM swan song, *The Thirteenth Chair*, she starred in two B's elsewhere in '38—*Sinners in Paradise* opposite John Boles at Universal and, with Preston Foster, *Army Girl* at Republic; that same year, leaving the screen for good, she starred on Broadway in *Here Come the Clowns*; marrying famed playwright Sidney *(Dead End)* Kingsley in '39 (no children), she last appeared on the stage in '43 in *The Patriots*, written by her husband, and never acted again.

MOVIE HIGHLIGHTS: *Sporting Blood, West of Broadway, Good Times, Beauty for Sale, Hell Below, When Ladies Meet, Hallelujah I'm a Bum, What Every Woman Knows, David Copperfield, Death on the Diamond, Age of Indiscretion, Piccadilly Jim, Pennies from Heaven, The Show-Off.*

Douglas Fairbanks Jr.

(b. Douglas Elton Ullman, Jr., Dec. 9, 1907, New York, N.Y.) Few stars other than his famous daredevil dad ever seemed to find such joy in his work, and be able to communicate it to the public; his handsome grin, blithe spirit, and dashing, debonair manner together made him forever likable and memorable; has also always had the gift of friendship; Mary Pickford was his adored stepmother for 15 years after he turned 12; as long as she lived—she died at 86—she was the first person he saw when visiting Hollywood, and he was always her Pickfair houseguest; he and Joan Crawford, the first of his two wives (1929–33), remained forever in touch, and on most cordial terms; and, in the 25 years he and second wife Mary Lee Epling Hartford lived in England, they were members of the queen's most intimate social circle; after attending military schools in New York and Los Angeles, he made his movie debut at 16—over his father's protests— in *Stephen Steps Out*; played leads in another 17 films of the '20s (*Stella*

Dallas, *The Barker*, *The Jazz Age*, etc.); truly came into his own in the '30s in swashbucklers *(The Prisoner of Zenda)*, gangster pix *(Little Caesar)*, tony comedies *(Having Wonderful Time)*, action epics *(Gunga Din)*; was versatile enough to take on any assignment, being adept at fencing, boxing, wrestling, singing, and playing piano; heroic roles were not restricted to the screen; commanding a flotilla of British raiding craft in WW II, he was in 20 major military engagements; was awarded the DSC and made an honorary Knight of the Order of the British Empire; married to his present wife since '39, he has three daughters: Daphne, Victoria, and Melissa; a biography of him, *Knight Errant*, was published in '55.

MOVIE HIGHLIGHTS: *Outward Bound, Party Girl, Morning Glory, Catherine the Great, Union Depot, Joy of Living, The Young in Heart, Rage of Paris, Rulers of the Sea, The Sun Never Sets, Angels Over Broadway, Safari, The Corsican Brothers, Sinbad the Sailor, The Exile, That Lady in Ermine, Mr. Drake's Duck, Ghost Story.*

Frances Farmer

(b. Frances Elena Farmer, Sept. 19, 1913, Seattle, Wash.; d. Aug. 1, 1970) Paramount's volatile, vastly talented (though ill-used), classically beautiful blonde star whose tormented life has been grist for the media in the '80s; her tragedy—alcoholism and seven harrowing years in the violent wards of Washington State Asylum (committed there by her wildly neurotic mother)—has been chronicled in plays, TV dramas, movies (portraying the star in *Frances* in '82, Jessica Lange rated an Oscar nomination as Best Actress), and books (the most believable by far being *Look Back in Love* by Edith Farmer Elliot, her sister); the sister contends, perhaps accurately, that the actress's "mental illness" was actually a misdiagnosed case of hypoglycemia, biochemical in nature, and could have been "cured and controlled through proper diagnosis and diet"; created her most memorable performance in '36, her first year on screen, in Goldwyn's *Come and Get It*, in a dual role—saloon singer–mother and her society-belle daughter; played leads in 14 films through 1942's *Son of Fury* with Tyrone Power but never had another role to equal it; harboring a violent hate for the "phoniness" of Hollywood and the studio system, she fled to Broadway in '37 and scored a rousing success in *Golden Boy*; after an aborted love affair with its author, Clifford Odets, she returned to Hollywood—to her husband, actor

Leif Erickson, whom she soon divorced, to her $200,000-a-year contract, to drunk and disorderly arrests, and a crack-up; recovered, she was on "The Ed Sullivan Show" as a folk singer, had two more failed marriages, played a character role in a B movie, *The Party Crashers* (at, ironically, Paramount), and finally emceed old movies on a TV show in Indianapolis.

MOVIE HIGHLIGHTS: *Too Many Parents, Border Flight, Rhythm on the Range, Exclusive, The Toast of New York, Ebb Tide, Ride a Crooked Mile, South of Pago Pago, World Premiere, Flowing Gold, Among the Living, Badlands of Dakota.*

Charles Farrell

(b. Charles Farrell, Aug. 9, 1901, Onset Bay, Maine) Rugged guy who rose from extra (in *Rosita*, '23) to star (*Sandy*, '26), and fooled everyone by not marrying Janet Gaynor (not that he didn't try—she changed her mind at the last minute and married someone else); they teamed so romantically in so many movies after 1927's *Seventh Heaven* that fans were confident their love was real; did 11 together (*Street Angel, Delicious*, etc.) before breaking up the act with 1934's *Change of Heart*; by then, the actor was well into a happy marriage with lovely actress Virginia Valli—wed in '31—that lasted until her death in '68; his friendship with Gaynor, though, persisted through the years and they lived not far from one another in Palm Springs; the son of a Boston movie house owner, he started in the theater—sweeping it and selling popcorn; after graduation from Boston University, he set out for Hollywood and, being big and good-looking (though devoid of acting training), made a rapid leap from bits to blockbuster fame; "Success came too soon for me," he said later. "I hadn't had the experience to go with the star status I suddenly acquired, which is one reason talking pictures frightened me"; nonetheless, his transition to talkies was an easy one; his popularity took a nosedive in the mid-'30s and, after a few B's, he tore up a $100,000 contract and took off to make pictures in Germany, Australia, France (*Liliom*), and England (*Scotland Yard Commands*); back in Hollywood in '38, he was in a handful of low-budget pix before quitting after 1942's *Deadly Game*; great new fame came later (1952–55) on TV as Gale Storm's silver-haired dad in "My Little Margie."

MOVIE HIGHLIGHTS: *City Girl, The Red Dance, Rough Riders, Sunny*

Side Up, Happy Days, High Society Blues, Merely Mary Ann, The Man Who Came Back, The First Year, Tess of the Storm Country, After Tomorrow, Wild Girl, Our Daily Bread, The Flying Doctor, Just Around the Corner, Convoy, Tail Spin, Treachery on the High Seas.

Glenda Farrell

(b. Glenda Farrell, June 30, 1904, Enid, Okla.; d. May 1, 1971) A gum-chewing blonde, with eyelashes long enough to sweep a street, she sprayed out side-splitters like a scattergun gone berserk; one of Warner Bros.' indispensibles in the '30s, she was often to be found in the "Gold Diggers" extravaganzas acting alongside best pal Joan Blondell; noting that she was that rare star who created a type, author Garson Kanin, her friend, has said, "She invented and developed that made-tough, uncompromising, knowing, wisecracking, undefeatable blonde"; started in '30 as Douglas Fairbanks Jr.'s dancer-sweetheart in *Little Caesar*, but her humor—as natural to her as breathing—soon surfaced; acting was her life: made her professional debut at 7 playing Little Eva in a stock company production of *Uncle Tom's Cabin*; a devout, lifelong Catholic, she was educated at Mount Carmel Academy in Wichita, then made her way to the New York stage via stock work in California; starred on Broadway after '29 in *Skidding* (debut), *Life Begins* (did the same role later on screen), and *On the Spot*, a great hit in which she was a gun moll, which took her to Hollywood; made 122 movies, the last being *Tiger by the Tail* ('69); created the memorable role of Torchy Blane, that dynamite newspaper reporter—hard-driving but soft-hearted—who always got her story but never got her man (police lieutenant Barton MacLane, her dream guy); played the part seven times (1936–39); eased gently into character roles when older; long the wife of Dr. Henry Ross, a West Point graduate, she is the only member of her profession whose grave is situated in the U.S. Military Academy's cemetery.

MOVIE HIGHLIGHTS: *I Am a Fugitive from a Chain Gang, Three On a Match, Lady for a Day, Personality Kid, Go Into Your Dance, A Man's Castle, Gold Diggers of 1935, Smart Blonde, Stolen Heaven, Blondes at Work, Torchy Blane in Chinatown, Johnny Eager, Talk of the Town, Twin Beds, Lulu Belle, Susan Slept Here, The Girl in the Red Velvet Swing.*

Alice Faye

(b. Alice Jeanne Leppert, May 5, 1912, New York, N.Y.) In her first nine movies, her studio presented her as a songbird carbon copy of Jean Harlow—platinum blonde with eyebrows razor-edge thin; softening process came in '36 with *Poor Little Rich Girl* and *Sing, Baby, Sing*, a vastly appealing personality emerged, the whole world fell in love with her, and a superstar was born; Henry King, her *In Old Chicago* director, has said her success secret was "a deep-seated human warmth, so genuine, so real that everyone felt it; it's truly a gift"; a star for 11 years, in 32 films, she introduced songs still sung around the globe ("You'll Never Know," "Hello, Frisco, Hello," etc.) and, in '38 and '39, was one of the Box Office Top Ten; born in Manhattan's "Hell's Kitchen," the daughter of a policeman, she crashed show business as a dancer at 13; later, hoofing in the chorus of *George White's Scandals*, she took her professional name—considering it lucky—from Frank Fay, then a top star; Rudy Vallee, star of this Broadway show, hired her to sing on his radio show, then in '34, when *Scandals* was filmed, he persuaded the studio to make her his leading lady; from '37 to '40 was married to tenor Tony Martin, her co-star in *You Can't Have Everything*, *Sing, Baby, Sing*, and *Sally, Irene and Mary*; long, happy marriage to orchestra leader Phil Harris began in '41 with two weddings—in Mexico in May, Galveston in Sept.; two daughters: Alice Jr., Phyllis; retired after a straight dramatic role in *Fallen Angel* ('45); returned to movies in '62 (mother role in the *State Fair* remake) and '78 *(The Magic of Lassie)*, and starred on Broadway in '74 in *Good News* with John Payne, her former leading man in musical movies.

MOVIE HIGHLIGHTS: *She Learned About Sailors, Every Night at Eight, King of Burlesque, On the Avenue, Wake Up and Sing, You're a Sweetheart, Alexander's Ragtime Band, Rose of Washington Square, Hollywood Cavalcade, Lillian Russell, Tin Pan Alley, Little Old New York, That Night in Rio, The Great American Broadcast, Hello, Frisco, Hello, The Gang's All Here.*

Stepin Fetchit

(b. Lincoln Theodore Perry, May 30, 1892, Key West, Fla.) Between '28 and '39, when his vogue ended, he was the top-billed, high-salaried black comic in 36 pictures, co-starring in four with Will Rogers (*David Harum*, *Steamboat 'Round the Bend*, etc.); in each he was the same—lanky, bald, shabbily dressed, simple-minded, whining, sleepy-eyed, clownish; with it all, though he was a great comedian, a master of stylization; contrary to prevailing opinion, he did not portray a placid "Tom"; black film historian Donald Bogle has noted that, instead, his characters "were coons, those lazy, forever-in-hot-water, natural-born comedian Negroes. Fetchit became the arch-coon, introducing to the screen a repertoire of antics and flamboyant poses that younger black comedians have used ever since"; speaking for himself, the actor said, "Like Charlie Chaplin, I played the part of a simple, sincere, honest, and lovable character who won sympathy from an audience by being tolerant of those who hurt him so that he could do good for those he loved"; in bios, he always cited his hobby as "making others happy"; playing the fool (to the chagrin of most blacks), he could laugh all the way to Hollywood's Bank of America; reportedly, he earned $1500 a week when black players as well known as Louise Beavers were paid less than $50 a day—and demanded that his Fox studio bosses pay his salary in cash; lived in grand style as a star, once employing 16 Chinese servants at his mansion and owning 12 luxurious cars, one a pink Cadillac; lost his fortune in the '40s; in Hollywood in '81, the National Film Society presented him the American Classic Screen Award and, putting aside his crutches to do the shuffle for which he was famous, the 89-year-old star received a deafening ovation.

MOVIE HIGHLIGHTS: *Hearts in Dixie, In Old Kentucky, Judge Priest, County Chairman, Carolina, Stand Up and Cheer, The World Moves On, The Virginia Judge, Charlie Chan in Egypt, Dimples, On the Avenue, Love Is News, The Galloping Ghost, Fifty Roads to Town, Zenobia;* later: *The Sun Shines Bright* ('53), *Amazing Grace* ('74).

W. C. Fields

(b. William Claude Dunkinfield, Feb. 10, 1879, Philadelphia, Pa.; d. Dec. 25, 1946) It was no gift to the world when this great cantankerous comedian—bibulous and bulbous-nosed—died on Christmas Day; hilariously for movie fans, he displayed, between 1915's *Pool Sharks* and *Sensations of 1945*, an unbridled loathing for cops, dogs, banks, preachers, and kids (though he left a large share of his $1.3 million estate to an orphanage); his hatred of authority figures started with his Cockney father, a fruit peddler and a bully, who beat him regularly before he ran away from home at 9; in his teens, having become a skillful juggler, he performed (soon adding jokes to his act) at carnivals, in circuses, vaudeville, and burlesque shows, eventually starring on Broadway in the Ziegfeld Follies; *You Can't Cheat an Honest Man* may have been the title of one of his hit movies, but he never believed it, for he was ever the accomplished con man; signing his Paramount contract, he demanded total script approval; for each picture, he would then secretly write several scripts, submit them under phony names, reject them, and collect his fee, and finally "approve" one; result: a windfall; the story that he spiked moppet star Baby LeRoy's milk with gin is true; so are reports of his own alcoholic intake—starting at breakfast, he often downed a fifth of gin daily; he was, he growled, "a reformed teetotaler"; was married early and briefly ("I believe in tying the marriage knot, as long as it's around the woman's neck"); actress Carlotta Monti, who later lived with him for years, penned the book *W. C. Fields & Me*, which was filmed, with Rod Steiger trying hard, and failing, to fill his spats.

MOVIE HIGHLIGHTS: *If I Had a Million, Tillie and Gus, Six of a Kind, You're Telling Me, The Old-Fashioned Way, It's a Gift, David Copperfield, Mississippi, Man on the Flying Trapeze, Poppy, The Bank Dick, My Little Chickadee, Never Give a Sucker an Even Break, Tales of Manhattan, Song of the Open Road.*

Geraldine Fitzgerald

(b. Geraldine Fitzgerald, Nov. 24, 1912, Dublin, Ireland) Arriving in Hollywood in the late '30s, after playing leads in English movies (*Mill on the Floss*, etc.), with a waystop on Broadway in *Heartbreak House*, the compelling green-eyed redhead announced that she meant to be a star—and immediately made good on her promise; in her first American movie, *Wuthering Heights*, she raced off with "most of the acting honors" (*New York Daily News*) and garnered an Oscar nomination as Best Support; starring roles followed in many films, all dramas, and many memorable now only for her beauty and intelligence; only in recent years, when she has played character parts, has her Gaelic gift of gaiety been allowed to shine; admitted early that she was "fearfully ambitious," an apparently inherited trait for her father was a brilliant barrister of Dublin; aspiring first to being a portrait painter, she studied at the Dublin School of Art, then was off to London where she modeled and failed as a commercial artist, finally returning to Ireland to win a scholarship at the Abbey Theater's School of Acting; made her professional debut at the Gate Theater as Isabella in *Wuthering Heights*, the same role that made her suddenly famous later in Hollywood; next made a number of British films, one being *Turn of the Tide*, which marked J. Arthur Rank's debut as a producer; career as a Hollywood star continued through *So Evil My Love* ('48); has since alternated between the stage, TV, and movies (*Arthur*, etc.); was first married (1936–46) to Edward Lindsay-Hogg; son Michael became an acclaimed TV director ("Brideshead Revisited"); has a daughter, Susan, by wealthy Stuart Scheftel, co-founder of New York's Pan-Am Building, her husband since '46.

MOVIE HIGHLIGHTS: *Dark Victory, Till We Meet Again, A Child Is Born, Shining Victory, The Gay Sisters, Watch on the Rhine, Wilson, Ladies Courageous, The Strange Affair of Uncle Harry, Nobody Lives Forever, Three Strangers, O.S.S., 10 North Frederick, The Pawnbroker, Rachel, Rachel, The Mango Tree.*

Errol Flynn

(b. Errol Leslie Flynn, June 20, 1909, Hobart, Tasmania; d. Oct. 14, 1959) *The Adventures of Robin Hood* captured for all time the essence of the screen persona of this prize package of a man—his devil-may-care charm, swashbuckling courage, athleticism, zest as a lover, and his immeasurable masculine beauty; the real man was not far removed from the one immortalized by the camera; his self-appraisal, like Robin's archery, was on the mark: "By instinct I'm an adventurer; by choice I'd like to be a writer; by pure, unadulterated luck I'm an actor"; when young, he fished for pearls in Tahiti and prospected for gold in New Zealand; he eventually published books, novels *(Beams End)* and an autobiography *(My Wicked, Wicked Ways)*; and, owning and sailing a schooner in the South Seas, he got into movies quite by accident—a director, meeting him as a real-life seaman, chose him, at 24, to play Fletcher Christian in an Australian film, *In the Wake of the Bounty*; next did a minor role in a British movie, *Murder at Monte Carlo*, prompting Warners to sign him to a $150-a-week contract; on board the liner to America, met French star Lili Damita, to whom he was later married (1935–40), tempestuously; son Sean became a news photographer, was taken prisoner by the Viet Cong in '71 and was never seen again; in '35 Warners, unable to get Robert Donat, gave Flynn the star-making title role in *Captain Blood* (almost lost it during production by his amateurish histrionics), and the rest was smooth sailing; second wife Nora Eddington (1943–49) presented him with two daughters, Deidre and Rory, and his third, Patrice Wymore (from '50 on), with another, Arnella Roma; lived as lavishly as an Arabian prince—died deeply in debt to the IRS.

MOVIE HIGHLIGHTS: *The Charge of the Light Brigade, Another Dawn, The Prince and the Pauper, The Sisters, Dawn Patrol, The Sea Hawk, Dodge City, The Private Lives of Elizabeth and Essex, Dive Bomber, They Died with Their Boots On, Gentleman Jim, Edge of Darkness, San Antonio, Cry Wolf, That Forsyte Woman, Rocky Mountain, Kim, The Sun Also Rises.*

Henry Fonda

(b. Henry Jaynes Fonda, May 16, 1905, Grand Island, Neb.; d. Aug. 12, 1982) Critics claimed this lanky Midwesterner presented to the world the true face of America; certainly no actor was better at playing the admirable or idealized American—the pioneer *(Drums Along the Mohawk)*, the countryman *(Way Down East)*, the Okie *(The Grapes of Wrath)*, the Western lawman *(My Darling Clementine)*, the man in uniform *(The Immortal Sergeant, Mister Roberts)*, the President *(Fail Safe, Young Mr. Lincoln)*; in the spring of his last year, for his performance in *On Golden Pond*, he received an Academy Award as Best Actor; though he'd been nominated just once before (for *The Grapes of Wrath*), and lost, this was not his first Oscar; in '81 had been presented a special Award for "a half-century of brilliant accomplishments and an enduring contribution to the art of motion pictures"; the son of a print-shop owner, he grew up in Omaha; in '25, working for an insurance company, he was urged to try acting at the local Community Playhouse by its director, Dorothy Brando, Marlon's mother; many plays later he joined the Cape Playhouse in Massachusetts; was on Broadway from '29 to '34, when success in the play *The Farmer Takes a Wife* took him to Hollywood to recreate the role, and an

69

80-picture career; cooperated fully with Howard Teichmann on his biography, *Fonda: My Life* ('81); said in the book's most revealing statement: "I don't really like myself. Never did. People mix me up with the characters I play. I'm not a great guy like Doug Roberts [in *Mister Roberts*]. I'd like to be but I'm not"; had five wives: Margaret Sullavan (1931–33), Frances Brokaw (1936–50; kids: Jane, Peter; committed suicide), Susan Blanchard (1950–56; adopted daughter: Amy); Afdera Franchetti (1957–62), Shirlee Adams (from '65 on).

MOVIE HIGHLIGHTS: *You Only Live Once, Slim, Trail of the Lonesome Pine, Jezebel, Jesse James, The Story of Alexander Graham Bell, Lillian Russell, The Lady Eve, The Male Animal, The Ox-Bow Incident, The Fugitive, Fort Apache, The Wrong Man, Twelve Angry Men, Advise and Consent, The Best Man, A Big Hand for the Little Lady, Madigan, Yours, Mine and Ours.*

Joan Fontaine

(b. Joan de Beauvoir de Havilland, Oct. 22, 1917, Tokyo, Japan) Escaping the shadow of sister Olivia de Havilland, who was famous first, required several seasons and two screen names; was billed Joan Burfield when cast in a minor role in her debut film, *No More Ladies* ('35), became Fontaine (stepfather's name) in her next, *Quality Street*; did leads in B's *(Maid's Night Out)*, played vacuous ingenues *(Gunga Din)*, and danced (briefly, badly) with Astaire in *A Damsel in Distress* before *Rebecca* made her a star, bringing a Best Actress Oscar nomination in '40; won her Oscar in '41 for *Suspicion* but still maintains "I should have got it the year before"; becoming famous in fragile femme roles gave fans a false impression of her; has been a licensed pilot, a champion balloonist, an expert rider, a prize-winning tuna fisherman, and a hole-in-one golfer, not to mention being a licensed interior decorator, a Cordon Bleu chef, and an author (her '78 autobiography, *No Bed of Roses*, told many amusing tales, including that of the loss of her virginity at 20 to much-older actor Conrad Nagel); has said of her varied interests: "If you keep marrying as I do, you learn everyone's hobby"; divorced four husbands: Brian Aherne (1939–43), producer William Dozier (1946–51; daughter: Deborah), producer Collier Young (1952–61), sportswriter Alfred Wright Jr. (1964–69); the decades-long feud with Olivia de Havilland is genuine, so much so that she hardly knows her sister's son and daughter; "My sister is a very peculiar lady," she says. "When we were young I wasn't allowed to talk to her friends. Now I'm not allowed to talk to her children, nor are they permitted to see me. This is the nature of the lady. Doesn't bother me at all."

MOVIE HIGHLIGHTS: *The Duke of West Point, Man of Conquest, The Women, This Above All, Frenchman's Creek, Jane Eyre, The Constant Nymph, The Emperor Waltz, Letter from an Unknown Woman, You Gotta Stay Happy, September Affair, Ivanhoe, Island in the Sun, Until They Sail, A Certain Smile, Tender Is the Night.*

Preston Foster

(b. Preston S. Foster, Aug. 24, 1900, Ocean City, N.J.; d. July 14, 1970) For cause, this curly-haired, two-fisted, blue-eyed actor always regarded *The Last Mile* ('32) as his lucky film; as a Broadway hit it made a star of Spencer Tracy while on the coast it brought Clark Gable his first major contract—and it established Preston Foster as a star of the first magnitude; originally under contract at Warners, he later starred at, literally, every studio in Hollywood; a high school dropout, he held various sales jobs before discovering he could cash in on his baritone voice; joined the Grand Opera Company of Philadelphia, where he sang many leading roles, and was soon a popular singer on radio and in vaudeville prior to playing dramatic leads on Broadway (1928–32) in *Congratulations, Adam Had Two Sons*, etc.; the oddity is that, as a screen star, even in such musicals as *The Harvey Girls*, he was rarely given a chance to sing; was typecast in rugged, serious roles like that of trenchcoated Dan Gallagher, the Irish revolutionaries' leader, in *The Informer* ('35), which remained his personal favorite of all the 95 movies in which he starred; his musical predilection was not to be forever denied; in the '50s, while starring in a dozen films and on TV as Capt. John Herrick, the modern tugboat skipper, in the popular "Waterfront" series, he finally had his career as a singer (and guitar player); in demand as a musical duo at parties, he and actress-wife Sheila D'Arcy took their act on the road and were soon barnstorming up to 28 weeks a year at fairs, auto shows, and clubs; also published many songs ("Two Shillelagh O'Sullivan," "Good Ship Lalapaloo," etc.); found it all a lot more fun than *I Am a Fugitive from a Chain Gang.*

71

MOVIE HIGHLIGHTS: *Life Begins, Dr. X, Wharf Angel, Heat Lightning, The Devil's Mate, The Last Days of Pompeii, Annie Oakley, The Plough and the Stars, White Banners, Submarine Patrol, 20,000 Men a Year, Geronimo, Northwest Mounted Police, Unfinished Business, My Friend Flicka, Guadalcanal Diary, Ramrod, Green Grass of Wyoming, The Big Cat, Chubasco.*

Kay Francis

(b. Katherine Edwina Gibbs, Jan. 13, 1899, Oklahoma City, Okla.; d. Aug. 26, 1968) Elegant, sophisticated brunette—with a cello voice and a husky laugh—who, often labeled "washed up," always bounced back; working girls aped her mannerisms and followed her every move in fan mags because, they thought, she was one of them; true, her first job was as a secretary—but as the social secretary of wealthy Mrs. W.K. Vanderbilt, arranging the lady's parties; learned her skills at the Katherine Gibbs Secretarial School, owned by her mother; her father was a well-heeled playboy and her birth occurred in Oklahoma only because he was there to buy polo ponies; grew up in luxury in Santa Barbara, L.A., Manhattan, and various European cities; tried being a society wife before deciding to act; professional name came from her first wealthy husband (1922–24), Dwight Francis; was first known as Katherine Francis on Broadway in '25 when she was the Player "Queen" in a modern version of *Hamlet*; William B. Gaston, a Boston blue-blood lawyer was (1926–28) her second millionaire groom; next (1929–30) was John Meehan, author of the play *Gentlemen of the Press*, which became her highly successful debut movie in '29; was last married (1931–33) to actor-director Kenneth MacKenna; starred in 68 movies (the best being *One Way Passage, The White Angel, In Name Only*), making 28 in the '30s at Warners, where her annual salary escalated to $227,000; was mostly seen as a "clothes horse" or in weepy mother-love melodramas; adoring canines, she said in a 1937 interview: "A dog has kindliness in his heart and dignity in his demeanor, the finest qualities anyone can have"; left most of her $1 million estate to the Seeing Eye Dog Foundation.

MOVIE HIGHLIGHTS: *Street of Chance, Raffles, Let's Go Native, House of Scandal, Trouble in Paradise, Cynara, Wonder Bar, Mandalay, Dr. Monica, Give Me Your Heart, Another Dawn, My Bill, Stolen Holi-*

72

day, Secrets of an Actress, First Lady, Comet Over Broadway, It's a Date, Little Men, Charley's Aunt, The Feminine Touch, Between Us Girls.

Clark Gable

(b. Clark William Gable, Feb. 1, 1901, Cadiz, Ohio; d. Nov. 16, 1960) The King they called him, and he was; was a towering screen presence, an incomparable mixture of masculine swagger, talent, and earthy charm; asked on "The David Frost Show" what was special about him, Joan Crawford answered aptly, albeit bluntly (and was bleeped): "He had balls"; won the Best Actor Oscar for *It Happened One Night* (which he was forced to make on loan-out to Columbia as "punishment" for demanding a wage hike at MGM); years later gave the statuette to the small son of a friend who thought it was a toy; when, shortly after Gable's death, his son John Clark, his only child, was born, the same person—now grown—brought the Oscar to the infant as a birth gift; hoped to win a second Academy Award, and was greatly disappointed not to, as Rhett Butler in GWTW; was in the Box Office Top Ten from '32 through '43 when, overage, he enlisted in the Air Force as a buck private; was back on the list 1947–49 and again in '55; had a varied background prior to going on the stage: timekeeper in a rubber factory, telephone lineman, newspaper ad salesman, worker in Oklahoma oil fields; portraying Killer Mears in the play *The Last Mile*, he was discovered by Lionel Barrymore, then directing films, who got him a test and contract at Metro that lasted 20 years; first movie: *The Painted Desert* ('30); was married five times: to drama teacher Josephine Dillon, wealthy Texan Ria Langham, star Carole Lombard, Lady Sylvia Ashley, actress Kay Williams, mother of his son, who became a race car driver.

MOVIE HIGHLIGHTS: *A Free Soul, Dance, Fool, Dance, Red Dust, China Seas, Mutiny on the Bounty, San Francisco, Test Pilot, Idiot's Delight, Boom Town, Honky Tonk, The Hucksters, Key to the City, Across the Wide Missouri, Mogambo, Teacher's Pet, The Misfits.*

Greta Garbo

(b. Greta Lovisa Gustafsson, Sept. 18, 1905, Stockholm, Sweden) Hauntingly lovely and regarded by legions as the Duse of the screen; sharing this opinion, Clarence Brown, who directed her greatest successes, has said: "She has this great appeal to the world because she expresses her emotions by *thinking* them. Garbo does not need gestures and movements to convey happiness, despair, hope and disappointment, joy or tragedy. She registers her feelings literally by radiating her thoughts to you"; was 14 when her father, a shopkeeper, died, leaving the family penniless; when working in the hat department of the Bergstrom department store, she was used as a hat model in newspaper ads; that led to a job in an advertising film that was seen by a Swedish comedy director, Eric Petscher, who gave her a small part in a movie, *Peter the Tramp*; this brought her to the attention of Mauritz Stiller, then Sweden's greatest director; becoming her mentor, he gave her the name Garbo, which he'd concocted much earlier awaiting the day he found a talent great enough to wear it; she starred for him, at 18, in *The Story of Gosta Berling*; offered an MGM contract, Stiller refused until they agreed to sign his discovery too; her first American film was *The Torrent* ('26), a silent of course, and fortunately, for she spoke not a word of English; first talkie: *Anna Christie*, which brought her an Oscar nomination, as did *Camille* and *Ninotchka*; retired at 36; in '54 was accorded a special Oscar "for her unforgettable performances."

MOVIE HIGHLIGHTS: *Flesh and the Devil, Love, The Temptress, The Divine Lady, The Kiss, Romance, Inspiration, Susan Lennox—Her Fall and Rise, Mata Hari, Grand Hotel, As You Desire Me, Queen Christina, The Painted Veil, Anna Karenina, Conquest, Two-Faced Woman.*

John Garfield

(b. Jacob Julius Garfinkle, March 4, 1912, New York, N.Y.; d. May 21, 1952) From the moment he entered the scene in *Four Daughters* ('38), this defiant yet vulnerable man was the antihero, the screen's first, setting the pattern for Bogart, Brando, Clift, Dean, Pacino; with him, it was not a role, but real; born in poverty on New York's Lower East Side, the son of a garment worker and a mother who died when he was 7, he was soon shipped up to the Bronx to live with a grudging uncle, sleeping on a cot in an unheated hall; a bright but incorrigible kid, he was rescued from what might well have been a life of crime by those who extended a helping hand; Angelo Patri, principal of P.S. 45 where Garfield was such a troublemaker, persuaded him to join the elocution class and debating team—within a year he'd won the *New York Times* oratorical medal in a citywide competition, a triumph for a lad who had stammered badly; deciding to act, he was advised by the great Jewish actor Jacob Ben-Ami to try to get into Maria Ouspenskaya's drama school; taken in by his fib that Ben-Ami had recommended it, Ouspenskaya gave him a two-year scholarship; a friendship with playwright Clifford Odets led to his becoming a member of the Group Theatre, where, after five years' stage experience, he became a star in Odets' *Golden Boy* ('37); went directly to screen fame at Warners, studio of earthy dramas, the ideal spot for a guy who, as critic Archer Winsten noted, was "fate's whipping boy, a personification of the bloody but unbowed hero, and the embittered voice of the dispossessed"; he and Hedy Lamarr were regarded as the great movie discoveries of '38; though a man of many affairs, he was wed to first sweetheart Roberta Mann from '33 on; both his children, Katharine Ann (now Julie) and John David, became actors, fulfilling a wish he'd expressed in 1944 when they were young.

MOVIE HIGHLIGHTS: *They Made Me a Criminal, Dust Be My Destiny, Juarez, Four Wives, Blackwell's Island, Castle on the Hudson, East of the River, The Sea Wolf, Out of the Fog, Tortilla Flat, The Fallen Sparrow, Destination Tokyo, Pride of the Marines, Humoresque, The Postman Always Rings Twice, Gentleman's Agreement, Body and Soul, Force of Evil, The Breaking Point.*

Judy Garland

(b. Frances Gumm, June 10, 1922, Grand Rapids, Minn.; d. June 22, 1969) "You Made Me Love You" she sang, and that was precisely the effect she had on an audience from her first feature, *Pigskin Parade* ('36), to her last, *I Could Go On Singing* ('63); still-mourning millions wish that her "song" could have gone on forever; this small (4'11") person possessed a magic that, in films and on records, is eternal; parents were vaudevillians billed as Jack and Virginia Lee; father sang in the act a song he'd written, "I Will Come Back," which, in Judy's final years, she used as the sign-off on her CBS television series; began singing on stage at 3 with older sisters Virginia and Suzanne; at 11 was on a bill at Chicago's Oriental Theater with comedian George Jessel who urged a name change to "Garland," after New York newspaper critic Robert Garland who was backstage that night; she personally picked "Judy"—the title of a Hoagy Carmichael song she loved; "discovered" at 13 by Hollywood agent Al Rosen, she was turned down by RKO, Columbia, and Paramount; at Metro, Louis B. Mayer listened to her sing "Zing! Went the Strings of my Heart" and signed her immediately; fame, fortune, and nervous breakdowns followed; her long tenure as an "overworked" MGM star ("pills to make me sleep, pills to wake me up"), she later complained bitterly, destroyed her health; when 15 was told by Hollywood astrologer Blanca Holmes she'd "be married many times"; had five husbands: David Rose, Vincente Minnelli (father of Liza), Sid Luft (father of Lorna and Joey), Mark Herron, Mickey Deans; was Oscar-nominated as Best Actress for A *Star Is Born* and as Best Support for *Judgment at Nuremberg*.

MOVIE HIGHLIGHTS: *Broadway Melody of 1938, Love Finds Andy Hardy, The Wizard of Oz, Babes in Arms, Strike Up the Band, For Me and My Gal, Girl Crazy, Meet Me in St. Louis, The Clock, The Harvey Girls, Easter Parade, Words and Music, Summer Stock.*

Janet Gaynor

(b. Laura Gainor, Oct. 6, 1906, Philadelphia, Pa.; d. Sept. 14, 1984) Winsome, petite (5'), and greatly gifted heroine who won the first Best Actress Oscar for her work in three 1927–28 silents: *Seventh Heaven, Street Angel, Sunrise*; with a charming voice ideally suited to talkies, she sailed on as a much-loved star through 1938's *The Young in Heart*; nominated for another Oscar for A *Star Is Born*, she was the most popular actress on the screen in '34 and had also been one of the Box Office Top Ten for two years previously; lived a true rags-to-riches story; was an $18-a-week typist in a San Francisco shoe store at 17, a movie extra at 18, a bit player at 19, and, at 20, the leading lady in *The Johnstown Flood*; fans adored it when she was teamed romantically (in many) with handsome Charles Farrell; denying it then, she admitted, decades later, "we were lovers," adding, "Charlie pressed me to marry him, but we had too many differences"; he loved parties and "wild weekends" at Hearst's San Simeon ranch, while she was "not a party girl"; the upshot: "I married a San Francisco attorney, just to get away from Charlie. It was a disaster"; that first groom was Lydell Peck (1929–33); in '39, quitting movies, she married MGM's famed fashion designer (Gilbert) Adrian, the happy union lasting until his death in '59; son Robin became a TV exec; looking back, she said: "Most people stress the unhappiness in their careers, but mine was glorious, a happy career. But it ended and I went into another life"; was wed from '64 on to stage producer Paul Gregory; returned to movies just once, to play a mother in *Bernardene* ('57); starred on Broadway in '80 in *Harold and Maude*, which failed, but one critic noted she'd managed to "preserve her sweetness down the years" and that "her eyes still possess an ingenue's twinkle."

MOVIE HIGHLIGHTS: *Lucky Star, Sunny Side Up, Happy Days, Delicious, Daddy Long Legs, Merely Mary Ann, State Fair, Adorable, Carolina, Paddy the Next Best Thing, Change of Heart, The Farmer Takes a Wife, Servants' Entrance, One More Spring, Small Town Girl, Three Loves Has Nancy.*

James Gleason

(b. James Gleason, May 23, 1882, New York, N.Y.; d. April 12, 1959) Pugnacious little Irishman who talked tough (always out of the side of his mouth and usually hiding a heart of gold) while playing reporters, detectives, cabbies, etc.; rated a Best Supporting Oscar nomination as Robert Montgomery's prizefighter manager in *Here Comes Mr. Jordan*; was nothing if not consistent—played humorously waspish characters and his real-life hobby was raising bees; fans may well recall the low-budget "Higgins Family" comedy series he did at Republic (*My Wife's Relations, Money to Burn,* etc.), co-starring his wife, Lucille (Webster) and son, only child, Russell Gleason (who died in 1945, at 37, in a fall from a hotel window); of theatrical parents (mother was stage actress Mina Crolius Gleason), who operated the Liberty Theater in Oakland, Calif., he was on the stage from childhood; his many military roles in movies were type-casting; as a volunteer, he'd fought in both the Spanish-American War and WW I; between them, he had acted in stock with his wife (were married from 1905 until her death in '47) and, following The Great War, he was on Broadway in *The Five Million*; following his screen debut in Constance Talmadge's *Polly of the Follies* ('22), he spent the next six years on Broadway as a director (*The Butter and Egg Man*), playwright (six plays), and star of comedies (two of which, *Is Zat So?* and *The Shannons of Broadway*, he also wrote); returned to Hollywood as a scriptwriter (*The Broadway Melody*), actor, and sometime director (1935's *Hot Tip*, in which he also starred); his 100-plus movie career continued without a break from 1928's *The Count of Ten* through 1958's *The Last Hurrah*.

MOVIE HIGHLIGHTS: *Puttin' on the Ritz, Swellhead, Sweepstakes, A Free Soul, Orders Is Orders, Billion Dollar Scandal, West Point of the Air, Murder on the Bridle Path, The Ex-Mrs. Bradford, The Plot Thickens, On Your Toes, Meet John Doe, My Gal Sal, Footlight Serenade, Crash Dive, A Guy Named Joe, A Tree Grows in Brooklyn, The Bishop's Wife.*

Paulette Goddard

(b. Pauline Levy, June 3, 1911, Whitestone, N.Y.) Insouciant, irrepressible, and in comedies (*The Kid from Spain, The Ghost Breakers*, et al.), this sexy, dark-haired gamine was something else; no matter that she may be a bit older than she admits, she was forever young at heart; that much was true right from her bit-part debut in a '29 Laurel and Hardy talkie short, *Berth Marks*; had been on the stage as a Ziegfeld beauty as early as 1926 in *No Foolin'*; a publicity natural, she drew attention to herself in her early movietown years by cruising down Sunset Boulevard in an open Duesenberg, dressed all in black, carrying one red rose and a lap dog; it was no problem attracting men (or collecting baubles) and it was jested in Hollywood that her necklaces were made of her old engagement rings; four men managed to sweep her to the altar: Edgar James (1931–32), Charlie Chaplin (1933–42), Burgess Meredith (1944–50), novelist Erich Maria Remarque (maintaining separate residences, they were married from '58 until his death in '70); played minor roles in movies (*Kid Millions, Roman Scandals*, etc.) until, in '36, Chaplin made her a star in his *Modern Times*; claims that the role of the waif "was absolutely me—there is something in my character of the barefoot gamine"; was the front contender for GWTW's Scarlett O'Hara until producer David O. Selznick, fearing negative publicity if it wasn't true, demanded proof that she and Chaplin were married—which she never supplied; after director George Cukor let her claw it out in a catfight with Rosalind Russell in *The Women*, her career as an ace comedienne was solidly launched—but her single Oscar nomination (as Best Support) came in a WW II drama, *So Proudly We Hail*.

MOVIE HIGHLIGHTS: *Dramatic School, Young in Heart, The Cat and the Canary, Northwest Mounted Police, The Great Dictator, Hold Back the Dawn, Nothing But the Truth, Reap the Wild Wind, The Lady Has Plans, I Love a Soldier, The Crystal Ball, Standing Room Only, Kitty, Unconquered, Diary of a Chambermaid, My Favorite Brunette.*

Cary Grant

(b. Archibald Alexander Leach, Jan. 18, 1904, Bristol, England) A "10" in every category and loaded with TLC—talent, looks, charm—he brought a special spark to dozens of movies in the '30s (and subsequent decades); was ever the hero as romantic comedian, with a poise and mid-Atlantic accent that made him seem equally at home in Manhattan, Monte Carlo, or Madagascar; his light touch, unmatched by any other movie male, once prompted director Michael Curtiz to say, "Some actors squeeze a line to death—Cary tickles it into life"; the sophisticated man-about-town he played, perfected and became was a self-creation; his childhood was traumatic; the son of a cockney clothes presser, he was 10 when his mother, suffering a nervous breakdown, was institutionalized (did not see her again for more than 20 years, until after he had become famous); attended Fairfield Academy on a scholarship until he was expelled in his teens as "incorrigible"; ran off and joined Bob Pender's acrobatic troupe, traveling all over England and finally America with them as a "tumbler, eccentric dancer, and clown"; stayed in New York when the troupe returned home, working first as a billboard-carrying stilt walker at Coney Island; as Archie Leach, was a singer in Broadway musicals of the '20s (*Golden Dawn, Boom Boom* with Jeanette MacDonald, etc.); in '31 was a lead in *Nikki*, playing a man named Cary Lockwood, which gave him his movie name (Paramount moguls came up with "Grant," after Fox tested and rejected him, saying, "Good-looking. Neck too thick. No chance at all"); played a cuckolded Olympics javelin thrower in his debut film, *This Is the Night* ('32); four wives divorced him: Virginia Cherrill, Barbara Hutton, Betsy Drake, Dyan Cannon (one child: Jennifer); at 72 wed Barbara Harris, a 30-year-old British journalist.

MOVIE HIGHLIGHTS: *Blonde Venus, Sinners in the Sun, Madame Butterfly, She Done Him Wrong, I'm No Angel, Spitfire, Thirty Day Princess, Sylvia Scarlet, Suez, Topper, The Awful Truth, Holiday, Bringing Up Baby, Only Angels Have Wings, Gunga Din, His Girl Friday, The Philadelphia Story, Penny Serenade, Suspicion, Notorious, The Bishop's Wife, To Catch a Thief, An Affair to Remember, That Touch of Mink.*

Richard Greene

(b. Richard Greene, Aug. 25, 1918, Plymouth, England) His time in Hollywood was brief (1938–40) but of sufficient duration for him to star romantically in 10 top-budget films and, thanks to his spectacular good looks (black curly hair, flashing blue eyes, and dimples), cause a cascade of fan mail at 20th Century–Fox; discovered on stage in London, in *French Without Tears*, he passed a screen test with flying colors and was hastened to Hollywood, where he promptly learned the unusual ways movies are made; met at the airport the morning he arrived, he was whisked to the studio soundstage where *Four Men and a Prayer* was already in production; thrust before the cameras, he found himself gazing into the eyes of Loretta Young, whom he'd seen on screen but never in person, and murmuring, "I love you, you know I love you"; other movie love scenes followed—with Alice Faye, Sonja Henie, Brenda Joyce, etc.—and a real-life engagement, which did not lead to marriage, to beautifully blonde Virginia Field; what the studio always endeavored to soft-pedal was his extreme youth—except for Nancy Kelly and Shirley Temple, all the femme stars with whom he acted were older than he; went back to England in '40, enlisted in the British armed forces and served until medically discharged in '44; returned to Hollywood three years later with his then wife, Patricia Medina (div. '51) and starred (at his old studio) in *Forever Amber*, followed by more films in both America and England, but he never again generated the same excitement among movie fans; became a huge TV favorite, though, starring (1955–60) in the "Adventures of Robin Hood" series; remarried (wealthily), he breeds thoroughbreds on a large farm in Ireland.

MOVIE HIGHLIGHTS: *Kentucky, My Lucky Star, Submarine Patrol, The Little Princess, The Hound of the Baskervilles, Here I Am a Stranger, Stanley and Livingstone, Little Old New York, I Was an Adventuress, Flying Fortress, The Fan, Desert Hawk, Lorna Doone, Rogue's March, The Black Castle, Captain Scarlett, Sword of Sherwood Forest.*

Virginia Grey

(b. Virginia Grey, March 22, 1917, Los Angeles, Calif.) Delicate blonde beauty who was an MGM fixture from '36 to '43 and later, as a freelancer, was the leading lady in dozens; the daughter of Ray Grey, a Mack Sennett comedy director, she made her movie debut at 9 as Little Eva in Universal's *Uncle Tom's Cabin*; other juvenile roles followed in *Heart to Heart, Jazz Mad, The Michigan Kid*; earliest ambition was to have a medical career and, when 15, worked for a while as a student nurse at City Hospital in Glendale, Calif.; at 16 was a $50-a-week chorus girl at Warner Bros.; was next a stand-in for Madge Evans and Florence Rice before getting her own chance at leads; early on she played floozies ("always a girl with a problem") before winning roles as a mirthful, well-adjusted young woman; Clark Gable, whom she supported in *Test Pilot* and *Idiot's Delight*, was her first champion at MGM; after Carole Lombard's death, and after Gable returned from the war, all Hollywood predicted—erroneously—that she would be his next wife, as they were long inseparable; never married, she has gone on record as saying (but never about Gable or earlier love Richard Arlen), "Hollywood men are a lot of phony balonies"; in '55 she returned to playing a "shady lady," in *The Rose Tattoo*, snagging the most brilliant notices of her career; producer Ross Hunter, claiming she's "my good luck charm," insists that she appear in all his movies (*Portrait in Black, Back Street, Airport*, etc.); often works on stage now; a realist, and frank, she says, "I consider myself a professional who acts, not to express my soul or elevate the cinema, but to entertain and get paid for it."

MOVIE HIGHLIGHTS: *Old Hutch, Dramatic School, The Women, Thunder Afloat, Another Thin Man, The Big Store, Whistling in the Dark, Sweet Rosie O'Grady, Unconquered, The Bullfighter and the Lady, The Hardys Ride High, Jeanne Eagels, Love Has Many Faces.*

Sigrid Gurie

(b. Sigrid Gurie Haukelid, May 18, 1911, Brooklyn, N.Y.; d. Aug. 14, 1969) In 1938, thanks to Sam Goldwyn, who discovered her (at a dinner party in London), her name was on everyone's lips and photos displaying her exotic beauty plastered the pages of magazines; convinced she was a "new" Garbo, the producer spent months and a fortune grooming her for stardom, keeping her tucked away in a hillside house, guarded, forbidden to meet the press or even any movie people; after starring her opposite Gary Cooper in *The Adventures of Marco Polo*, which flopped, he became quickly disenchanted; news reporters had a field day gleefully revealing what she'd failed to tell Goldwyn—that, while indeed Norwegian, and Oslo-reared, her birthplace was Brooklyn, and her "extensive" stage experience in Norway was largely imaginary; she had taken this gamble as she and her then husband were having a thin time and she badly needed work; Goldwyn was further angered when she risked the public's disfavor by divorcing her husband and marrying a Hollywood doctor; producer Walter Wanger then chose her to star as Charles Boyer's half-caste love in *Algiers*; in one *Algiers* scene, Boyer, as master thief Pepe le Moko, offers her, then quickly withdraws, a jeweled ring he has stolen, saying, "No, this ring should be worn by an old, fat woman"; she then begs, "Give it to me, Pepe, I'll be fat someday"; each year after this film, she became increasingly heavy as movie roles became fewer; finally, weighing near 200 pounds, she was told by an astrologer: "Your fame was meant to be brief, and great, which it was. It will not return. But happiness awaits you still in another country"; lived the rest of her life in Mexico—presumably happy.

MOVIE HIGHLIGHTS: *Forgotten Women, Rio, Three Faces West, Voice in the Wind* (a minor classic; her finest performance), *Dark Streets of Cairo, Enemy of Women, Sofia, Sword of the Avenger.*

Jack Haley

(b. John Joseph Haley, Aug. 10, 1899, Boston, Mass.; d. June 6, 1979) Happy-faced guy who won his most famous role, The Tin Man in *The Wizard of Oz*, by default (Buddy Ebsen, originally cast, proved allergic to the metallic makeup and had to withdraw); son Jack Jr., the writer-producer-director of *That's Entertainment*, etc., once humorously explained that he never became an actor because "I didn't want to clank in my father's bootsteps"; his big song in *The Wizard of Oz* was "If I Only Had a Heart," but he actually had a great one—his philanthropies were such that the Catholic Church made him a Knight of Malta, an honor held then by only two other actors, Danny Thomas and Pat O'Brien; went from vaudeville (song-and-dance man) to Broadway where, in the '20s, he starred in *Good News, Gay Paree, Round the Town*, etc.; made one movie in '30, *Follow Thru*, based on his stage musical hit; when the notices went to romantic leads Buddy Rogers and Nancy Carroll, it was back to the stage (*Free for All, Take a Chance*, etc.) until he returned to Hollywood for good in 1933's *Sitting Pretty* with Jack Oakie; major fame came his way three years later when he stole *Wake Up and Live* from the likes of Alice Faye and Walter Winchell; a 20th Century–Fox star before and after MGM borrowed him for *The Wizard of Oz*, he was later a freelancer until '49 when, after *Make Mine Laughs*, he retired; said, "A smart performer knows when to get off. It wasn't a wrench leaving movies. I don't believe there's no business like show business—it was just a business with me"; made a million in real estate and other interests; returned to movies once, in '69, to play a farmer in *Norwood*, at the behest of the director—his son.

MOVIE HIGHLIGHTS: *Mr. Broadway, The Girl Friend, Redheads on Parade, Coronado, Poor Little Rich Girl, Pick a Star, Rebecca of Sunnybrook Farm, Alexander's Ragtime Band, Thanks for Everything, Moon Over Miami, Navy Blues, Higher and Higher, Scared Stiff, Sing Your Way Home, One Body Too Many, Vacation in Reno, People Are Funny.*

Ann Harding

(b. Dorothy Walton Gatley, Aug. 7, 1901, Fort Sam Houston, San Antonio, Texas; d. Sept. 1, 1981) Patrician beauty, wearing minimal makeup and her silver-blonde hair in a bun, who reigned for years as queen of the RKO-Pathe lot; the daughter of an Army career officer, she was educated at posh Bryn Mawr, worked briefly for an insurance firm in New York, then went on the stage there, first with the Provincetown Players; took her professional name from President Harding; was a major star on Broadway throughout the '20s, being a particular hit in *Tarnish* and *The Trial of Mary Dugan*, and often acting with Harry Bannister; wed in '26, they went to Hollywood in '29 and were together in *Her Private Affair* and *The Girl of the Golden West*, but her fame far outstripped his; two years after their '32 divorce, he attempted to smear her reputation and win custody of their daughter, Jane; failed at both; she started in movies—*Paris Bound* was first—at $3,500 a week which, thanks to her enormous popularity (especially with femme fans), soon escalated to $6,000; became stereotyped on screen as the victim who triumphed over her oppressors by the sheer force of her nobility; said one critic, "She is so filled with spiritual sweetness that she ends up making you just a trifle resentful of so much greatness of soul"; after becoming the wife of symphony conductor Werner Janssen in '37 (divorced in '63), she was off the screen until '42, appearing most successfully on Broadway in *Candida*; returned as a character star, playing most notably the wife of Ambassador Joseph E. Davies (Walter

Huston) in *Mission to Moscow*, and that of Justice Oliver Wendell Holmes Jr. (Louis Calhern) in *The Magnificent Yankee*; left movies in '56; last acted on Broadway in '64.

MOVIE HIGHLIGHTS: *Holiday, East Lynne, Devotion, The Conquerors, The Animal Kingdom, The Life of Vergie Winters, The Fountain, Biography of a Bachelor Girl, Peter Ibbetson, Enchanted April, Gallant Lady, The Lady Consents, Stella Dallas, Eyes in the Night, The Male Animal, The North Star, Janie, The Man in the Gray Flannel Suit.*

Jean Harlow

(b. Harlean Carpenter, March 3, 1911, Kansas City, Mo.; d. June 7, 1937) MGM's great Platinum Blonde who was usually cast as a lovable heart-of-gold tramp; studio colleagues who knew and loved her (Myrna Loy, Maureen O'Sullivan et al.) maintain it was not typecasting, and were incensed when, in '61, a scandalous book titled *Jean Harlow: An Intimate Biography* was published, based largely on the alleged reminiscences of her onetime agent, Arthur Landau; Dr. Mont Clair Carpenter, her Kansas dentist-father (lived to be 96), surfaced and sued for $3 million, but lost; siding with the doctor, Tay Garnett, who directed her in *China Seas* and knew her intimately, said, "She was just a happy-go-lucky actress whose morals would have stood up against those of any devastatingly pretty girl"; engaged to William Powell when uremic poisoning snuffed out her life, she'd had three husbands; at 16, attending exclusive Ferry Hall in Lake Forest, Ill., she eloped with millionaire playboy Charles McGrew; divorced four years later, in '31, she married MGM exec Paul Bern, who committed suicide (creating a still-reverberating scandal) soon after their '32 wedding, and then was the wife (1933–35) of cinematographer Hal Rosson; had started as an extra (taking her divorced mother's maiden name); was then in Hal Roach comedy shorts for almost two years; became an overnight worldwide sensation in 1929's *Hell's Angels* when, midway in its production as a silent, producer Howard Hughes chose to make it as a talkie; took Norwegian-accented Greta Nissen out of the lead and gave it to Harlow; Metro quickly snapped up her contract and stood back to watch studio coffers overflow with gold; schoolmate Evelyn F. Scott wrote after the star's death: "So she stayed young, and can be seen without any blurring by age of that sultry face and sashaying figure—without any dimming of that blinding hair."

MOVIE HIGHLIGHTS: *Public Enemy, Goldie, Platinum Blonde, Red-Headed Woman, Red Dust, Dinner at 8, Bombshell, The Girl from Missouri, Reckless, Riffraff, Libeled Lady, Wife vs. Secretary, Suzy, Personal Property, Saratoga.*

Louis Hayward

(b. Charles Louis Hayward, March 19, 1909, Johannesburg, South Africa) Fine actor (and the first of Ida Lupino's husbands) whose best outings may have been *The Man in the Iron Mask* and *My Son, My Son*, but he wasn't quite conventionally handsome enough to make it to the top rung; educated in France, this son of a banker went to England in '28 to study drama before appearing on the London stage in *The Church Mouse, The Vinegar Tree*, etc.; following his screen debut in 1932's *Self-Made Lady*, he starred in several British films, including *Sorrell and Son* and *Chelsea Life*; MGM talent scouts discovered him on Broadway in *Point Valaine*; *The Flame Within* marked his auspicious start in American movies in '35; said a leading critic of his performance, "Taking a role that might easily have been played like a love-sick personality boy, he injected it with a magnificent soul-stirring feeling"; resisting playing thankless juvenile roles offered him at Metro, he soon moved on to RKO, where he remained under contract through the '30s; it is generally believed that George Sanders created the role of "The Saint," but Hayward played it first, in 1938's *The Saint in New York*, and last, in 1954's *The Saint's Girl Friday*; fans were puzzled to spot him as an "extra" in the ball sequence in Orson Welles' *The Magnificent Ambersons*—the fact is that his entire performance, as with various other parts of this epic, was left on the cutting-room floor; after *Ladies in Retirement* ('41), the only one in which he and Ida Lupino co-starred, was off the screen for four years; serving heroically as a U.S. Marines captain (combat photographer) in WW II, he was in the first wave of fighting men to land on the beach at Tarawa; also saw service on Guadalcanal and the Atlantic patrol; was awarded the Bronze Star and a Presidential Unit Citation.

MOVIE HIGHLIGHTS: *Anthony Adverse, The Luckiest Girl in the World, The Woman I Love, Duke of West Point, The Rage of Paris, Dance, Girl, Dance, The Son of Monte Cristo, And Then There Were None, Young Widow, The Saxon Charm, The Strange Woman, Ruthless, The Black Arrow, Walk a Crooked Mile, The Search for Bridie Murphy, Chuka.*

Sonja Henie

(b. Sonja Henie, April 8, 1913, Oslo, Norway; d. Oct. 12, 1969) Blonde ice-skating champion whose Olympic gold medals (won in '28, '32, and '36) translated into millions of greenbacks for 20th Century–Fox—and herself; behind those matching dimples and that baby-faced innocence was a rapid calculator mind; spoke four languages (Norwegian, French, English, and German) and in each of them, when the subject was business, the first question she asked was, "How much money is there in this for me?"; Hollywood moguls became interested in her when her final Olympic Games performance was filmed completely for a Pete Smith short, *Sports on Ice*; they blanched, but gave in, when she demanded $75,000 for her first picture and $100,000 for the second; pirouetted her perky-pouty way immediately into moviegoers' hearts and the Box Office Top Ten ('37, '38, '39) and soon was being paid a half-million a year; in her debut movie, *One in a Million* ('36), the second femme lead was played by Arline Judge, whose soon-to-be ex, playboy Dan Topping, became Henie's first husband (1940–46); two other millionaires followed him: Winthrop Gardiner (1949–55) and Norwegian Niels Onsted (from '56 on); when new in Hollywood, her studio highly publicized a romance (phony) between Tyrone Power and herself ("We had to consult the gossip columns every day to see if we were still in love or not"); made ice-skating movies so "in" that MGM even starred Joan Crawford, who couldn't skate a lick, in *Ice Follies of 1939*, with other studios also following suit; was such an all-round sports figure that she won two dozen trophies in skiing competitions and a few others for tennis; the daughter of a well-known skater, Wilhelm Henie, she began studying ballet at 4 (continued all her life), took up skating at 8 and, at 10, skated off with the Open Championship of Norway.

MOVIE HIGHLIGHTS: *Thin Ice, Happy Landing, My Lucky Star, Everything Happens at Night, Second Fiddle, Sun Valley Serenade, Iceland, Wintertime, It's a Pleasure, The Countess of Monte Cristo.*

Katharine Hepburn

(b. Katharine Houghton Hepburn, Nov. 8, 1907, Hartford, Conn.) A star of "records"; has received more Oscar nominations than anyone—*On Golden Pond* marked her 12th; the only player to date to win four Academy

Awards (and was not on hand to receive any personally), for *Morning Glory*, *The Lion in Winter*, *On Golden Pond*, *Guess Who's Coming to Dinner*; the latter marked her ninth and final teaming with Spencer Tracy, her real-life love of two-and-a-half decades; the others: *Woman of the Year* ('42, their first), *Keeper of the Flame*, *Without Love*, *Sea of Grass*, *State of the Union*, *Adam's Rib*, *Pat and Mike*, *The Desk Set*; shrugs off her Oscars, saying, "I don't take honors too seriously. You might deserve a prize if you lead an honorable life. But a prize for acting?"; curiously, she's been in the Box Office Top Ten just once, in '69, but, during the Hepburn–Tracy heyday, he was regularly on the list; George Cukor, her director nine times (more than any other), discovered her in '32 for *A Bill of Divorcement* and, after viewing her screen test, declared, "It's really foul. She looks like a boa constrictor on a fast. But she's marvelous. She'll be greater than Garbo"; they remained the closest of friends until his death and he forever maintained he'd been right on all counts; the daughter (and second of six children) of a wealthy surgeon dad and a crusading suffragette mother, she was graduated from exclusive Bryn Mawr in '28; made her Broadway debut in November of that year, in *These Days*, which lasted eight performances; but was launched on an unprecedented career of triumphs in movies (40-plus), plays (almost 20), radio, and TV dramas; was married once, briefly when young, to Ludlow Ogden Smith, Philadelphia socialite.

MOVIE HIGHLIGHTS: *Little Women*, *Alice Adams*, *Stage Door*, *Bringing Up Baby*, *Holiday*, *The Philadelphia Story*, *African Queen*, *Summertime*, *The Rainmaker*, *Suddenly Last Summer*.

Jean Hersholt

(b. Jean Hersholt, July 12, 1886, Copenhagen, Denmark; d. June 2, 1956) In the late 1930s, this beloved actor could truthfully boast of being the oldest veteran movie player, when not much past the age of 50; was in European films for a half-dozen years before making his Hollywood debut as a contract actor, at $15 a week, at the old Thomas Ince Studios, which he—a stickler for detail—would note "was on March 6, 1913"; in all that time he was under contract to one studio or another except for a single four-month period—and he had "made pictures for every major Hollywood company, past or present"; Mary Pickford's *Tess of the Storm Country* ('22) made him a "name"; soon signed a Universal contract (going from

$1,250 to $3,000 a week), then it was on to MGM, where the sky was the limit and the workload heavy; one year there ('32), he made 10 films, including classics like *Emma* and *Grand Hotel*, plus another two on loan-out; at the same time, he was on the board of directors of two Hollywood banks and the advisory board of the Beverly Hills Chamber of Commerce; founded the Motion Picture Relief Fund, which has benefitted thousands of needy or ill persons in the industry; while its president, he and other Fund leaders were accorded, in '39, an honorary Oscar; in '49, he received a personal special Academy Award "for distinguished service to the motion picture industry"; the Jean Hersholt Humanitarian Award was created in his honor in '56; a villain early on, he made so convincing a switch to sympathetic parts that, finally, fans thought of him mainly as kindly "Dr. Christian," a role he played in six 1939–41 movies and on radio from 1937 to '53.

MOVIE HIGHLIGHTS: *Hell's Hinges, Greed, Stella Dallas, So Big, Don Q* (silents), *The Sin of Madelon Claudet, Susan Lennox—Her Fall and Rise, The Lullaby, Beast of the City, The Mask of Fu Manchu, Dinner at Eight, Men in White, The Painted Veil, The Cat and the Fiddle, The Country Doctor, One in a Million, Seventh Heaven, Alexander's Ragtime Band, Heidi, Happy Landing, I'll Give a Million, Meet Dr. Christian.*

Wendy Hiller

(b. Wendy Margaret Hiller, Aug. 15, 1912, Bramhall, Cheshire, England) If she had never made another picture after 1938's *Pygmalion*, screen immortality still would have remained hers for putting on celluloid the definitive portrayal of Eliza Doolittle; performance rated her a Best Actress Oscar nomination; had played the role on stage, greatly impressing George Bernard Shaw, who proclaimed her his favorite actress and demanded that she play Eliza in the film; the playwright, incidentally, was just as strenuously opposed to the casting of Leslie Howard as Professor Henry Higgins, insisting that Higgins should not be a matinee idol but a "heavy"; producer Gabriel Pascal not only stuck to his guns but gave the movie a romantic ending (unlike the play) that pleased audiences and even, finally, Shaw himself; the actress had been seen earlier in just one British film, *Lancashire Luck*, written by playwright Ronald Gow, who became her husband; made her stage debut at 18 with the Manchester Repertory Theatre; at 23, she scored an instantaneous success in her first London play, *Love on the Dole*, repeating the triumph the following year in New York; though she won the Best Supporting Actress Oscar in *Separate Tables* and was nominated in the same category in *A Man for All Seasons*, her career emphasis has always been on the stage; with the Old Vic and other companies in England and America, she has played the greatest roles in classics by Shakespeare, Chekhov, O'Neill, and O'Casey; primarily in honor of her work in theater, she was awarded the Order of the British Empire in '71 and, four years later, made Dame, the female equivalent, of course, of knighthood.

MOVIE HIGHLIGHTS: *Major Barbara, I Know Where I'm Going, Single Handed, Outcast of the Islands, Sailor of the King, Something of Value, How to Murder a Rich Uncle, Sons and Lovers, Toys in the Attic, David Copperfield, Murder on the Orient Express, Voyage of the Damned, The Cat and the Canary, The Elephant Man, Making Love.*

Jack Holt

(b. Charles John Holt, May 31, 1888, Winchester, Va.; d. Jan. 18, 1951) When great Western stars and two-fisted adventure heroes are being talked about, this guy with the steely gaze is always one of the first mentioned; while keeping a low profile privately, he was highly visible and ever in the thick of the action for 36 screen years, in more than 200 pictures from 1915's *A Cigarette—That's All* to *Across the Wide Missouri*, released after his death; the son of an Episcopal minister, he was educated at Trinity School in New York and the Virginia Military Institute; led an adventurous life—prospecting for gold in Alaska, working as a cowpuncher on Northwestern ranches— before traveling the country for four years with a troupe of actors; entered movies as a stunt man; first assignment: riding a horse over a 30-foot cliff into a river; a 1916 Universal serial, *Liberty, A Daughter of the U.S.A.*, made him a star overnight; throughout the '20s, playing rugged he-men, he was a Paramount powerhouse; talkies proved no problem for he possessed a rich, strong voice; his commanding screen presence marked him as a straight-shooting leader, whether in cowboy duds or military garb; an authority on horseflesh, he enlisted in the U.S. Cavalry during WW II (at 54), serving first as a horse buyer and, when the Cavalry was mechanized, with the Remount Division at Fort Reno; discharged as a major after two and a half years, he then was in *They Were Expendable*—as a general; married to Margaret Woods from '16 on, he was the father of Jennifer Holt, a popular heroine in Westerns, and Tim, who became a top Western star in his own right.

MOVIE HIGHLIGHTS: *Call of the North, North of the Rio Grande, The Tiger's Claw, Light of Western Stars, Wild Horse Mesa* (silents), *Hell's Island, Dirigible, Fifty Fathoms Deep, Border Legion, The Littlest Rebel, San Francisco, Crash Donovan, Outlaws of the Orient, Trapped by G-Men, Roaring Timber, Trapped in the Sky, Thunder Birds, Holt of the Secret Service* (serial), *The Cat People, Arizona Ranger, Treasure of the Sierra Madre.*

Miriam Hopkins

(b. Ellen Miriam Hopkins, Oct. 18, 1901, Bainbridge, Ga.; d. Oct. 8, 1972) A temperamental blonde with a Dixie-tinted drawl, she was feisty, flighty, and forever fascinating—but some brittle quality about her precluded her becoming a star adored by movie fans; born into wealth and well-educated (Vermont's Goddard Seminary; Syracuse University), she studied dancing with Russian teachers in New York before becoming a chorus girl (decked out as a water lily) in the first *Music Box Revue* in '21, followed by more musicals; turned dramatic in '25 in *Puppets* and the critics were merciless ("Miss Hopkins was super-childish . . . so pit-a-pat and goo-goo . . . "); got rave notices the following year as the rich girl in *An American Tragedy*; in '28 was the star of a stock company in Rochester, N.Y., where the ingenue was a newcomer named Bette Davis; they would meet again—blazingly; between '30 and '34, Hopkins was a top-salaried Paramount star, giving brilliant performances in *Trouble in Paradise* and *Design for Living*, but chilly ones in most; admittedly was a poor judge of movie roles—turned down both *Twentieth Century* and *It Happened One Night*; returned to Broadway to star in *Jezebel* (she got scathing reviews; play flopped); after Bette Davis (to Hopkins' fury) won an Oscar in the role, Warners co-starred the two in *The Old Maid* and *Old Acquaintance*, during both of which Hopkins waged a one-sided, spiteful feud with Davis, who has said, "She was too good an actress to indulge herself in jealousy of another performer. . . . She finally ruined her career because of this"; divorced four husbands: actor Brandon Peters (1926–31), playwright Austin

Parker (1931–32), director Anatole Litvak (1937–39), newspaperman Raymond Brock (1945–51).

MOVIE HIGHLIGHTS: *Fast and Loose, The Smiling Lieutenant, Dr. Jekyll and Mr. Hyde, The Story of Temple Drake, The World and the Flesh, Two Kinds of Women, She Loves Me Not, The Richest Girl in the World, Becky Sharp, Splendor, Barbary Coast, These Three, Men Are Not Gods, Woman Chases Man, Virginia City, The Lady with Red Hair, The Heiress, The Mating Season, Carrie, The Children's Hour, The Chase.*

Leslie Howard

(b. Leslie Howard Stainer, April 3, 1893, London, England; d. June 1, 1943) Scarlett O'Hara was not alone in panting after Ashley Wilkes; millions of other femmes were equally captivated by this character's gentle-spoken alter ego; a number of them may have found their affections reciprocated for, despite being well-married (from '16 on to Ruth Evelyn Martin), he was privately reputed in Hollywood to be the town's ace ladies' man; the son of a Hungarian father, a lowly paid stockbroker's aide, he was briefly a bank clerk and, for three years, was in a WW I cavalry regiment before being wounded in the battle at Bethune; back home, he landed a small role in a touring company of *Peg o' My Heart* ('17); made his reputation as a stage actor in '20 in *Mr. Pym Passes By* in London; remained behind the footlights—mostly in New York—for a full decade until, at 37, he starred in his first movie, *Outward Bound* (salary $5,000 a week); of his films, he personally liked best *Berkeley Square* and *Pygmalion* (for both of which he was Oscar-nominated as Best Actor), *The Petrified Forest*, and *The Scarlet Pimpernel*; each reflected his understated charm and formidable skill as a romantic actor; did not like the part of Ashley Wilkes in GWTW (never bothered to read the book) and only agreed to do it after David O. Selznick agreed to allow him to direct films, which never happened; WW II interfered and he returned to England, where he directed and acted in propaganda films; on a mission for the British Council in '43, he was aboard a commercial Lisbon–London airliner that Nazi aircraft shot down, believing Prime Minister Winston Churchill was also a passenger; was the father of two; Ronald became an actor and Leslie Ruth penned his biography, *A Quite Remarkable Father.*

91

MOVIE HIGHLIGHTS: *A Free Soul, Never the Twain Shall Meet, Devotion, Reserved for Ladies, The Animal Kingdom, Smilin' Through, Secrets, British Agent, Captured, Of Human Bondage, The Lady Is Willing, Romeo and Juliet, It's Love I'm After, Stand-In, Intermezzo, Pimpernel Smith, Spitfire.*

Rochelle Hudson

(b. Rochelle Hudson, March 6, 1916, Oklahoma City, Okla.; d. Jan. 17, 1972) Even not-quite-stars "had faces then," and hers was indeed one of the loveliest; was long on the brink of big-league fame at 20th Century-Fox, utterly winning when somebody's sweetheart in A's and admirably able when starring in low-budget films; her made-for-marquees name was real—her long eyelashes weren't; had a cattle rancher father and, not surprisingly, an ambitious "stage mother"; so it was piano lessons at 3, speech lessons at 6, dancing lessons— in Hollywood—at 11, and, when 14 (pretending to be 16), an RKO contract and her movie debut in Edna May Oliver's *Laugh and Get Rich*; beloved comedian Will Rogers, also from Oklahoma, took a personal interest in her future and persuaded Fox to put her under contract; was in four of the films of "Uncle Bill" (as she called him): *Mr. Skitch* (as his daughter), *Judge Priest*, etc.; was a fixture, and a busy one, at Fox (and elsewhere on loan-out) from '33 through '38; was occasionally allowed to showcase her excellent singing voice (in *She Had to Eat*, etc.); bored with saccharine-sweet roles ("I'm sick of waving the Janet Gaynor banner"), she fought for more dramatic parts but never got them, even when a freelance; during WW II, when wed to naval reservist Harold Thompson, she was gone from Hollywood for years; reporter Kirk Crivello later revealed this secret behind that mysterious disappearance: "Together they made several trips to Mexico on the pretext of fishing expeditions. Actually they were engaged in espionage for the U.S. government"; that marriage, as did two later ones—to sports writer Dick Hyland and Robert Mindel—ended in divorce.

MOVIE HIGHLIGHTS: *Wild Boys of the Road, Dr. Bull, She Done Him Wrong, Imitation of Life, The Mighty Barnum, Life Begins at 40, Curly Top, Way Down East, Show Them No Mercy, Les Miserables, The Music Goes 'Round, Reunion, Poppy, Mr. Moto Takes a Vacation, Pride of the Navy, Convicted Women, Meet Boston Blackie, Rebel Without a Cause, Strait-Jacket.*

Ian Hunter

(b. Ian Hunter, June 13, 1900, Kenilworth (near Capetown), South Africa; d. Sept. 24, 1975) Handsome, with an attractive, sympathetic voice, he had that air of charm and culture so typically British; for a decade (starting in '35) was one of Hollywood's busiest—and usually pipe-smoking and tweedy—actors, though most often losing the girl in the last reel; lived his first 14 years, the fourth son of a well-to-do wine expert, in South Africa; during WW I, following his older brothers, he enlisted at 16 as a private in King Edward's Horse Brigade and was under fire in France for two years; began his career in English repertory theaters at 19, quickly becoming popular in romantic juvenile roles; married Casha Pringle at 26; two sons: Jolyon George and Robin Ian; Alfred Hitchcock introduced him to the screen in a British silent, *Downhill* ('27); then in many English films (*The Silver Spoons, The Church Mouse*, etc.) including two opposite the U.K.'s #1 song-dance favorite, Jessie Matthews—*There Goes the Bride* and *The Man from Toronto*; was lured to America by Warner Bros., where he co-starred most frequently with Kay Francis (*I Found Stella Parish, The White Angel, Stolen Holiday, Another Dawn*); less-famous brother Kenneth Hunter appeared with him in *The Adventures of Robin Hood* and *The Little Princess*, in which Ian was Shirley Temple's long-lost soldier-father; on screen was often to be found in drawing rooms, but away from the cameras he was an outdoorsman with a passion for golf, tennis, swimming, sailing; remains most memorable for his portrayal of the Christ-like Cambreau, that soul in all men, in Gable's *Strange Cargo*.

MOVIE HIGHLIGHTS: *Jalna, To Mary With Love, The Devil Is a Sissy, 52nd Street, The Sisters, Broadway Serenade, Yes, My Darling Daughter, Maisie, Tower of London, The Long Voyage Home, Bitter Sweet, Ziegfeld Girl, Dr. Jekyll and Mr. Hyde* (Tracy's version), *Smilin' Through, A Yank at Eton, Forever and a Day, Edward, My Son.*

Ruth Hussey

(b. Ruth Carol O'Rourke, Oct. 30, 1914, Providence, R.I.) Classy brunette leading lady whose best outings may have been as the sophisticated magazine photographer covering Hepburn's wedding in *The Philadelphia Story* (rated a Best Supporting Oscar nomination) and as Ray Milland's sister in the spinetingling *The Uninvited*; of a prominent New England family—father was president of a mail-order jewelry firm; graduated (degree in philosophy) from Pembroke College; began as a fashion commentator on local radio station KPRO (and continues to do commentating in shows staged by her Brentwood church); next studied drama at the University of Michigan and gained additional experience in summer stock at a theater in Northport, Mich.; a role in the road company of *The Old Maid* won her parts on Broadway in *Waiting for Lefty, Stevedore*, etc.; playing a lead (socialite Kay) in the road company of another show, *Dead End*, took her to Los Angeles and an MGM contract in '37; first movie: *The Big City*, supporting Spencer Tracy, with whom she soon co-starred in *Northwest Passage*; despite her adopted, attention-getting stage-screen name, chosen for just that purpose, Hollywood cast her only in ladylike roles, and often as a wife—Robert Young's in *H. M. Pulham, Esq.*, Van Heflin's in *Tennessee Johnson*, Clifton Webb's in *Stars and Stripes Forever*; became a wife really, for the first time and lastingly, on Aug. 10, 1942, when she married U.S. Army Lieutenant Robert Longenecker, once a radio producer who became a top Hollywood agent; three children: George Robert (jet pilot, Navy career officer), John William (filmmaker whose short, *The Resurrection of Broncho Billy*, won an Oscar), Mary Elizabeth.

MOVIE HIGHLIGHTS: *Man Proof, Honolulu, The Women, Susan and God, Another Thin Man, Our Wife, Bedtime Story, Flight Command, Marine Raiders, I, Jane Doe, The Great Gatsby* (Ladd version), *Mr. Music, The Lady Wants Mink*.

Walter Huston

(b. Walter Houghston, April 6, 1884, Toronto, Canada; d. April 7, 1950) Fans last saw him as the mighty cattle baron in *The Furies*, released four months after his death, and in which his final line of dialogue was most apt; gunned down and dying, he warns daughter Barbara Stanwyck that she must not pass his name on to his grandson because "it's too big a bag for him to carry, 'cause there'll never be another like me"; no matter who shared movie scenes with him, it was this compelling man who drew one's attention like a magnet; was Oscar-nominated as Best Actor for *Dodsworth* and *All That Money Can Buy* (a.k.a. *The Devil and Daniel Webster*), as Best Support for *Yankee Doodle Dandy*, and won in this category for

Treasure of the Sierra Madre; accepting his Oscar, he said, "A long time ago I brought up a boy and I told him one thing about the theater: 'Someday write a good part for your old man.' Well, by golly, he did!"; son John Huston scripted *Treasure of the Sierra Madre* and directed it, keeping his father in character as the grizzled old gold prospector by occasionally whispering, "Dad, that was a little too much like Walter Huston"; he had earlier written the movie *A House Divided* ('32) as a starring vehicle for his father; the son of a professional gambler, Walter tried the New York stage at 18, failed, returned home for an engineering career (1903–08); then went into vaudeville with first wife (1905–13) Rhea Gore (John's mother); second marriage ('14) to Bayonne Whipple also ended in divorce; was wed to actress Nan Sunderland from '31 on; was a major star on Broadway in the '20s (*The Barker, Congo*, etc.); starred in his first movie, *Gentlemen of the Press* ('29), and was bound for glory as one of the true originals of the screen.

MOVIE HIGHLIGHTS: *The Bishop's Candlesticks, The Lady Lies, The Virginian, Abraham Lincoln, The Star Witness, Rain, Night Court, Gabriel Over the White House, The Wet Parade, Ann Vickers, Hell Below, The Prizefighter and the Lady, Of Human Hearts, The Light That Failed, Edge of Darkness, The Outlaw, Mission to Moscow, Dragon Seed, And Then There Were None, Duel in the Sun, Summer Holiday.*

Rita Johnson

(b. Rita Johnson, Aug. 13, 1913, Worcester, Mass.; d. Oct. 31, 1965) Brittle blonde who generally played "other women," often rich bitches, but sometimes popped up as a loving mom (Roddy McDowall's in *My Friend Flicka*) or devoted wife (Tracy's in *Edison the Man*); trying out for—and never winning—roles in high school plays in her home town, she was informed by the drama coach that she had no future as an actress; worked as a waitress in her mother's tea room to pay for private dramatic lessons; landed small parts in a local civic repertory company with Rosalind Russell as visiting star (later supported Russell at Metro in *Man Proof*); next toured New England with a company that played in town halls and schoolhouses, followed by summer stock in Brookfield, Mass., with Eva Le Gallienne, Broadway (first an ingenue role in George M. Cohan's *If This Be Treason*), and many radio appearances; screen debut as an MGM contractee was in 1937's *London by Night*; never made it to top stardom; she and movie exec Stanley Kahn were divorced in '43, remarried the same year, divorced again in '47; on September 6, 1948,she was discovered unconscious, having suffered a head injury causing a blood clot that was removed in a delicate brain operation; found beside her was a hair drier and it was publicized that she'd been injured when it fell from a shelf; whispers spread through Hollywood, however, that her "accident" had actually been a Mafia-inflicted beating as she lately had been associated with a known mobster; made a few more films but never fully recovered; died—a charity case—in Los Angeles County General Hospital, where a spokesperson said a possible cause of death was cardiac arrest due to a head injury.

MOVIE HIGHLIGHTS: *A Letter of Introduction, Serenade, Honolulu, Congo Maisie, Forty Little Mothers, Here Comes Mr. Jordan, The Major and the Minor, They Won't Believe Me, The Big Clock, Sleep My Love, Susan Slept Here.*

Al Jolson

(b. Asa Yoelson, May 26, 1883, St. Petersburg, Russia; d. Oct. 23, 1950) "Wait a minute, wait a minute, you ain't heard nothing yet!"; the year: 1927, the picture: *The Jazz Singer*, the star: Al Jolson; for the first time movies "talked"—and "sang" ("Toot, Toot, Tootsie" was the first song heard); considering the star's place in screen history, the revolution he started, and the enthralled reaction of movie audiences, it comes as a shock to discover a critic of the time writing: "Neither a Broadway reputation nor 'Mammy' songs on the Vitaphone nor a good story can conceal the painful fact that Al Jolson is no movie actor"; as great an entertainer as he was, his sobs-and-songs routine quickly wore thin with moviegoers, and his rampant ego did not enhance his popularity with studio bosses, fans, or the press; denied reports that Warners had given him company stock to star in *The Jazz Singer*, adding bitterly, "I got my salary ($75,000), and that's all. I haven't made a penny out of this picture racket, not compared with what I used to make on the stage. Of course, I only started the whole talkie business and put the company on its feet . . . "; his parents, who brought him to America when an infant, wanted him to become a cantor in a synagogue but, running away from home, he joined a circus as a ballyhoo man; made his stage debut in 1899 in a mob scene in *Children of the*

Ghetto; next did a vaudeville act with brother Harry (who in '29 advertised—with scant success—in a Hollywood paper: "There Are Two Talented Jolsons"); started the black-face act that made him lastingly famous in 1906; had long been considered a has-been when his screen bio (starring Larry Parks), *The Jolson Story* ('46), made him popular all over again; for reasons of her own, Ruby Keeler, third of his four wives, would not let them use her name in the picture.

MOVIE HIGHLIGHTS: *The Singing Fool, Say It With Songs, Sonny Boy, Mammy, Big Boy, Wonder Bar, Hallelujah, I'm a Bum, Go Into Your Dance, The Singing Kid, Alexander's Ragtime Band, Rose of Washington Square, Swanee River, Hollywood Cavalcade.*

Allan Jones

(b. Don Diego Jones, Oct. 14, 1905. Scranton, Pa.) Virile, handsome, golden-voiced tenor—and father of singer Jack Jones—who was a popular MGM star from '35 through '38, before taking his tonsils and make-up kit to Paramount and Universal; realized at an early age that, poor though his family was, his voice represented an "inherited income"; sang with local church choirs then worked in Pennsylvania coal mines—his Welshman father, who had started as a slate picker, was foreman—to earn money to study music in Paris; eager to get to Europe, he worked double shifts—at 58 cents an hour; following his training abroad, he appeared in concert all over America before doing a lengthy stint at the St. Louis Municipal Opera, singing a different light opera each week; was starring on Broadway in '34 in *Bitter Sweet* when Metro talent scout Billy Grady discovered him for movies; as his contract with the Schubert Company had two years to go, he found himself paying $20,000 for the freedom to take a crack at Hollywood stardom; screen debut was simply singing a song in Harlow's *Reckless*; next co-starred (on loan-out) in *Show Boat* with Irene Dunne, then did a favor for a friend who did a bigger favor for him; producer Hunt Stromberg had completed filming the big production number in *The Great Ziegfeld*, with baritone Dennis Morgan (then Stanley Morner) singing "A Pretty Girl Is Like a Melody," when he was reminded that Ziegfeld's male singer was always a tenor; Jones dubbed the song—Stromberg reciprocated by casting him with Jeanette MacDonald in *The Firefly* (his big solo: "The Donkey Serenade"), which put him over the top; divorced from his first wife on July 25, 1936, he married actress Irene Hervey the next day; were married 21 years before they divorced.

MOVIE HIGHLIGHTS: A *Day at the Races, Everybody Sing, Rose Marie, Honeymoon in Bali, The Great Victor Herbert, The Boys from Syracuse, One Night in the Tropics, There's Magic in Music, Moonlight in Havana, When Johnny Comes Marching Home, Rhythm of the Islands, Crazy House, The Senorita from the West.*

Buck Jones

(b. Charles Frederick Gebhard, Dec. 12, 1888, Vincennes, Ind.; d. Nov. 30, 1942) Brawny and heroic, he headed all the cowboy stars at the box office in 1936 (first year of the poll) and, though unseated by Gene Autry, remained in the Top Ten in '37, '38, '39; donned spurs as a movie extra in 1917 in Tom Mix shoot-'em-ups; became King of the Cowboys at Fox in the '20s, overtaking both Mix and William S. Hart; no rhinestone cowboy, but the genuine article, he was just a lad when his father took the family to live on a ranch he'd bought in the Old Cherokee Outlet of Oklahoma; ranch hands nicknamed him "Buck" when he tried to ride a particularly cantankerous mule and was sent flying; enlisting in the U.S. Cavalry in his teens, he went with his troop to the Philippines, where for two years they fought Moro bandits; receiving a severe leg wound, he was honorably discharged in 1909; joined the military again the following year, when his injury healed, and served with the First Aero Squadron until '13; was next a rider with the Miller Brothers' 101 Ranch Wild West Show, where he fell in love with a 14-year-old equestrienne, Odelle Osborne; together they joined the Julia Allen Show and were married (Aug. 11, 1915) in Lima, Ohio, in a horseback ceremony in the circus tent; unlike many celluloid cowboys, he owned his horse, Silver; paid $100 for the beautiful gray stallion and rode him in tank-town shows and Ringling Bros. Circus before going into movies—at $5 a day; earned $4,000 a week at his peak; died a hero's death; at a party given in his honor for his war bond tours at Boston's Cocoanut Grove, a sudden fire erupted, killing 490 people; surviving witnesses reported that he could have escaped but went back into the club three times to rescue others—the third time the roof collapsed on him.

MOVIE HIGHLIGHTS: *The Lone Rider, Shadow Ranch, Riders of the Purple Sage, Branded, The Texas Ranger, McKenna of the Mounted, White Eagle, The Dawn Trail, Border Brigands, Silver Spurs, Sandflow, Boss of Lonely Valley, California Frontier, Wagons Westward.*

Boris Karloff

(b. William Henry Pratt, Nov. 23, 1887, Dulwich, England; d. Feb. 2, 1969) *Frankenstein* is everyone's reaction when his name is mentioned; actually, although he starred in dozens of horror flicks, he played Dr. Frankenstein's immortal monster (in a costume weighing 67 pounds) only three times—in *Frankenstein* ('31), *The Bride of Frankenstein* ('35), and *The Son of Frankenstein* ('39); was second choice for the part; Bela Lugosi rejected it because he wouldn't be recognized under the make-up; a generous man, as well as a cultured, gentle-spoken one, he gave most of the credit for his success in *Frankenstein* to make-up wizard Jack Pierce, "the real star of the picture, who created a monster that made audiences react with sympathy as well as horror"; one of eight children in a middle-class English family, he was educated at King's College and, at 21, sailed for Canada where he worked as a $10-a-month farm hand; began acting in small repertory companies there in 1913; had a 53-year movie career, starting in *The Dumb Girl of Portici* in '16; took his screen name from a seventeenth-century ancestor who came of Russian stock; played bits in movies for 15 years (while also working as a ditchdigger and truck driver) until Columbia signed him to repeat a role he'd played on stage, the killer in *Criminal Code*, which made him a "name"; his fame in villainous or monster roles proved the wisdom of his friend Lon Chaney, the silents' great "bogeyman," who advised: "Find something no one else can or will do—the secret of success in movies lies in being different from anyone else"; played many varieties of "bad guys": Chinese *(The Mask of Fu Manchu)*, Indian (the savage Chief Guyasuta in *Unconquered*), etc.; had three wives: Helen Soule (1923–28), Dorothy Stine (1929–46), Evelyn Helmore (from '46 on).

MOVIE HIGHLIGHTS: *Five-Star Final, Scarface, The Mad Genius, The Mummy, The Old Dark House, The Lost Patrol, The Black Cat, The House of Rothschild, The Raven, The Walking Dead, Mr. Wong—Detective,*

Tower of London, Devil's Island, The Man They Could Not Hang, The Body Snatcher, Tap Roots, Black Sabbath.

Ruby Keeler

(b. Ruby Ethel Keeler, Aug. 25, 1909, Halifax, Nova Scotia) "You're going out a youngster, but you've *got* to come back a star," hardboiled director Warner Baxter snarls at Ruby Keeler, the trembling chorus girl he sends on stage to substitute for the leading lady in *42nd Street*; tapping her heart out, she did, doubly, in the story and for real; the oldest of six children, she grew up in the tenements of New York's East Side (father worked for the Knickerbocker Ice Co.), and at 13 (claimed to be 16) was hoofing in the chorus of *The Rise of Rosie O'Reilly* on Broadway; soon discovered by Florenz Ziegfeld, she starred for him in such successes as *Whoopee* and *Show Girl*; in Hollywood, dancing on stage at the Egyptian Theater, she got a screen test, but no contract, at Fox; perhaps at the behest of her then husband, Al Jolson, a Warners star, Jack Warner saw the test and—as in the plots of her movies—decided she was just the girl for the studio's musicals; her sudden fame as the song-dance queen of the WB lot (usually in the arms of crooning Dick Powell), just as Jolson's popularity was beginning to wane, did little to help their marriage; millions flocked to see the one movie they made together, *Go Into Your Dance*, but were a bit disgruntled since he dominated the film while she was shunted into the shadows; divorced in '39, she complained to the court that Jolson "ridiculed" her; later had a most happy 28-year marriage to Pasadena broker John Lowe, who died in '69; their children (Kathleen, Christine, Theresa, John Jr.) were the main reason she refused to be portrayed in *The Jolson Story*; producer Sidney Skolsky has quoted her as saying of her ex: "I don't like him. I don't want my children to grow up someday and maybe see the picture and know I was married to a man like that"; in '71, after 41 years away, made a glorious comeback on Broadway in *No, No, Nanette*.

MOVIE HIGHLIGHTS: *Gold Diggers of 1933, Footlight Parade, Dames, Flirtation Walk, Shipmates Forever, Colleen, Ready, Willing and Able, Mother Carey's Chickens, Sweetheart of the Campus.*

Patsy Kelly

(b. Sarah Veronica Rose Kelly, Jan. 21, 1910, Brooklyn, N.Y.; d. Sept. 24, 1981) In an era when movies had no shortage of memorable character stars, dumpy, saucer-eyed Patsy Kelly—tough in looks and talk—had no peer in the wisecracks department; her acidulous charm was everywhere; going to one of her feature films, fans were likely to be treated, as well, to one of the 40 hilarious Hal Roach two-reelers in which she starred, first with Thelma Todd, then Pert Kelton, and finally Lyda Roberti; began her career at 17, tap-dancing in a chorus line behind headliner Frank Fay at the Palace; never married, she was engaged once, for one month, to Frank Fay—till she lost him to stage newcomer Barbara Stanwyck; was shortly a featured comedienne on Broadway in *Wonder Bar* and *Three Cheers*; made her film debut in '33 in *Going Hollywood* and, throughout the '30s, she could take the silliest script and, magically, make it scintillate (many of her best smart quips were ad libs); suddenly, in 1943 the red carpet was pulled right out from under her; reportedly, too, a drinking problem played a part in her downfall; for the next 17 seasons, not one movie role ("Those were the years when I could do nothing right"); she survived, thanks to radio, TV, and close friend Tallulah Bankhead, who gave her moral support and a role in *Dear Charles*, a play the star played repeatedly in stock; even after returning to Hollywood in *Please Don't Eat the Daisies*, she was less than besieged with other offers; at 61, she scored hugely on Broadway (winning a Tony) as the tap-dancing maid in *No, No, Nanette* with Ruby Keeler, her childhood friend, and later co-starred on stage with Debbie Reynolds in *Irene*; calling it "a miracle," she said, "I think people are starved for happy endings—I know I was."

MOVIE HIGHLIGHTS: *The Girl from Missouri, The Countess of Monte Carlo, Page Miss Glory, Go Into Your Dance, Thanks a Million, Every Night at Eight, Pigskin Parade, Sing, Baby, Sing, Pick a Star, Wake Up and Live, There Goes My Heart, Merrily We Live, The Cowboy and the Lady, Ever Since Eve, Topper Returns, Playmates, Ladies' Day, The Naked Kiss, Rosemary's Baby.*

Guy Kibbee

(b. Guy Bridges Kibbee, March 6, 1882, El Paso, Texas; d. May 24, 1956) Plump, twinkly-eyed little baldie with gray fringe who, possessing a rollicking good nature off screen, could play everything from bigtime crooks (the governor, harried by his eight kids, in *Mr. Smith Goes to Washington*) to folksy smalltime editors *(Our Town)*; model for the latter role was his father, the editor of the newspaper in Roswell, New Mexico, where the actor spent his youth—before running away at 14 to go on the stage; in his busiest year on screen, 1932, appeared in 20 films (managed a mere 12 the following season); made it to Hollywood shortly before his 50th birthday, after scoring a hit on Broadway in *The Torch Song*; debut character role was in William Powell's *Man of the World*; was first at Warners for seven years, then at Metro for four before turning freelance; while reeling in major movie roles, he was, away from the cameras, an enthusiastic fisherman; other outside interest: a successful printing shop (had once spent a four-year professional lull working in a San Francisco printing firm); was the proud owner of a fine horse ranch in the San Fernando Valley, where he lived with wife Esther Reed and their children, Shirley Ann and Guy Jr.; was married earlier (1918–23) to Helen Shea, by whom he had two sons, Robert Joseph and John Patrick; character actor Milton Kibbee was his brother; gregarious and a "joiner," he was a member of many clubs— the Lambs, the Bohemian, the Lakeside Golf Club, etc.; many fans may recall him best as the star of the "Scattergood Baines" series at RKO.

MOVIE HIGHLIGHTS: *42nd Street, Rain, So Big, Gold Diggers of 1933, Footlight Parade, Lady for a Day, Babbitt, Little Lord Fauntleroy, Captain January, Three Comrades, Joy of Living, Babes in Arms, It Started with Eve, Whistling in Dixie, Girl Crazy, Fort Apache.*

Patric Knowles

(b. Reginald Lawrence Knowles, Nov. 11, 1911, Horsforth, England) Tall (6′2″) and handsome, with green eyes, a splendid physique, and charm to spare, the Yorkshireman had everything pal Errol Flynn had—except his luck in starring vehicles; made up for that by playing leads in many more films and by having a full, happy life (two children who have made him proud and one wife, actress Enid Percival, whom he married in '35); the son of an Oxford publisher, he was born on the eleventh hour of the eleventh day of the eleventh month of the eleventh year; after attending Oxford University, he worked briefly as an ad designer for his father's firm before going on the stage; was "Patrick" at the start but changed that at the recommendation of a psychic who assured him he'd have better luck without the "k"; joined Agnew McMasters's Shakespearean Players, appearing first at Dublin's Abbey Theatre; after more stage experience, he made his screen debut at 23 in a movie made in Ireland, *Irish Hearts*, going on to roles in such British films as *A Student's Romance* and *Mister Hobo*; two years later was in Hollywood, under contract at Warners and co-starring with look-alike Errol Flynn (playing his brother) in *The Charge of the Light Brigade*; was again with Flynn (godfather of his son Michael) in *The Adventures of Robin Hood*, *The Sisters*, and *Four's a Crowd*; an expert pilot, he enlisted in the Royal Canadian Air Force in '40 and served as a flight instructor; honorably discharged for medical reasons, he promptly joined the U.S. Air Force where he performed the same duty; served as honorary mayor of Tarzana, Calif., became wealthy via business interests (gas docks, apartments, etc.), and published a successful novel, *Even Steven*.

MOVIE HIGHLIGHTS: *Give Me Your Heart, It's Love I'm After, The Patient in Room 18, Five Came Back, Torchy Blane in Chinatown, Another Thin Man, A Bill of Divorcement, How Green Was My Valley, Lady in a Jam, Forever and a Day, Kitty, Masquerade in Mexico, Of Human Bondage, Dream Girl, Monsieur Beaucaire, O.S.S., The Bride Wore Boots, Band of Angels, Auntie Mame.*

Miliza Korjus

(b. Miliza Korjus, Aug. 17, 1902, Warsaw, Poland; d. Aug. 26, 1980) Blonde and beefy Continental coloratura whom MGM trimmed down (by 45 pounds), corseted tightly, and presented glamorously in 1938's *The Great Waltz*; her flutelike voice, coupled with a certain flirtatious flounce in white frills, brought her an Academy Award nomination as Best Support; terming her a "kind of Mae West with a concealed steam whistle," one critic accurately predicted, "Hollywood won't quite know what to do with her and she'll be put back on the shelf"; never made another American movie, though it's reported that, when living in Mexico in the '40s, she starred in a Spanish musical film, *Caballeria del Imperio*; trained for a music career in the Conservatory at Moscow, after attending schools in many cities—Kiev, Vienna, Dresden, Hamburg, etc.; her great fame in Europe was gained at the Berlin State Opera, where she became a prime favorite starring in such operas as *The Magic Flute* and *Rigoletto*; her avowed favorite operatic character was Gilda, and it was her unfulfilled ambition of portraying her on screen; a recording of one of her opera performances brought her to the attention of MGM's Irving G. Thalberg, who spent a year convincing her to sign a movie contract; Hollywood career was cut short by an automobile accident in '40 that caused her to be hospitalized for many months; became, almost certainly because of her aborted screen career, a cult figure; made her New York concert debut at Carnegie Hall in '44; returned to Hollywood and lived there, rarely appearing on stage, for the rest of her life; continued to record, mainly for Venus Recording Company of America; one of her final albums, appropriately, was *Night in Vienna with Johann Strauss*—recorded at her West Los Angeles home with a pet canary, William, trilling along in the background; to the end, spoke of making a screen comeback.

MOVIE HIGHLIGHT: *The Great Waltz.*

Arthur Lake

(b. Arthur Silverlake, April 17, 1905, Corbin, Ky.) Long-memoried fans of the comedy star know that long before he became *Blondie's* befuddled "Dagwood Bumstead," he had created another comic-strip character on the screen; that was in a 1928 silent, *Harold Teen*; said one critic: "Arthur Lake walks away with the honors as Harold"; it can't be denied that *Blondie* ('38) lastingly changed his professional life; except for five comedies he made in 1943–45, when Columbia felt the series was played out, and one movie in '48 *(Sixteen Fathoms Deep)*, he was permanently locked in as bowtied, squeaky-voiced, forever-late-to-work "Dagwood"; played the part opposite "Blondie" Penny Singleton in all 28 of the comedies, through 1950's *Blondie's Hero* and *Beware of Blondie*, which marked his departure from the screen; starred in the *Blondie* radio show from '39 to '50; reprised his role on TV in '57 in a short-lived NBC series, with the late Pamela Britton as "Blondie"; also did another television series, "Meet the Family," co-starring his real-life wife, Patricia Van Cleve, who is, of course, blonde (and even played "Blondie" for a while with him on radio); their '37 wedding was an elaborate affair taking place at Hearst's fabled San Simeon (the only one ever performed there), as the bride's aunt, Marion Davies, was the publisher's longtime companion; the son of circus acrobats, Lake was first on stage as an infant in *Uncle Tom's Cabin*; was part of his father's act between the ages of 3 and 13; made his movie debut at 19 in *When Love Is Young* and was continuously on the screen, usually in juvenile leads, for the next 26 years; starred first for Universal in a series of comedy shorts; like "Dagwood," he is the father of a son (Arthur Jr.) and a daughter (Marion).

MOVIE HIGHLIGHTS: *Skinner's Dress Suit, The Cradle Snatchers, Irresistible Love* (silents), *Lilac Time, On With the Show, Cheer Up and Smile, Tanned Legs, Midshipman Jack, Orchids for You, I Cover Chinatown, Annapolis Salute, Topper, Everybody's Doing It, There Goes My Heart, Sailor's Holiday, Three Is a Family.*

The Lane Sisters

Lola (b. Dorothy Mullican, May 21, 1907, Marcy, Ind.; d. June 22, 1981), **Rosemary** (b. Rosemary Mullican, April 4, 1913, Indianola, Iowa; d. Nov. 25, 1974), **Priscilla** (b. Priscilla Mullican, June 12, 1917, Indianola, Iowa) Lola, who began in vaudeville and was discovered on stage when playing with George Jessel in *The War Song*, made it to the screen first—in 1929's *Speakeasy*; Rosemary and Priscilla, who sang together on radio with Fred Waring's Pennsylvanians, made their joint debut as members of the Waring troupe in 1937's *Varsity Show*; realizing their starring potential, Warner Bros. quickly put them under contract, while also adding Lola to the studio roster; promoting Priscilla to be Wayne Morris' leading lady in *Love, Honor and Behave*, they paired Lola and Rosemary in *Hollywood Hotel*; the three finally got together, charmingly and most successfully, in 1938's *Four Daughters* (the fourth "sister" being Gale Page), which, to satisfy moviegoers' demands, was followed in '39 by *Daughters Courageous* and *Four Wives*, then, in '41, *Four Mothers*; went separate ways afterwards, leaving fans with rather special memories of them as a group; Rosemary, twice married and divorced, starred on Broadway in *Best Foot Forward*, then in B musicals, and left the screen in '45. . . . Four times divorced (first from Lew Ayres), Lola retired in '46, was later successful in real estate, and was last married to lawyer Robert Hanlon. . . . Continuing to play leads until '48, Priscilla, who was wed for one day in

'39 to director Orin Haglund, had a happy marriage from '43 on to the late Joseph A. Howard, a bombardier pilot who became a wealthy building contractor, lived in New Hampshire and became the mother of four—two sons, two daughters.

MOVIE HIGHLIGHTS: **Lola:** *The Costello Murder Case, Woman Condemned, His Night Out, Marked Woman, Torchy Blane in Panama, Zanzibar, Gangs of Chicago, Mystery Ship;* **Rosemary:** *Gold Diggers in Paris, The Oklahoma Kid, Blackwell's Island, The Return of Dr. X, The Boys from Syracuse, Harvest Melody, Trocadero;* **Priscilla:** *Brother Rat, Yes, My Darling Daughter, The Roaring Twenties, Dust Be My Destiny, Blues in the Night, Saboteur, Arsenic and Old Lace.*

Charles Laughton

(b. Charles Laughton, July 1, 1899, Scarborough, England; d. Dec. 15, 1962) A heavyweight in size and talent, he won a Best Actor Oscar for *The Private Life of Henry VIII* ('33), his first time in competition, and was later nominated in the same category for *Mutiny on the Bounty* and *Witness for the Prosecution;* recalled having been plump, homely, sensitive, lonely, and "different" as a child; grew up in the north of England, the son of a hotel proprietor, in a stern, staid middle-class environment offering little freedom, except in one's imagination; such a set of facts, he said, contributed to his need to act; before going to the Royal Academy of Dramatic Arts (won a gold medal there), he first attended Stonyhurst College, went to London to learn the hotel business at Claridge's (working as a reception clerk provided ample opportunity to study a wide variety of human characteristics), and served during WW I with the Seventh North Hampshire Regiment; first appeared on the London stage at the Barnes Theatre on April 28, 1926, in *The Government Inspector,* followed by more plays in England and America; in '29 made his movie debut, playing (brilliantly) a drunk in *Piccadilly,* starring Gilda Gray, and he married actress Elsa Lanchester, his wife for 33 years; were often together on screen (*Rembrandt, The Beachcomber,* etc.); 14 years after his death, she assisted on the book *Charles Laughton: An Intimate Biography;* revealed in it that she learned about his homosexuality only years after they wed; remained together because of mutual interests (cooking, cats, gardening, acting) but theirs was an "open" marriage ("We both needed other company. I met his young men, and I had a young man around, and Charles didn't even argue").

MOVIE HIGHLIGHTS: *Comets, Down River* (English films), *Payment Deferred, Island of Lost Souls, If I Had a Million, Sign of the Cross, The Old Dark House, Les Miserables, The Barretts of Wimpole Street, Ruggles of Red Gap, Jamaica Inn, The Hunchback of Notre Dame, They Knew What They Wanted, This Land Is Mine, The Suspect, The Canterville Ghost, Captain Kidd, The Paradine Case, The Big Clock, Hobson's Choice, Spartacus.*

Laurel and Hardy

Stan Laurel (b. Arthur Stanley Jefferson, June 16, 1890, Ulverston, England; d. Feb. 23, 1965) and **Oliver Hardy** (b. Oliver Norvell Hardy, Jan. 18, 1892, Atlanta, Ga.; d. Aug. 7, 1957) The Sons of the Desert, a large club with members of many nationalities, meets regularly (in the summer of '84 at Stan Laurel's birthplace) to honor the memory and humor of what was perhaps the best-loved male comedy team in movie history; the derbied pair—moon-faced Ollie with his moustache and short fuse and Stan, the befuddled "cry baby"—did not start as a twosome; ditching plans to be an attorney, Hardy went on the stage then made his movie debut in '13 *(Outwitting Dad)*; was in many early silents, often being teamed with partners (Jimmy Aubrey, Billy Ruge, Larry Semon) in one- or two-reel comedies; first on stage in 1903 in England, with the Juvenile Pantomime Co., Stan Laurel came to the U.S. in 1910, billed as star Charlie Chaplin's understudy, with the Fred Karno Boys; troupe lost its mainstay when Chaplin chose to go to Hollywood; Laurel was in vaudeville until '17, when Chaplin urged him to give movies a try; made his screen debut in *Nuts in May*, which was followed by dozens, including *Lucky Dog* ('18) and *With Love and Hisses* ('27), in which Laurel was the featured comic and Hardy played minor roles; producer Hal Roach was inspired to team them later in '27; the short in which fans first saw them: *The Second Hundred Years*; after scores of two-reelers, began starring in features in the early '30s; were vastly popular in 27 through *The Bullfighters* ('45); Laurel, regarded as the "inventive one" (even by Hardy), was accorded a special Oscar in '60 "for his creative pioneering in the field of cinema comedy."

MOVIE HIGHLIGHTS: *The Rogue Song, Pardon Us, Pack Up Your Troubles, The Devil's Brother, Sons of the Desert, Babes in Toyland* (a.k.a. *The March of the Wooden Soldiers*), *Bonnie Scotland, The Bohemian Girl, Our Relations, Way Out West, Swiss Miss, Pick a Star, The Flying Deuces, A Chump at Oxford, Saps at Sea, Air Raid Wardens, The Dancing Masters, Jitterbugs, The Big Noise.*

Andrea Leeds

(b. Antoinette Lees, Aug. 18, 1914, Butte, Mont.; d. May 21, 1984) An auburn-haired beauty—full-lipped, brown-eyed, and sweet of face—she played an aspiring actress, Kay, who committed suicide, in *Stage Door* and was Oscar-nominated as Best Support; was much like Olivia de Havilland in both looks and style, and at one time was a leading contender for Melanie in *GWTW*; the daughter of an English mining engineer, she won her bachelor's degree at UCLA, planning to be a screenwriter, before being persuaded to turn actress; was given a screen test by director William Howard, who showed it to director Howard Hawks, who put her under personal contract and showed the test to producer Sam Goldwyn, who bought out the contract and promptly cast her as Edward Arnold's daughter in *Come and Get It*; a hit in this, she incurred Goldwyn's wrath next by refusing to appear in Miriam Hopkins' *Woman Chases Man* (a singularly silly comedy); as "punishment," he loaned her to RKO for a small, "unimportant" role in *Stage Door*—which won high praise from fans and critics; announced early that she meant to marry, stop acting, and rear a family; left the screen, after leads in nine films, in '40 when she became the wife of Robert Stewart Howard, a young Palm Springs millionaire whose family owned the famous racehorse Seabiscuit; had a son and daughter, R.S. Howard Jr. and Leeann; profoundly religious, she was a person of exceptional character—accepting life's bounties with gratitude and its severest blows with indomitable grace; her one marriage ended with the death of her husband in '62 and her daughter, a young beauty, died of cancer in '71; in the unadorned manner that marked, and made memorable, her work on the screen, she said at the time, "So I have had a share in unhappiness, but I have also been blessed in many ways."

MOVIE HIGHLIGHTS: *The Goldwyn Follies, Youth Takes a Fling, A Letter of Introduction, They Shall Have Music, The Real Glory, Swanee River, Earthbound.*

Vivien Leigh

(b. Vivian Mary Hartley, Nov. 5, 1913, Darjeeling, India; d. July 8, 1967) Exquisite in looks, and an artist to her fingertips, she twice adapted her English accent to play Southern women and both times, in these, her only Academy Award nominations, won the Best Actress Oscar—for *Gone With the Wind* and *A Streetcar Named Desire*; it is surprising to note that she had been in more pictures (11), all made in England, before *GWTW* then she was after portraying Scarlett O'Hara (only eight, and three of them were British-made films); from the time this daughter of a wealthy English stockbroker was 7, when she announced intentions of becoming an actress, the stage was her first love; later, between films, she devoted far more time and energy to the theater, usually starring in the classics; made her screen debut, as Vivian Leigh, in a minor 1934 comedy, *Things Are Looking Up*; name change to "Vivien" came the next year when in a play; risked scandal by following Laurence Olivier (with whom she fell in love while co-starring in 1937's *Fire Over England*) to Hollywood when he played Heathcliff in *Wuthering Heights*; each had left behind a spouse and a child; she had been wed since '32 to barrister Herbert Leigh Holman, by whom, the following year, she had a daughter, Suzanne; obtaining divorces, she and Olivier married in California in '40 and co-starred in the movie *That Hamilton Woman* before returning to England, where they remained for the duration; repeatedly together on stage—until '60, when he asked for a divorce—they never again teamed for a movie; was long plagued by precarious health—mental (had a nervous breakdown while filming *Elephant Walk* in '53; was replaced by Elizabeth Taylor) and physical (tuberculosis, diagnosed in '45, finally claimed her life).

MOVIE HIGHLIGHTS: *The Village Square, Look Up and Laugh, Gentleman's Agreement, First and Last, Dark Journey, Storm in a Teacup, Sidewalks of London, A Yank at Oxford* (all made in England), *Waterloo Bridge, Caesar and Cleopatra, Anna Karenina, The Deep Blue Sea, The Roman Spring of Mrs. Stone, Ship of Fools.*

Margaret Lindsay

(b. Margaret Kies, Sept. 19, 1910; Dubuque, Iowa; d. May 8, 1981) Brunette with a winning smile and breezy personality who took a roundabout route to become one of Warners' most durable (1933–40) leading ladies; between her '31 graduation from the American Academy of Dramatic Arts and a trio of forgettable B's at Universal, she was on stage in London in *Death Takes a Holiday*; in '33, eager to play the ingenue lead—an English girl—in the movie *Cavalcade*, she landed it by successfully passing herself off as Surrey-born; that memorable performance brought her long-term contract at WB, where she had top roles in more than 50 movies; played opposite all the studio's major male stars: James Cagney *(G-Men)*, Pat O'Brien *(Public Enemy's Wife)*, Errol Flynn *(Green Light)*, etc.; often cast as the "other woman" in Bette Davis vehicles *(Hard Luck Dame, Bordertown, Jezebel)*, she also occasionally inherited one of Davis' castoffs *(Garden of the Moon)*; during the '30s was one of Hollywood's most avidly pursued "bachelor girls" (as the phrase then went), and for a while was engaged to actor William Lundigan but the wedding never took place; remained single to the end; between '40 and '42, in Columbia's popular "Ellery Queen" series, she was a charming fixture as the sleuth's indispensable secretary, "Nikki Porter"; played the part four times opposite Ralph Bellamy and another three with his successor, William Gargan; was steadily on screen through '48 but only infrequently afterwards; last acted in '74, in a one-day stint as Fred MacMurray's secretary in an unsold TV pilot, "The Chadwicks"; seeing the single episode on television, lifelong fans were struck by how little the years had changed her.

MOVIE HIGHLIGHTS: *Voltaire, Lady Killer, Devil Dogs of the Air, Dangerous, The Frisco Kid, The Case of the Curious Bride, Slim, Gold Is Where You Find It, There's That Woman Again, Sinner Take All, 20,000 Men a Year, House of the Seven Gables, Ellery Queen's Penthouse Mystery, The Spoilers, Cass Timberlane.*

Carole Lombard

(b. Jane Alice Peters, Oct, 6, 1908, Fort Wayne, Ind.; d. Jan. 16, 1942) Soon after Pearl Harbor, the colorful, vibrant star answered the call to promote Defense Bonds in the home town that she had left at 7 to go to California with her family; this time, returning to Hollywood after selling $2 million in bonds, she perished in a mountaintop plane crash and was mourned as a national heroine; at 33, she had been in movies 22 years,

110

having made her debut in a child role in a Monte Blue silent, *A Perfect Crime*; ironically, for someone whose greater fame rests on her genius for madcap comedy (*My Man Godfrey*, which rated her an Oscar nomination, and others), and who had a natural gift for laughter, her life was less than cloud-free; in a near-fatal car crash at 18, she was thrown through a glass windshield; the resulting facial scar, from the left corner of her mouth to her eye, had to be artfully camouflaged with make-up throughout her career; her first marriage, to William Powell (1931–33), ended in divorce; and she was engaged to singer-actor Russ Columbo when, in '34, he was accidentally shot to death; friends have said that, except for her childhood, the lengthiest completely happy time in her life was when she and Clark Gable fell in love and then, in '39, were married; hit her stride as a star (earning $487,000 a year) in the mid-1930s when, by sheer vitality and a keen intelligence, she made screwball comedy an intelligent art; said one critic: "Her best work comes close to having something of the acid-etched savagery that Swift brought to literature, but there is always the rich sense of fun to temper the sharpness of the comment"; President Roosevelt spoke for the world when, in a wire to Clark Gable, he said: "She is and always will be a star, one we shall never forget nor cease to be grateful to."

MOVIE HIGHLIGHTS: *Dynamite, Safety in Numbers, No One Man, The Match King, The Eagle and the Hawk, Bolero, We're Not Dressing, Now and Forever, Twentieth Century, Rumba, Hands Across the Table, The Princess Comes Across, Swing High, Swing Low, Nothing Sacred, True Confession, Made for Each Other, In Name Only, Vigil in the Night, They Knew What They Wanted, Mr. and Mrs. North, To Be or Not to Be.*

Peter Lorre

(b. Ladislav Loewenstein, June 26, 1904, Rozsahegy, Hungary; d. March 23, 1964) Owl-eyed, small-sized menace who knew how to make a whisper more arresting than a gunshot; was a popular light comedian on stage in Berlin and Vienna before director Fritz Lang cast him as a child murderer in the German-made *M* ('31); this debut movie, bringing fame, shaped his entire professional future; Hitchcock insisted on him for a villainous role in the original *The Man Who Knew Too Much* ('34), Lorre's first in English; the director discovered that he "had a very sharp sense of humor" and was a trifle eccentric ("They called him 'the walking overcoat' because he went around in a long coat that came down to his feet"); arriving in Hollywood in '35 to star as a creepy doctor in MGM's *Mad Love*, he was next under contract at 20th Century–Fox (mainly starring in the "Mr. Moto" series) before settling in at Warner Bros.; started at WB with a gem: perfumed, effeminate little Joel Cairo in *The Maltese Falcon*; won a reputation as the most outrageous practical joker on the lot; once as a busload of studio tourists lumbered past, he grabbed unsuspecting George Raft in a passionate embrace and kissed him squarely on the lips; as Raft spluttered in disgust, he shrugged and said, "I just thought we should give those poor creeps a little fun"; first wife (married in 1933) Celia Lovsky (Cecilia Lovovsky), a major European stage star, gave up her career at his insistence when they went to Hollywood; resumed it as a character actress after he asked for a divorce in '44 to wed Kaaren Verne, a blonde leading lady at Warners; they, too, divorced and from '52 on, he was married to Anne Marie Brenning; their daughter, Catharine, was his only child.

MOVIE HIGHLIGHTS: *Crime and Punishment, Nancy Steele Is Missing, Mr. Moto's Gamble, Lancer Spy, The Face Behind the Mask, Casablanca, The Constant Nymph, Passage to Marseilles, The Mask of Dimitrios, Arsenic and Old Lace, Hotel Berlin, Three Strangers, The Beast with Five Fingers, The Verdict, Rope of Sand, Beat the Devil, Voyage to the Bottom of the Sea.*

Edmund Lowe

(b. Edmund Dantes Lowe, March 3, 1890, San Jose, Calif.; d. April 21, 1971) Two highly disparate images persist of this handsome star whose career spanned more than four decades—from 1918's *Viva La France!* to 1960's *Heller in Pink Tights*; there's hardboiled Sergeant Quirt who wrangled ("Sez you!"—"Yeah! Sez me!") with Captain Flagg (Victor McLaglen), usually over women, in *What Price Glory* and its sequels; on the other hand is the man in the dinner jacket, gleaming black hair plastered tight against his skull and a perfectly manicured moustache, the ultimate in suavity; back of both images was a man of some brilliance; the son of a lawyer-judge (and one of 13 children), he won his Master's degree at Santa Clara University at 19, then was on the faculty of the school for a year before going on the stage; became a matinee idol in the '20s when making love to smoldering Pola Negri in *East of Suez*; his drawing-room manners served him well in scores of starring roles in the '30s and '40s; fans were charmed by his elegance but not everyone was—film historian William K. Everson, for one, has noted: "Whether he was playing Chandu the Magician or Philo Vance [in 1936's *The Garden Murder Case*], he was always exactly the same: the veneer was polished but there was no subtlety or differentiation between roles beneath it"; equally debonair in private life, he lived on a large Hollywood estate, entertained lavishly, and took vast pride in his reputation as a fashionplate; divorced by Esther Miller, he was wed to actress Lilyan Tashman for 10 years until her death in '34, and was later divorced by Rita Kaufman, whom he married in '35.

MOVIE HIGHLIGHTS: *In Old Arizona, The Cockeyed World, Born Reckless, Don't Bet on Women, Misleading Lady, Her Bodyguard, Dinner at Eight, Let's Fall in Love, The Best Man Wins, King Solomon of Broadway, Mad Holiday, The Girl on the Front Page, Espionage, Everyday's a Holiday, Murder on the Diamond, Secrets of a Nurse, I Love You Again, Call Out the Marines.*

Myrna Loy

(b. Myrna Williams, Aug. 2, 1905, Raidersburg, Mont.) Everything about this delightful redhead is unique—her freckles, quirky voice, tip-tilted nose, offhand style (acts as though no camera is anywhere around), and, most of all, her gaiety; entered movies, the protogée of Rudolph Valentino and his wife, Natacha Rambova, in Oriental roles, hence her screen surname; as for "Myrna," her cattleman father, traveling on a train once before she was born, saw it painted on a small railroad station and decided it was an appropriately charming name for a daughter; studied to be a sculptor and dancer, and was an artists' model before, at 19, beginning to play bits in movies, the first of which was *Pretty Ladies*; in many silents: *Cave Man, Ben Hur, Don Juan, Across the Pacific*, etc.; first lead was as a Chinese maiden in 1928's *Crimson City*; thanks to many happily-wed roles, particularly those with William Powell in the "Thin Man" series and numerous other comedies, she soon became known as the movies' "Perfect Wife"; privately, the label may have jinxed her; had four husbands (no children), each of whom she divorced: producer Arthur Hornblow Jr., John Hertz Jr., writer-producer Gene Markey, and Howland Sargeant; in the Box Office Top Ten in '37 and '38; after a long list of romantic leads, segued easily, in her early 40s, into mother roles in *The Best Years of Our Lives*, *Cheaper by the Dozen*, etc.; debuted on Broadway in '43 in *Button Your Lip*; in her late 50s carved an entirely new career on stage, touring in *Marriage-Go-Round* and *Barefoot in the Park* (won Chicago's prized Sarah Siddons Award), before returning to Broadway.

MOVIE HIGHLIGHTS: *Arrowsmith*, *When Ladies Meet*, *Broadway Bill*, *Wife vs. Secretary*, *The Great Ziegfeld*, *Test Pilot*, *Too Hot to Handle*, *The Rains Came*, *Love Crazy*, *The Bachelor and the Bobby-Soxer*, *Mr. Blandings Builds His Dream House*, *The Red Pony*, *From the Terrace*.

Bela Lugosi

(b. Bela Blasko, Oct. 20, 1882, Lugos, Hungary; d. Aug. 16, 1956) Universal's horror flicks would never have been the same without the man whose "Dracula" sucked the blood of lovely heroines and pumped new life into a faltering studio; women, for a fact, did not find unappealing this well-read, gentle-spoken man with the prominent widow's peak, satanic face, and piercing blue eyes; besides a once well-publicized romance with flapper Clara Bow, he was married five times; was divorced in short order by the first three of his wives: Ilona Szmik (a young woman in Hungary), Ilona von Montagh (a Hungarian actress in New York), and Beatrice Weeks (a San Francisco socialite; left him after three days); for 20 years (1933–53), until they divorced, he was wed to Lillian Arch (mother of his only child, Bela George Lugosi, who is now a prominent California attorney); in '55 was married to Hope Linninger; took his stage name, of course, from the village where he was born; the son of a baker who became president of the town bank, he ran away from home at 12, when his father died; worked in coal mines, as a riveter on bridges, as a machinist in a railway repair shop; finally, as he had a fine lyric baritone, he was persuaded by his sister's husband—director of a little theater—to sing in the chorus there; soon was acting in provincial theaters throughout Hungary, experiencing, too, "long chains of love affairs"; with 11 years' training, he was invited to join Hungary's Royal National Theatre, where he quickly became its leading actor, starring in *Romeo and Juliet*, *Hamlet*, etc.; sentenced to death for his part in Count Karolyi's revolution of 1918, he escaped to Austria and, finally, in '21, made it to New York; first played Dracula, triumphantly, on Broadway in '27.

MOVIE HIGHLIGHTS: *The Black Camel, White Zombie, Murders in the Rue Morgue, Island of Lost Souls, The Black Cat, The Raven, Phantom Ship, Son of Frankenstein, The Gorilla, Ninotchka, The Devil Bat, The Wolf Man, The Night Monster, Return of the Vampire, The Body Snatcher, Bride of the Monster, The Shadow Creeps.*

Jeanette MacDonald

(b. Jeanette Anne MacDonald, June 18, 1903, Philadelphia, Pa.; d. Jan. 14, 1965) Metro's titian-haired songbird enjoyed a lengthy career in Broadway musicals *(Sunny Days, Yes, Yes, Yvette, Angela)* before debuting in movies in '29 opposite Maurice Chevalier, in *The Love Parade*; they sang together in three more, and she also duetted with Dennis King in *The Vagabond King*, before signing with MGM in '34; that studio first paired her musically with Ramon Novarro in *The Cat and the Fiddle*; struck gold the next year when she and Nelson Eddy matched notes in *Naughty Marietta*, followed by *Rose Marie* and *Maytime*; moviegoers cried "foul" when Metro next had her singing romantically in the arms of Allan Jones in *The Firefly*; reunited, the MacDonald–Eddy duo enchanted millions in six more tune-filled movies, occasionally going off to warble solo in other films, before splitting up permanently after 1942's *I Married an Angel*; her delicious comedy talent was allowed to atrophy after her early movies with Chevalier, though it surfaced unexpectedly in flashes in *The Firefly* and *San Francisco*; had a steely will—was called, behind her back, "The Iron Butterfly"; on June 16, 1937, at the Wilshire Methodist Church, she became the bride of star Gene Raymond; Nelson Eddy sang ("I Love You Truly" and "O Perfect Love"); among the bridesmaids in this social event of the season were Ginger Rogers, Fay Wray, and Jeanette's sister, comedienne Marie (Blossom Rock) Blake; MacDonald and Raymond remained lastingly a love match.

MOVIE HIGHLIGHTS: *Love Me Tonight, The Lottery Bride, One Hour with You, The Merry Widow, Girl of the Golden West, Sweethearts, Broadway Serenade, New Moon, Bitter Sweet, Smilin' Through* (with Gene Raymond), *Cairo, Three Darling Daughters, The Sun Comes Up* (her last, in '49).

Fred MacMurray

(b. Frederick MacMurray Jr., Aug. 30, 1907, Kankakee, Ill.) With black curly hair and a handsome grin, this brawny guy looked for years like some recent BMOC at a Midwestern university—which was true when a screen newcomer; had studied for two years at little Carroll College, nearby Beaver Dam, Wis., which was his mother's home town, where he grew up in near-poverty; parents had divorced soon after he was born (birthplace was an accident as his concert violinist father was only playing a one-night stand there); worked as a teenager in a pea cannery and a factory; attended college on a football scholarship (played center), singing and playing sax in local dance bands to earn pocket change; next was with professional orchestras in Chicago and Hollywood where, in '29, he worked as a day laborer also and as a movie extra (*Girls Gone Wild* starring Sue Carol); went on stage in New York with the California Collegians band before landing a part in a revue, *Three's a Crowd*; was soon cast in a lead on Broadway in *Roberta*, which won him a Paramount contract in '34; loaned out to RKO, he made his debut as a movie actor in *Grand Old Girl* starring May Robson, then returned to his home studio and was properly, romantically launched as Claudette Colbert's co-star in *The Gilded Lily*; his smile and friendly, unassuming manner made him an instant hit with fans; called his success "pure, dumb luck"; remained at Paramount 11 years, earning one year $419,166 (fourth highest salary in the U.S.), while frugally getting by on $35 a week spending money; was married to former *Roberta* showgirl Lillian Lamont from '36 until her death in '53 (two adopted children: Susan and Robert); has been wed to June Haver since '54 (adopted twin daughters: Laurie and Kathryn).

MOVIE HIGHLIGHTS: *Hands Across the Table, Alice Adams, Trail of the Lonesome Pine, The Texas Rangers, Maid of Salem, True Confession, Swing High, Swing Low, Men With Wings, Sing You Sinners, Cafe Society, Honeymoon in Bali, Too Many Husbands, Virginia, Remember the Night, Dive Bomber, Take a Letter, Darling, No Time for Love, Double Indemnity, Practically Yours, The Egg and I, The Caine Mutiny, The Absent-Minded Professor.*

Fredric March

(b. Frederick Ernest McIntyre Bickel, Aug. 31, 1897, Racine, Wis.; d. April 14, 1975) Motion picture stardom was, for him, inevitable; started in talkies with a decade of stage experience and every gift the Thespic gods can bestow: superb speaking voice and a fine face and physique, not to mention talent; the winner, eventually, of two Best Actor Oscars (*Dr. Jekyll and Mr. Hyde, The Best Years of Our Lives*), he has been hailed by many as the greatest American actor on the screen; certainly, none was more versatile—traveled easily between tragedy and comedy, modern and costume dramas; oddly, he got off to a most inauspicious start; in his debut movie, *The Dummy* ('29), he had major billing and a minor role, and *Variety's* critic noted that "he doesn't get a single closeup and remains a zero throughout"; rave reviews didn't come until he played the flamboyant, John Barrymore-like movie idol, Tony Cavendish, in *The Royal Family of Broadway* (his 14th picture), which rated him an Oscar nomination, as did, later, *A Star Is Born* and *Death of a Salesman*; the son of a small-scale manufacturer, he left the University of Wisconsin, where he studied economics and acted in plays, in his junior year; served a year in the Army then toiled briefly as a teller in a Manhattan bank before deciding to act; in 1920, while working as an extra in New York-made movies (first: *Paying the Piper*) and as a photographer's model, he landed a small part in a Broadway drama, *Deburau*, billed as Frederick Bickell; did many other roles before and after '24, when he concocted his new monicker from his mother's maiden name, "Marcher"; an early marriage ('23) to stage actress Ellis Baker ended in divorce; from '27 on was married to Florence Eldridge, with whom he starred often on stage and screen (*Les Miserables, Mary of Scotland*, etc.); two adopted children: Penelope and Anthony.

MOVIE HIGHLIGHTS: *The Wild Party, Sarah and Son, My Sin, Sign of the Cross, Smilin' Through, Design for Living, Death Takes a Holiday, The Affairs of Cellini, The Barretts of Wimpole Street, The Dark Angel, Anna Karenina, Anthony Adverse, Nothing Sacred, The Buccaneer, Susan and God, One Foot in Heaven, So Ends Our Night, I Married a Witch, Inherit the Wind.*

Herbert Marshall

(b. Herbert Marshall, May 23, 1890, London, England; d. Jan. 22, 1966) For good cause, this aristocratic Britisher—smooth as Steuben's finest crystal—was most often photographed either standing or sitting; had lost a leg fighting in the Great War and his artificial one (about which he was somewhat sensitive) sometimes creaked a bit, driving soundmen wild; Joan Fontaine reports that, while co-starring with him in *Ivy*, she committed one of her most embarrassing gaffes by whispering to him as a famous gossip columnist appeared on the set: "Don't look now—if she joins us, she'll talk your leg off!"; educated at St. Mary's College, Harlow, he was an accountant for a short while before going on the stage in 1911 *(The Adventures of Lady Ursula)*; played important roles on British and American stages both before and after WW I; began on screen in England in '28 *(Dawn, Mumsie)*; in Hollywood after '29, he starred first with Jeanne Eagels in *The Letter* (repeated the husband role 11 years later opposite Bette Davis); his second movie here, *Secrets of a Secretary* with Claudette Colbert, made him a matinee idol, which he continued to be until '40; played fathers of daughters more often than not after that: Shirley Temple's in *Kathleen*, Laraine Day's in *Foreign Correspondent*, Teresa Wright's in *The Little Foxes*, Maureen O'Hara's in *A Bill of Divorcement*; had two daughters of his own: Sarah, who became an actress, by Edna Best (married 1928–40), and Anne by Lee Russell (1940–46); prior to these wives was married (1915–28) to Mollie Maitland and, following them, to Boots Mallory (died in '58) and, in '60, to Dee Kahmann.

MOVIE HIGHLIGHTS: *Blonde Venus, Trouble in Paradise, The Painted Veil, Rip Tide, The Good Fairy, Accent on Youth, The Dark Angel, Four Frightened People, The Lady Consents, A Woman Rebels, Till We Meet Again, Girls' Dormitory, Angel, Breakfast for Two, Mad About Music, Always Goodbye, Zaza, Marie Antoinette, The Moon and Sixpence, The Enchanted Cottage, The Razor's Edge.*

The Marx Brothers

Groucho (b. Julius Henry Marx, Oct. 2, 1890, New York, N.Y.; d. Aug. 19, 1977), **Chico** (b. Leonard Marx, March 22, 1887, New York, N.Y.; d. Oct. 11, 1961), **Harpo** (b. Adolph Arthur Marx, Nov. 23, 1888, New

York, N.Y.; d. Sept. 28, 1964), and **Zeppo** (b. Herbert Marx, Feb. 25, 1901, New York, N.Y.; d. Nov. 29, 1979) All four brothers were in their first five movies; Zeppo, who became an actors' agent, was absent in their other eight together; the fifth brother, Gummo (r.n. Milton; also an agent), was in vaudeville with them but never in pictures; all were trained for the stage by their ambitious mother, Minnie; all went through years of trial-and-error in show biz prior to WW I, not to mention odd jobs (Harpo being a bellhop at New York's Plaza Hotel, Groucho driving a grocery wagon in Colorado, etc.); during the war Harpo saw overseas service with the Seventh Regiment of New York; end of the war saw the formation of the antic quartet of Groucho-Chico-Harpo-Zeppo, forever contemptuous of authority in its patented, hilariously irreverent efforts to dismantle the establishment; starred on stage for two years in *I'll Say She Is*, followed by the shows *The Cocoanuts* and *Animal Crackers*, both of which they transferred to the screen, the first in '29; private lives: Groucho was divorced from dancer Ruth Johnson (son Arthur, daughter Miriam), actress Kay Gorcey (daughter Melinda), and actress Eden Hartford. . . . Chico was divorced from dancer Betty Karp (daughter Maxine) and married Mary DiVithas. . . . Harpo wed actress Susan Fleming, lastingly, in '36 (sons William, Alexander, James; daughter Minny). . . . Zeppo, who did straight romantic scenes in their movies, was divorced from Marion Benda (two adopted kids), and Barbara Blakely (who later married Frank Sinatra).

MOVIE HIGHLIGHTS: *The Cocoanuts, Animal Crackers, Monkey Business, Horse Feathers, Duck Soup* (all with Zeppo), *A Night at the Opera, A Day at the Races, Room Service, At the Circus, Go West, The Big Store, A Night in Casablanca, Love Happy.*

Joel McCrea

(b. Joel Albert McCrea, Nov. 5, 1905, South Pasadena, Calif.) A stalwart, amiable, masculine screen presence, stamped almost visibly "Made in the U.S.A.," he was a most deceptive actor; hardly seeming to shift gears, he was equally at home in sophisticated comedy *(The Palm Beach Story)* and stark drama *(Private Worlds)*; his understated performances were quite enough to take him from minor roles to stardom, and make him, a veteran of nearly 90 films, a very rich man (estimated wealth: $50 million-plus); has said, "The best advice I ever had came from my friend Will Rogers, who told me, 'No matter how much you make, you ought to save half of it,' and I've always tried to follow that"; Jody, one of his three sons by Frances Dee (married since '33), says, "He's a Scotsman—not one to throw money around"; his preference for Western roles (and ranching, his present occupation) came naturally as his ancestors were California pioneers; one grandfather was a '49 gold prospector, the other fought Apache Indians and drove a stagecoach in the Pacific Southwest; his earliest screen idol was William S. Hart ("I'd try to imitate him and ride just like him"); when a teenager was one of the few male students at the exclusive Hollywood School for Girls, attending class alongside Jean Harlow; planned early to be an actor; while at Pomona College (graduated in '28), he did plays, worked as an extra in silent movies, and once stunt-doubled on horseback for Greta Garbo (in *The Torrent*); starred from '30 (*The Silver Horde* was his first romantic lead) through '62's *Ride the High Country*; came back (regretted it) in '75 for *Mustang Country*; has more friends than he has millions; one of them, Ginger Rogers, explains why: "Joe truly loves everybody. He expects to find the best in everyone he meets, and he does."

MOVIE HIGHLIGHTS: *Lightnin', Lost Squadron, Bird of Paradise, Our Betters, Splendor, These Three, Barbary Coast, Banjo on My Knee, Come and Get It, Dead End, Wells Fargo, Three Blind Mice, Union Pacific, The Primrose Path, Foreign Correspondent, Sullivan's Travels, The More the Merrier, Buffalo Bill, The Virginian, The Great Man's Lady, Saddle Tramp, Stars in My Crown.*

Hattie McDaniel

(b. Hattie McDaniel, June 10, 1895, Wichita, Kans.; d. Oct. 26, 1952) Playing Scarlett O'Hara's "Mammy" in *Gone With The Wind*, she made history three ways: was the first black player to be nominated for an Oscar, the first to win (Best Support), and the first ever to sit down at an Academy Awards dinner; it is further claimed that she was the first female of her race to sing on radio, in the '20s, with Prof. George Morrison's all-black orchestra; the 13th child of a Baptist minister, she was inspired to go into show business in '16 by winning a gold medal in dramatic art presented by Denver's White Women's Christian Temperance Union; sang with bands and was in vaudeville, but there were lean times also; in Milwaukee once, when no theatrical bookings were to be had, she worked as a maid in the ladies' room of Sam Pick's Suburban Inn; a cross-country tour in *Show Boat* took her to Hollywood in the '20s; small movie jobs came along occasionally, but in between, when the going was bad, she took in washing; devoutly religious (a tithing member of Los Angeles' Independent Church of Christ), she never doubted that the breaks would eventually come; after *The Golden West*, a '32 George O'Brien Western, she never again had to take in washing; before GWTW, had important roles in 38 films and, after it, another 19; won the "Mammy" role over many contenders, including Louise Beavers and Hattie Noel; had to abandon her Kansas accent for a Deep South drawl ("Effen you don' care 'bout how folks talks 'bout dis fambly, Ah does!") and patterned her speech after her late father, the son of a Virginia-born slave; character actor Sam McDaniel, with whom she worked in *Hearts Divided* and *The Great Lie*, was her brother.

MOVIE HIGHLIGHTS: *I'm No Angel, Judge Priest, Alice Adams, The Little Colonel, China Seas, Gentle Julia, Can This Be Dixie?, Valiant Is the Word for Carrie, Show Boat, Racing Lady, Saratoga, True Confession, Nothing Sacred, The Shopworn Angel, The Mad Miss Manton, The Shining Hour, Maryland, The Male Animal, In This Our Life, Janie, Song of the South, Mr. Blandings Builds His Dream House.*

Spanky McFarland

(b. George Robert Phillips McFarland, Oct. 2, 1928, Dallas, Tex.) For a decade after '32, this chubby brown-eyed lad was easily the most famous and best-loved of all the "Our Gang" kids; made his professional debut as a tyke when he was the model for a poster advertising a Texas-made bread; proved so appealing to the public that the company produced an advertising film starring him; when an aunt sent a print of the film to Hal Roach in Hollywood, the producer signed him at once to a contract; starred in 95 "Our Gang" comedies; his debut when barely 3: "Free Eats"; his second short was titled simply "Spanky"; "Unexpected Riches" was his swan song in the series; was the same spunky, feisty kid off screen as on; one reporter wrote of him when he was 7: "Spanky still gets spanked occasionally. Sometimes for swearing . . . the kid star has picked up an impressive vocabulary somewhere"; he has said he acquired it "by osmosis" from his dad; last acted in a '43 feature at Republic, *Johnny Doughboy*, with "Our

Gang" pal Carl "Alfalfa" Switzer; after service in the Air Force (where he got his high school diploma via correspondence courses), he found Hollywood had no place for him; tried many occupations: hosted a TV show in Tulsa (showing "Our Gang" comedies), owned a restaurant, sold insurance and autos, was the state sales manager for a wine company in Oklahoma; now, still stocky and short, he again lives in Dallas and is the area manager of the commercial contract division of Philco-Ford television; long married to his second wife, Doris, he has a grown son, Verne, and daughter, Betsy; of his child star years, he told the authors of the book *Our Gang:* "I wouldn't take a million dollars for the experience, and I wouldn't take a penny to do it again. If I knew then what I know now . . . I would have finished school and gone to college, and by now I'd be the president of some corporation."

MOVIE HIGHLIGHTS: *Day of Reckoning, Miss Fane's Baby Is Stolen, Kentucky Kernels, O'Shaughnessy's Boy, The Trail of the Lonesome Pine, Varsity Show, Peck's Bad Boy with the Circus.*

Victor McLaglen

(b. Victor McLaglen, Dec. 11, 1886, Tunbridge Wells, Kent, England; d. Nov. 7, 1959) A giant of a man, he starred often for John Ford, and the director knew how to get the best from him; won the Best Actor Oscar for *The Informer* as brawling, drunken Gypo Nolan who, in the Irish rebellion, betrays his best friend for 20 pounds; was Oscar-nominated as Best Support in *The Quiet Man*; both were Ford films; so were others of his: *Wee Willie Winkie, Fort Apache, The Lost Patrol,* etc.; the son of a Church of England bishop, he ran away from home at an early age to join the army; later led an adventurous life in various parts of the world as a silver prospector, physical culture advisor to the Rajah of Akolkot in India, professional strong man, model for statues of Hercules and Adonis, and boxer; best known feat in the ring with Jack Johnson, then the world's heavyweight champ; "Stand up and fight" was, in all areas, his lifelong motto; broke into British films as a star (in 1920's *Call of the Road*); went to Hollywood in '24 to star in *The Beloved Brute*, a Vitagraph Western; highlight of his silent career came with *What Price Glory* ('26), as the Marines' hilariously combative Captain Flagg, the character he played often and, finally, in the talkies *The Cockeyed World* and *Sez You, Sez Me;*

financially astute, he parlayed his hefty movie earnings into a fortune via Hollywood's Athletic Center, which he owned; from '18 until her death in '42, he was married to Enid Lamont; two children: Sheila and Andrew; divorced by his second wife, he was last married ('48) to Margaret Humphrey; last starred in 1957's *The Abductors*—directed by his son.

MOVIE HIGHLIGHTS: *The Glorious Adventure, The Unholy Three, Beau Geste, Winds of Chance, A Girl in Every Port* (silents), *King of the Khyber Rifles, Dishonored, Rackety Rax, Under Two Flags, The Magnificent Brute, Mary of Scotland, Klondike Annie, This Is My Affair, Gunga Din, Captain Fury, Rio, China Girl, Call Out the Marines, The Foxes of Harrow, She Wore a Yellow Ribbon, Rio Grande, Fair Wind to Java, Many Rivers to Cross, Trouble in the Glen.*

Adolphe Menjou

(b. Adolphe Jean Menjou, Feb. 18, 1890, Pittsburgh, Pa.; d. Oct. 29, 1963) Moustachioed and debonair, he was one of Hollywood's best—and best-dressed (titled his autobiography *It Took Nine Tailors*); was on screen in nearly 150 movies from '14 *(The Man Behind the Door)* to '60 *(Pollyanna)*; not a large man (5'8", 145 lbs.), he managed by his intense energy and sheer force of personality to dominate any scene in which he played; the son of immigrant parents (mother was Irish; father, a restaurateur, came from France), he was a graduate of Culver Military Academy and Cornell University; went directly on the stage despite family opposition and then, two years later, into movies; became a major star in '23 in *A Woman of Paris*; remained a matinee idol to the end of the decade when studio moguls too hastily proclaimed him "washed-up"; multilingual, he then starred in Hollywood's foreign-language versions of pictures headlining others in English; did Paul Lukas's *Slightly Scarlet* in both Spanish *(Amore Audaz)* and French *(L'Enigmatique Monsieur Parkes)*; even made a German version of *The March of Time (Wir Um Schalten auf Hollywood)*, a film so dreadful in its English edition that MGM never released it; made an astonishing comeback as tough, salty city editor Walter Burns in *The Front Page* ('31) and was rewarded with a Best Actor Oscar nomination; first wife Katherine Tinsley (married 1920) divorced him in '26; was next married (1927–33) to Kathryn Carver, his leading lady in silents *(Service for Ladies, Serenade*, etc.); in her divorce suit, she testified he'd said he loved "money more than anything else"; from '34 on was wed to actress Verree Teasdale.

MOVIE HIGHLIGHTS: *The Kiss, Marquis Preferred, Fashions in Love, Morocco, Forbidden, Bachelor's Affairs, A Farewell to Arms, Morning Glory, Gold Diggers of 1935, A Star Is Born, One Hundred Men and a Girl, One in a Million, Stage Door, A Letter of Introduction, Golden Boy, A Bill of Divorcement, Roxie Hart, You Were Never Lovelier, The Hucksters, State of the Union, To Please a Lady, Paths of Glory.*

Ray Milland

(b. Reginald Alfred John Truscott-Jones, Jan. 3, 1905, Neath, Wales) After being a crack rifle shot in the Household Cavalry in England, he arrived in Hollywood in '30 and promptly scored a bull's-eye; came equipped with experience in Britain on the stage and in movies (*The Flying Scotsman*, etc.), and a readymade screen name (a variation of his stepfather's, Mullane); at Paramount for 15 years (1934–49), he gave persuasive performances in every sort of movie: comedies (*Easy Living, The Major and the Minor*), costume dramas (*Reap the Wild Wind*), "sarong" epics with Lamour (*Her Jungle Love*), suspense films (*Bulldog Drummond Escapes, The Uninvited*), Westerns (*Copper Canyon*), military flicks (*Beau Geste, I Wanted Wings*); the role he approached with the greatest trepidation, alcoholic Don Birnham in *The Lost Weekend*, won him an Academy Award—and playing it brought on such severe depression that, he has said, his marriage was threatened; but this one marriage of his, beginning in '32, survived; in later years, he and wife Muriel experienced stark tragedy together—their son Daniel, then 41, shot himself to death in 1981; their only other child is daughter Victoria; in the '50s, Milland branched out and directed several movies in which he also acted (*The Girl in the Red Velvet Swing, Lisbon*, etc.); also starred in two TV series: "Meet Mr. Nutley" and "Markham"; made his Broadway debut at 60, triumphantly, in the mystery drama *Hostile Witness*, which he later filmed; in '70, played, sans toupee, the first of many character roles, in *Love Story*; published his humorously ironic autobiography, *Wide-Eyed in Babylon* in '74; a realist, he says: "My philosophy is do what you can with what you've got. I know actors from my generation who cry, 'Why don't they send me any scripts?' I tell them, 'Because you still think of yourself as a leading man. You're 68, not 28. Face it.'"

MOVIE HIGHLIGHTS: *Blonde Crazy, Ambassador Bill, We're Not Dressing, Bolero, The Gilded Lily, The Glass Key, The Big Broadcast of 1937, Jungle Princess, Three Smart Girls, Men With Wings, Arise My Love, Skylark, The Doctor Takes a Wife, Lady in the Dark, Ministry of Fear, Kitty, Golden Earrings, The Big Clock, A Life of Her Own, Rhubarb, The Thief, Dial "M" for Murder.*

Robert Montgomery

(b. Henry Montgomery Jr., May 21, 1904, Beacon, N.Y.; d. Sept. 27, 1981) Achieving fame on Broadway at 20, he became an MGM luminary at 25 and for the next decade grabbed the best parts for a breezy, dinner-jacketed man-about-town, to the despair of rivals Franchot Tone and Robert Young; role was typecasting for this son of the v.p. of the New York Rubber Co.; after private tutoring, attended a fashionable prep school (Pawling) and was further educated in France, England, Switzerland, and Germany; all changed when he was 16 and his father died, leaving the family penniless; went to work as a mechanics' helper on a railroad, then was a deckhand on a Standard Oil tanker before drifting into acting; did bits on stage, had a year's seasoning with a Rochester (N.Y.) stock company, finally scored a solid hit in New York in *Possession*; first movie, in '29, was *So This Is College*; two years and 14 pictures later was elevated to stardom in *Shipmates*; departed from top-hat roles in '37 by persuading Metro to allow him to play a baby-faced murderer in *Night Must Fall*, which brought his first Best Actor Oscar nomination (lost to Tracy in *Captains Courageous*); nominated again four years later as sax-playing boxer Joe Pendleton in *Here Comes Mr. Jordan*, he lost to Gary Cooper's *Sergeant York*; was in the U.S. Navy throughout WW II, emerging with the rank of Lt. Commander and a Bronze Star; four-time president of the Screen Actors Guild; directed (first) *Lady in the Lake*; had an Elizabeth "fixation": was married for 22 years (until they divorced) to stage actress Elizabeth Allan (not the British star); daughter Elizabeth became a star; was last wed, from '50 on, to socialite Elizabeth Grant Harkness.

MOVIE HIGHLIGHTS: *The Divorcee, Let Us Be Gay, Faithless, Letty Lynton, When Ladies Meet, Private Lives, Riptide, Biography of a Bachelor Girl, The Last of Mrs. Cheyney, Yellow Jack, Mr. and Mrs. Smith, They Were Expendable, June Bride.*

(b. Grace Moore, Dec. 5, 1901, Jellico, Tenn.; d. Jan. 26, 1947) Golden-haired, golden-voiced soprano from the Met who introduced opera to the movie masses and, with a transparently superior air, usually gave the impression that she was slumming; a volatile personality (never denied she was "difficult"), she was also shrewd; while her first three movies (all in '30) were artistic successes but box office failures, she was certain she had a winner in her next, *One Night of Love* ('34); halfway through its production, though, Columbia studio topper Harry Cohn decided to cut out the opera scenes because they were too expensive; they stayed in because she paid for them out of her own pocket—in exchange for 50 percent of the movie's profits; the deal made her a millionaire; a true prima donna, she lived a life of opulence, owning villas in Italy and Cannes and a palatial home in Hollywood where she gave sumptuous parties for the music world's elite; in deluxe style, she traveled all over the globe accompanied by an entourage—chauffeur, chef, secretary, personal maid—and appeared before all the crowned heads of Europe; "I already had some of the fame," she said, "but Hollywood gave me the rich lace trimmings, the royal robes, the furs, the jewels, the international celebrity"; the daughter of a millionaire banker who gave her an exclusive education but forbade her to go into show business, she ran away from home, got a job singing at the Black Cat Cafe in New York's Greenwich Village and paid for opera training with her own earnings; next was in touring revues (first song she ever sang on stage: "First You Wiggle and Then You Waggle") and in Broadway musicals (*Hitchy-Koo*, *Up in the Clouds*); twice rejected in Metropolitan auditions, she was finally signed by the opera company and made her debut there in '28 as Mimi in *La Boheme*; from '30 until her death—in a plane crash—was married to Spanish actor Valentin Parera.

MOVIE HIGHLIGHTS: A *Lady's Morals*, *New Moon*, *Love Me Forever*, *The King Steps Out*, *I'll Take Romance*, *When You're in Love*, *Louise*.

Frank Morgan

(b. Francis Philip Wupperman, June 1, 1890, New York, N.Y.; d. Sept. 18, 1949) Stuttering, stammering, decidedly nonplussed scene-stealer who brightened scores of MGM movies; may be most fondly recalled in the title role of *The Wizard of Oz*—but got his Best Actor Oscar nomination for *The Affairs of Cellini* and a Best Support nomination for *Tortilla Flat*; was famous at the studio for his "Morganisms"—word-pictures of his fellow stars: The Marx Bros. ("What happens as you come out of the ether"), Jack Benny ("The guy who sold you the Brooklyn Bridge"), Wallace Beery ("A fight club when the crowd is gone"); was of the wealthy Wupperman family of Angostura Bitters fame (jested: "Bitters runs in our family; it will run in almost any family if you give it a chance, but we own the copyright"); dropped out of Cornell; sold tooth brushes door-to-door, real estate, and ad space in the *Boston Traveler*; was next a cowpuncher on a western ranch, a hobo, and a stoker on a New Orleans-to-New York tramp steamer before following older brother Ralph Morgan on the stage, even assuming his adopted name; success in a vaudeville sketch led to Broadway (*Topaze*, *The Firebrand*, etc.) and New York-made silent movies (first, in '17, *The Girl Philippa*, as Anita Stewart's handsome leading man); as amusing off screen as on, he often quipped: "I have had a lot of lives in my time, and, for that matter, I've had a lot of times in my life"; the father of two, he was long and happily married to Alma Muller; the public never saw his final performance; as Buffalo Bill in *Annie Get Your Gun*, he had filmed all the musical sequences with Judy Garland; she suffered a nervous breakdown and he died before production resumed with Betty Hutton and Louis Calhern in their roles.

MOVIE HIGHLIGHTS: *Reunion in Vienna, Bombshell, The Good Fairy, Naughty Marietta, Dimples, Saratoga, Rosalie, The Shop Around the Corner, The Mortal Storm, Boom Town, Honky Tonk, The Human Comedy, The White Cliffs of Dover, Green Dolphin Street, Key to the City.*

Chester Morris

(b. John Chester Brooks Morris, Feb. 16, 1901, New York, N.Y.; d. Sept. 11, 1970) Compact (5'8") and dynamic, this square-jawed star with the distinctive black patent-leather hair started off with a bang—winning a Best Actor Oscar nomination for his debut movie, *Alibi* ('29); after a few other major-league films, though, including his lifelong favorite, *The Big House*, which he regarded as "the best prison picture ever made," his 20-year Hollywood career found him typecast as a charming tough guy in B's; starred in 41 movies in the '30s, some of the best being *Red-Headed*

Woman, *The Miracle Man*, and *Five Came Back*; achieved his greatest popularity in the '40s as "Boston Blackie," the ex-safecracker turned good-guy sleuth; played the role 13 times (1941–49), from *Meet Boston Blackie* to *Boston Blackie's Chinese Venture*; "The series helped me to decide to leave Hollywood," he said. "After that, a producer wouldn't put me in an 'A' movie even if I paid for the privilege. The only thing I could do was get out and go back to the theater"; the son of theatrical parents, he had started on Broadway at 16, alongside Lionel Barrymore, in *The Copperhead*; also acting from an early age were his sister, Wilhelmina, and his brothers, Adrian and Gordon; after returning to the stage, he starred in hits like *Blue Denim*, *Advise and Consent*, and *The Subject Was Roses*; went back to Hollywood for just three more movies: *Unchained* ('55), *The She-Creature* ('56), and *The Great White Hope* ('70), playing the black heavyweight champ's manager; by his first wife, Suzanne Kilborn (1927–38), he was the father of two: Brooks and Cynthia; was wed from '40 on to Lillian Barker, by whom he had a son, Kenton; continued to act on stage even after becoming fatally ill.

MOVIE HIGHLIGHTS: *The Divorcee, The Bat Whispers, Cock of the Air, Corsair, King for a Night, Gift of Gab, Princess O'Hara, Society Doctor, Three Godfathers, The Devil's Playground, Law of the Underworld, Smashing the Racket, Thunder Afloat, Blind Alley, The Marines Fly High, Aerial Gunner, Tornado, High Explosive, Thunderbolt.*

Paul Muni

(b. Muni Weisenfreund, Sept. 22, 1895, Lemberg, Austria; d. Aug. 25, 1967) A titan, he was that rare star of whom it could be said that he never struck a false note; false faces, however, he wore—more accurately "hid behind"—as Zola, Juarez, Pasteur, for he felt better able to portray a character when outfitted with wigs and feature-altering make-up; one early movie, *Seven Faces*, was made solely to exploit his ability to create seven vastly different personalities via make-up wizardry; born to poor Jewish theatrical parents, he was brought to America at four and accompanied them on cross-country tours to small Yiddish theaters; went on stage at 11 and performed more than 300 different roles in Yiddish—always elderly character roles—before he spoke a word of English on a Broadway stage; that was in '26 when he starred in *We Americans*; first movie: *The Valiant*

('29), a flop, though it got him an Oscar nomination; first hit: as Capone-like gangster Tony Camonte in *Scarface* ('32); began his prestigious reign later that year at Warners, where he held the whip hand—rated a princely salary, was soon billed *Mr.* Paul Muni, and had final choice on all roles; when he insisted on making *The Story of Louis Pasteur*, Warners did the picture on a minimal budget ($330,000), using only leftover sets; he won the Best Actor Oscar and the movie made a mint; maintaining he was "an actor, not a reformer," he nevertheless demanded roles designed to "arouse the world against all sorts of evils"; was married from '21 on to actress Bella Finkel, and the two erected a high wall between themselves and Hollywood; his "art" was his life, and such an unswervingly aloof man was he that his brother-in-law, writer Abem Finkel, once lightly said, "In all the years I've been in the family, I've never known him to go to the bathroom."

MOVIE HIGHLIGHTS: *I Am a Fugitive from a Chain Gang, The World Changes, Bordertown, Dr. Socrates, Black Fury, The Good Earth, The Woman I Love, The Life of Emile Zola, We Are Not Alone, Hudson's Bay, Commandos Strike at Dawn, A Song to Remember, Counter-Attack, Angel on My Shoulder, Stranger on the Prowl, The Last Angry Man.*

George Murphy

(b. George Lloyd Murphy, July 4, 1902, New Haven, Conn.) Dapper, with a friendly, blue-eyed Irish mug, he made the journey from a Pennsylvania coal mine to being an ace song-and-dance man at Metro (the first ever, on stage or screen, to partner Eleanor Powell—in *Broadway Melody of 1938*), to playing Ronald Reagan's dad in *This Is the Army*, to being elected U.S. Senator (Rep.) from California; his was no rags-to-riches story, though; was the son of famed Olympic and University of Pennsylvania coach Michael Charles Murphy; was educated in prep schools and at Yale, where he studied engineering, hence his coal mine stint—learning the industry from the ground up; injured there, he was a Wall Street runner before falling in love with aspiring dancer Juliette Johnson; after teaching him to dance, they were a famous team at night spots all over the world—the Mayfair in London, the Opera Club in Paris, and the Lido in Manhattan; retiring soon after their marriage on December 28, 1926, at the Little Church Around the Corner in N.Y., she presented him with a son, Dennis, and a daughter, Melissa, and remained his wife until her death in '73; at 26, he began starring in Broadway musicals: *Good News, Of Thee I Sing, Roberta*, etc.; screen debut: *Kid Millions* ('34); danced with Shirley Temple *(Little Miss Broadway)*, Lana Turner *(Two Girls on Broadway)*, Judy Garland *(Little Nellie Kelly)*, Nancy Kelly *(Show Business)*; best dramatic outings: *Bataan* and *Battleground*; received a special Oscar in '50 "for his services in interpreting the film industry to the country at large"; published his lighthearted autobiography, *Say . . . Didn't You Used to Be George Murphy?*, in '70.

MOVIE HIGHLIGHTS: *The Navy Steps Out, You're a Sweetheart, Hold That Coed, Tom, Dick and Harry, Ringside Maisie, For Me and My Gal, The Powers Girl, Having a Wonderful Crime, Tenth Avenue Angel, It's a Big Country, Walk East on Beacon.*

David Niven

(b. James David Graham Niven, March 1, 1909, Kirriemuir, Scotland; d. July 29, 1983) Star whose sparkling wit and blithe spirit made and kept him popular with fans and colleagues for a half century; a general's son, he was schooled for the army at Stowe and Sandhurst, then spent two years in Malta as an officer in the Royal Light Highland Infantry; was next a lumberjack in Canada and a London wine merchant's rep in New York City; arriving in Hollywood in the mid-1930s with no acting experience, he worked as an extra; appeared first as a Mexican wrapped in a rug in a "Hopalong Cassidy" flick; socially, was an immediate success, being dashing, debonair, single, and a top polo player and cricketer; was soon given a contract by Sam Goldwyn as Merle Oberon, Niven's love at the time, was a Goldwyn star with a bit of clout; debuted as a Goldwyn star in *Dodsworth* ('36); first review: "All we can say about this actor is that he is tall, dark, and not the slightest bit handsome"; career was put on ice, after many starring roles, for several years after 1939's *Raffles*; commissioned a Second Lieutenant in the British Army, he served with the Rifle Brigade then with the Commandos, assigned to the super-secret Phantom Reconnaissance Regiment; was promoted to Colonel early in '44 and transferred to the British Liberation Army where he served until Germany's surrender; was the author of a novel, *Round the Rugged Rocks*, and two breezy best-selling memoirs, *The Moon's a Balloon* and *Bring on the Empty Horses*; his best role, in *Separate Tables*, won him an Oscar because, he modestly insisted, "two young ladies, Deborah Kerr and Wendy Hiller [his co-stars], cried so well."

MOVIE HIGHLIGHTS: *Barbary Coast, Thank You, Jeeves, Beloved Enemy, The Charge of the Light Brigade, The Prisoner of Zenda, Four Men and a Prayer, Three Blind Mice, Dawn Patrol, Bachelor Mother, Eternally Yours, Wuthering Heights, The Real Glory, Spitfire, Stairway to Heaven, The Bishop's Wife, The Moon Is Blue, Oh Men! Oh Women!, Please Don't Eat the Daisies, The Guns of Navarone.*

Jack Oakie

(b. Lewis Delaney Offield, Nov. 12, 1903, Sedalia, Mo.; d. Jan. 23, 1978) Moon-faced comedian, master of the triple-take, whose special genius was making movie fans regard him as a friend; an exuberant, gregarious soul, he lived his life by the catch-phrase "It's all in fun"; starting in Laura La Plante's *Finders Keepers* in '28, he starred for four decades before retiring voluntarily; snagged a Best Supporting Oscar nomination for *The Great Dictator*, as swaggering Napaloni (read "Mussolini"), Dictator of Bacteria; always said his greatest thrill was when Chaplin called and offered him the part; had been the partner (1919–27) of vaudeville star Lulu McConnell, appearing with her cross-country in two-a-day shows and on Broadway in *Artists and Models* and *Innocent Eyes*; his home town designated the house in which he was born a civic historical landmark, but he grew up, after age 5, in Muskogee, Okla.; friends tagged him "Oakie" when he entered show business, giving him his stage moniker (never legally adopted it); credited his early leading ladies (Clara Bow, Evelyn Brent, et al.) with teaching him the movie tricks of the trade and helping him become a star; had a phenomenal memory—could recall the titles, plots, songs, co-stars, bit players, even the names of the animals, in every movie he ever made; starred first, for nine years, at Paramount, and the friends he made there—Buddy Rogers, Mary Brian, Dorothy Lamour, etc.—remained forever his friends; divorced from Ziegfeld Follies beauty Venita Varden, he was wed for 30 years to actress Victoria Horne; lived on a vast estate in the San Fernando Valley and was one of Hollywood's wealthiest stars, confiding this secret: "I bought AT&T stock when it was American Smoke Signal and General Electric when it was called General Candle."

MOVIE HIGHLIGHTS: *The Wild Party, Sweetie, The Sap from Syra-cuse, Social Lion, Hit the Deck, June Moon, The Touchdown, Once in a Lifetime, Million Dollar Legs, If I Had a Million, College Humor, Call of the Wild, King of Burlesque, Champagne Waltz, Radio City Revels, Hit-ting a New High, Affairs of Annabel, Tin Pan Alley, Navy Blues, Hello, Frisco, Hello, It Happened Tomorrow, The Merry Monahans, The Rat Race, Lover Come Back.*

Merle Oberon

(b. Queenie Thompson, Feb. 19, 1911, Calcutta, India; d. Nov. 23, 1979) Exotically beautiful, sloe-eyed star who artfully hid her lowly beginnings for a lifetime, abetted by vast charm, an army of loyal friends, and an air—painstakingly acquired—of being to the manor born; the phony story peddled by studio publicists: she was born Estelle Merle O'Brien-Thompson in Tasmania, the daughter of a British army officer (who died before her birth) and an English mother who gave her an exclusive educa-tion in India before, at 17 in London, she captivated British society and decided to become an actress; the true story: born in Calcutta (never saw Tasmania), she was Eurasian, a half-caste, the illegitimate daughter (a "chi-chi," as the contemptuous expression was) of an Indian mother and an English Tommy (she never knew him) whose name, he said, was Thompson; a famous British jockey took her to England as his "protegee" when 17; movie producer Alexander Korda soon became enamored of her and, eradicating all trace of her past, became the Svengali to her Galatea; she brought her mother to London, passing her off as her servant; was posed beautifully in early movies but given little dialogue to say until, like Eliza Doolittle, she learned to speak the King's English properly; buying half her contract, Hollywood's Sam Goldwyn made her an international star; was nominated for an Oscar for *The Dark Angel* ('35); was married first to Alexander Korda (1939–45) becoming, when he was knighted, a Lady; later husbands: cinematographer Lucien Ballard, millionaire Bruno Pag-liai, and actor Robert Wolders (who was 29 years her junior); generous to many in life, she left in her will $1 million to the Motion Picture Country Home & Hospital.

MOVIE HIGHLIGHTS: *The Private Life of Henry VIII, These Three, Beloved Enemy, The Divorce of Lady X, The Cowboy and the Lady,*

Wuthering Heights, Over the Moon, Till We Meet Again, Affectionately Yours, Lydia, First Comes Courage, The Lodger, A Song to Remember, Hangover Square, This Love of Ours, Temptation, Dark Waters, Desiree, Hotel, Interval.

Pat O'Brien

(b. William Joseph Patrick O'Brien, Nov. 11, 1899, Milwaukee, Wis.; d. Oct. 15, 1983) No one played crusading newsmen *(Final Edition)*, or football coaches *(Knute Rockne—All-American)*, or Irish priests *(Fighting Father Dunne)* more convincingly than this staccato-voiced, rough-barked but big-hearted star; pressed to name his favorite of the 115 movies in which he starred, he would cite *Oil for the Lamps of China* and *The Iron Major* and then, always, plump for *Knute Rockne*; "He was not only a great coach but also an extraordinary human being, and I felt privileged, humble, trying to convey the glory and the humanness that was 'Rock.' And there were frightening moments when I briefly felt as if I were Knute Rockne"; in later years, in the star's successful nightclub act, Rockne's inspiring locker-room speech was ever the highlight of his performance; became a topflight star, after several minor films, in *The Front Page* ('31), getting the role by a fluke; producer Howard Hughes signed him to play fast-spieling reporter Hildy Johnson thinking he'd done the part on Broadway, when actually he had played the managing editor; had been a law major at Marquette before he and boyhood pal Spencer Tracy, who served together in the Navy during WW I, elected to study acting at the American Academy of Dramatic Arts; stock company jobs led, in the '20s, to Broadway (*Gertie, Henry, Behave!*, etc.); was a front-rank fixture at Warners for eight years (1933–40) and a ringleader of the studio's so-called "Irish Mafia" (James Cagney, Frank McHugh, Allen Jenkins, etc.); was reunited with Cagney in his final film, 1981's *Ragtime*; he and his one wife (from '31 on), Eloise Taylor, who finally acted alongside him on stage, were the parents of four: Mavourneen, Sean, Terence Kevin, and Kathleen.

MOVIE HIGHLIGHTS: *Flying High, Hell's House, Air Mail, Bombshell, Here Comes the Navy, Twenty Million Sweethearts, Flirtation Walk, Devil Dogs of the Air, Ceiling Zero, China Clipper, San Quentin, Submarine D-1, Boy Meets Girl, Angels With Dirty Faces, Indianapolis Speedway,*

The Fighting 69th, Till We Meet Again, Bombardier, His Butler's Sister, Marine Raiders, Crack-Up, The Last Hurrah, Billy Jack Goes to Washington, The End.

Warner Oland

(b. Johann Olande, Oct. 3, 1880, Umea, Vesterbotten, Sweden; d. Aug. 6, 1938) "Charlie Chan" he was, 16 times (1931–38), and the best of them, but Chinese, obviously not; more, having been brought to America as a child, he spoke with no foreign accent at all, though he did speak many languages; to friends, he was "Jack"; played Chan sans make-up, "becoming" Chinese simply by growing a tuft of chin-whiskers, combing the ends of his eyebrows up and the tips of his moustache down, then narrowing his eyes; during his heyday, he owned a 7,000-acre island, Palmetto de la Virgin, off the West Coast of Mexico, where he raised cattle and cocoanuts; also had mansions in Beverly Hills, Santa Barbara, and Boston; an intellectual lurked behind the mask of Earl Derr Biggers' great detective; Boston-educated and widely read, especially in philosophy, he was a student of classical music, an art connoisseur and painter, and a translator of Strindberg plays; a stage veteran, he began acting in silents in 1909, usually playing Orientals, and was often cast in villainous parts in Pearl White serials; among his atypical roles was that of Jolson's cantor father in *The Jazz Singer*; often, like Chan, he spoke in epigrams, a favorite being "Life is a circle that looks like a straight line"; was married from '08 until '37, when she sued for separate maintenance, to painter Edith Shearn, daughter of one of Back Bay Boston's oldest families; had many screen "sons" but no children, though he adored them; when youngsters visited, he might sing them the Chinese lullaby "Princess Ming Toy," from one of his "Chan" pictures, or delight them by dressing in a ceremonial robe and doing a samurai dance, flashing tablespoons for swords.

MOVIE HIGHLIGHTS: *The Serpent, Patria* (serial), *The Fatal Ring* (serial), *The Yellow Arm* (serial), *East Is West, Don Q, Tell It to the Marines, The Scarlet Lady* (all silents), *The Return of Dr. Fu Manchu, The Black Camel, Dishonored, Charlie Chan Carries On, The Son-Daughter, Mandalay, Before Dawn, Bulldog Drummond Strikes Back, The Painted Veil, Werewolf of London, Shanghai, Charlie Chan at the Circus, Charlie Chan at the Olympics.*

Maureen O'Sullivan

(b. Maureen Paula O'Sullivan, May 17, 1911, Royle, Ireland) Decades later (she last played the part in '42), the brunette Irish colleen remains, of them all, Tarzan's most memorable Jane; opposite Johnny Weissmuller, she did the role six times, from 1932's *Tarzan the Ape Man* to *Tarzan's New York Adventure*; recalls Weissmuller as "an amiable piece of beefcake, a likeable, overgrown child"; the daughter of a major of the Connaught Rangers in Ireland, she was educated at convents in Dublin and London and at finishing school in Paris; made her movie debut at 19 in *Song of My Heart*, opposite famous tenor John McCormack; was married for 26 years, until his death, to writer-producer-director John Farrow; at the time of their September 12, 1936, wedding they vowed they'd have 10 children; had seven—six of whom, including actresses Tisa and Mia Farrow, are still living (their firstborn, Michael Damien, 28, was killed in a private-plane crash in '58); off the screen for six years, she returned in '48 to star in *The Big Clock*, directed by her husband; left movies, permanently, she believed, after 1958's *Wild Heritage*; at 51, carved an entirely new career on Broadway, making her debut in the hit comedy *Never Too Late*; was both funny and touching as a New England matron who finds herself pregnant at a most unseemly age; repeated the role, triumphantly, in the '65 movie version after a many-months stint as co-host of TV's "Today" show; later Broadway successes: *No Sex Please, We're British* and *Morning's at Seven*; active in many Catholic and Jewish charitable organizations; in August '83 married James Cushing, president of a Schenectady (N.Y.) construction firm.

MOVIE HIGHLIGHTS: *Just Imagine, Tugboat Annie, The Barretts of Wimpole Street, David Copperfield, Anna Karenina, A Day at the Races, A Yank at Oxford, The Crowd Roars, Pride and Prejudice, Maisie Was a Lady, All I Desire.*

Jean Parker

(b. Luis Stephanie Zelinska, Aug. 11, 1915, Butte, Mont.) As a Pasadena high school girl, this auburn-haired beauty with the angelic smile painted a prize-winning poster publicizing the 1932 Olympics; attracted by a photo of her that appeared in the Los Angeles papers, Louis B. Mayer's secretary,

Ida Koverman, whose instincts he trusted, got her an MGM contract; concocting a phony "real" name and birthplace—Lois Mae Green, born in Deer Lodge, Mont.—she made her debut at 17 in a Jackie Cooper movie, *Divorce in the Family*; her elfin charms, not the least of which was a unique, breathless voice, quickly made her a fan favorite; career peaked early: *Little Women* (flawless as the tragic Beth), *Sequoia* (first starring role), Frank Capra's *Lady for a Day*, *Caravan* opposite Charles Boyer, Rene Clair's *The Ghost Goes West*, a classic, co-starring romantically with Robert Donat; angered by her '36 elopement with New York newspaper man George McDonald (divorced in '40), Louis B. Mayer dropped her option; much of the rest of her career, totaling 72 movies (last: 1966's *Apache Uprising*) was spent in B's; best were the many high-powered Pine-Thomas low-budgeters of the '40s (*Torpedo Boat*, *Alaska Highway*, etc.); married and divorced three later husbands: radio news commentator Douglas Dawson (1941–43), foreign correspondent Dr. Curtis Grotter (1944–49), the late actor Robert Lowery (1950–57), by whom she had a son, Robert Hanks Jr. (b. 1952); had a highly successful career on stage in the '40s and '50s, starring on Broadway and on tour in *Born Yesterday*, *Loco*, *Burlesque*, and *Dream Girl*; not surprisingly, since no young woman in movies had a lovelier face and figure, she has retained her beauty; in recent years has been kept busy by agents and studios as a coach for young players being groomed for fame.

MOVIE HIGHLIGHTS: *Rasputin and the Empress*, *Gabriel Over the White House*, *What Price Innocence*, *Have a Heart*, *Limehouse Blues*, *Princess O'Hara*, *Murder in the Fleet*, *The Texas Rangers*, *The Arkansas Traveler*, *Romance of the Limberlost*, *Zenobia*, *Power Dive*, *The Pittsburgh Kid*, *Hello Annapolis*, *High Explosive*, *Bluebeard*, *The Gunfighter*, *Black Tuesday*.

Gail Patrick

(b. Margaret Fitzgerald, June 20, 1911, Birmingham, Ala.; d. July 6, 1980) Wicked woman!; for 15 of Hollywood's Golden Years, between 1933's *Mysterious Rider* and 1948's *Inside Story*, she fascinated moviegoers like a cobra ready to strike; with icy charm, that insinuating voice and raven-black hair, center-parted with widow's peak, she was forever finagling to snare some other woman's man; offscreen, she had husbands of her own—four—none of whom she took from anyone: restaurateur Bob (Brown Derby) Cobb (1936–40), Navy lieutenant Arnold White (1944–46), ad exec Cornwall Jackson (1947–68), with whom she adopted a son and daughter, Tom and Jennifer, and Illinois businessman John E. Velde Jr. (from '74 on); ice water did not actually flow in her veins; one of Hollywood's most philanthropic and best-loved citizens, she worked for such worthy organizations as the Christmas Seal campaign, of which she was once national chairman; after receiving her bachelor's degree at Howard College, she matriculated as a law student at the University of Alabama, then was catapulted into pictures via Paramount's nationwide talent search for the movies' ideal "Panther Woman"; failed to win the role but landed a contract at the studio and went further indeed than the newcomer, Kathleen Burke, who starred as the "Panther Woman" in *Island of Lost Souls*; starting her at $75-a-week, Paramount spent $1500 correcting her teeth, well preparing her for meaty roles that lay ahead; was such a willing publicity subject (balked only at leg art) that the company's clipping bureau revealed in '37 that she received more square inches of newsprint space than any contractee at the studio; quitting movies finally, she became executive producer of the vastly popular "Perry Mason" TV series.

MOVIE HIGHLIGHTS: *Mama Loves Papa, The Cradle Song, If I Had a Million, Death Takes a Holiday, Murder at the Vanities, Rumba, Mississippi, The Big Broadcast of 1936, No More Ladies, My Man Godfrey, Stage Door, Artists and Models, Mad About Music, Man of Conquest, My Favorite Wife, Love Crazy, The Doctor Takes a Wife, We Were Dancing, Hit Parade of 1943, Up in Mabel's Room, Claudia and David.*

Dick Powell

(b. Richard Ewing Powell, Nov. 14, 1904, Mt. View, Ark.; d. Jan. 2, 1963) Curly-haired Warner Bros. tenor, crooning often into the pearly ears of Ruby Keeler, who surprised all by becoming, in the '40s, one of the screen's ace tough guys (*Murder, My Sweet*, etc.); a natural-born singer ("Casey Jones," he recalled, was the first song he ever sang, at 5), he sang in hometown choirs and at funerals before going into radio in his 20s; began his movie career in '32 in Will Rogers' *Too Busy to Work*, in a nonsinging role; went directly to Warners, where he remained through '39, making his studio debut in support of Lee Tracy in *Blessed Event*, playing a band leader and singing his first screen song, "I'm Making Hay in the Moonlight"; *42nd Street* made him an overnight star when his salary was $95-a-week; was in the Box Office Top Ten in '35 and '36, by which time, after a score of musicals, he was protesting, "I'm not a kid any more but I'm still playing boy scouts"; married Joan Blondell in '36, adopted her son by a previous marriage, Norman, and had a daughter, Ellen; divorced in '45 after co-starring in many films, including the prophetically titled *I Want a Divorce*; had been married earlier ('25) to hometown sweetheart Mildred Maund, who disapproved of his show business aspirations and divorced him in '33; from '45 on was married to June Allyson, with whom he had a son, Richard, and adopted a daughter, Pamela; it was an up-and-down marriage, as the actress disclosed in her '82 autobiography *June Allyson*; did more musicals at Paramount *(Happy Go Lucky, Riding High)* before going freelance in straight dramas; directed several films, including Allyson's *You Can't Run Away from It*; was finally one-third owner of Four Star, a prosperous television production company.

MOVIE HIGHLIGHTS: *Footlight Parade, Dames, The King's Vacation, Flirtation Walk, Wonder Bar, Twenty Million Sweethearts, Shipmates Forever, Gold Diggers of 1935, Colleen, Varsity Show, The Singing Marine, On the Avenue, Christmas in July, It Happened Tomorrow, Johnny O'Clock, Cornered, Pitfall, Station West, Mrs. Mike, The Bad and the Beautiful.*

Eleanor Powell

(b. Eleanor Torrey Powell, Nov. 21, 1912, Springfield, Mass.; d. Feb. 11, 1982) "The World's Greatest Female Tap Dancer" (an honor accorded her in '28 by the Dancing Masters of America) began dancing professionally at 13; fresh from Broadway musical triumphs *(Fine and Dandy, Hot-Cha,* etc.), she entered movies sans fanfare in Fox's *George White's Scandals of 1935*; in a minor role (billed seventh), but with a big production number, she put her best foot forward and stole the movie from star Alice Faye; before its release, MGM tested her for a dance cameo in *Broadway Melody of 1936*, but, after seeing the test, Louis B. Mayer assigned her the lead; for the next seven years her lavishly mounted musicals were catnip for the masses, sending enrollments skyrocketing at dancing schools across the land; the roster of her films, though, is astonishingly small—after becoming a star, she headlined in only 12, and two of these (*Thousands Cheer* and, in '50, *The Duchess of Idaho*) were guest-star stints; married Glenn Ford, her only husband, in '43 and soon gave up her career to make a home for him and their only child, Peter; came out of retirement in '61, two years after divorcing Ford, at the behest of her then 15-year-old son, who had never seen her dance professionally except in movies; for three years, before hanging up her dancing shoes forever, she was a sensation at top clubs in Las Vegas and Manhattan (the Latin Quarter) and on TV ("Hollywood Palace," "The Perry Como Show," etc.), and even gave a command performance in Monaco for Princess Grace; a Presbyterian Sunday School teacher, she was the host (1953–56) of an NBC-TV religious series, "Faith of Our Children," which won five Emmys.

MOVIE HIGHLIGHTS: *Born to Dance, Rosalie, Broadway Melody of 1938, Honolulu, Broadway Melody of 1940, Lady Be Good, Ship Ahoy!, I Dood It, Sensations of 1945.*

William Powell

(b. William Horatio Powell, July 28, 1892, Pittsburgh, Pa.; d. March 5, 1984) In 33 years of stardom (34 silents, 62 talkies), there was no other star quite like him—the polished sophisticate whose gentlemanly elegance unfailingly showed off to perfection an endless list of lovely leading ladies: Kay Francis, Hedy Lamarr, Joan Crawford, Rosalind Russell, Irene Dunne, Annabella, etc.; among the many others were Carole Lombard (in *Man of the World, My Man Godfrey*), his wife (second) for two years after '31, and Jean Harlow (in *Reckless, Libeled Lady*), his lost love whose untimely death at 26 devastated him; then, of course, there was Myrna Loy; moviegoers demanded to see them together repeatedly; were the incomparable Nick and Nora Charles, the wealthy mystery-solving twosome, in six "Thin Man" comedies and also did another seven pictures as a romantic team; deciding at 18 to become an actor, he worked at the Home Telephone Co. in Kansas City, where his family had moved, for $50 a month to earn tuition money to attend the American Academy of Dramatic Arts in New York; that proved too slow so a wealthy aunt came through with a loan—which took him 13 years to repay; was six years on Broadway before making his first movie, *A Society Exile* ('19); was initially a villain in silents; talkie debut: 1929's *Interference* with Evelyn Brent and Doris Kenyon; was three times nominated for the Best Actor Oscar: *The Thin Man* (lost, ironically, to Gable, who later wed Lombard), *My Man Godfrey, Life With Father* (lost to pal Ronald Colman, on whose yacht he had spent a month in seclusion after Jean Harlow's death); was married from '40 to the end to starlet Diana Lewis.

MOVIE HIGHLIGHTS: *The Canary Murder Case, One Way Passage, Manhattan Melodrama, Evelyn Prentice, The Great Ziegfeld, I Love You Again, The Ex-Mrs. Bradford, Love Crazy, Crossroads, The Heavenly Body, The Senator Was Indiscreet, Mr. Peabody and the Mermaid, Mr. Roberts.*

George Raft

(b. George Ranft, Sept. 24, 1903, New York, N.Y.; d. Nov. 24, 1980) Sleek and dark, he was a guy from Hell's Kitchen who might have become a notorious hood (was an intimate of many in the mob) but, instead, became one of Hollywood's most famous figures, helping create the myth of the gangster as culture hero; other male stars were awed by his off-screen reputation as a stud, one, it was claimed, of phenomenal staying power and nature's gifts; among the many glamour queens counted (by others, never himself) as his conquests: Betty Grable, Norma Shearer, Carole Lombard, Marilyn Monroe, Marlene Dietrich (once slugged it out over her with Edward G. Robinson); had, admittedly, been a gigolo and taxi-dancer in Manhattan speakeasies prior to crashing the movies in '29 in *Queen of the Night Clubs*; picture starred Texas Guinan and he'd been the bouncer at her club in New York; 1932's *Scarface*, introducing the nickel-flipping bit that became his trademark, made him a star; almost lost the part of gunman Gino Rinaldi because, unaware that she was producer Howard Hughes' girl friend, he'd made a big play for the beautiful Billie Dove; an untutored actor, he never ventured far from his own personality in playing a character and used that yardstick in choosing his roles; even his wardrobe— pearl-gray hat, long-roll collar, high-rise pants—seldom varied from film to film, unless he was in prison stripes *(Each Dawn I Die)* or a workman's garb *(They Drive by Night)*; was portrayed by Ray Danton in 1961's *The George Raft Story*; starred in more than 70 movies; last did a cameo, as himself, in 1978's *Sextette*, starring Mae West, a lifelong pal after he was the leading man in her debut movie, *Night After Night* ('32); an extraordinarily generous man, and a high stakes gambler, he died broke.

MOVIE HIGHLIGHTS: *Madame Racketeer, Night World, Undercover Man, The Bowery, Bolero, Limehouse Blues, The Glass Key, Every Night at Eight, Souls at Sea, You and Me, Spawn of the North, I Stole a Million, The House Across the Bay, Manpower, Mr. Ace, Nob Hill, Nocturne, Whistle Stop, Race Street, Lucky Nick Cain, Black Widow, Rogue Cop, Some Like It Hot.*

Luise Rainer

(b. Luise Rainer, Jan. 12, 1909, Vienna, Austria) Petite dramatic star, a discovery at 16 of stage director Max Reinhardt, she was the first to win two Best Actress Oscars, and in successive years (for *The Great Ziegfeld* and *The Good Earth*), a feat since repeated by Katharine Hepburn; *Ziegfeld* also won her the Foreign Press and New York Film Critics' Awards; claims her salary at Metro then was a mere $250 a week; said once, on TV's "Merv Griffin Show," "I always considered myself the world's worst actress"; certain detractors agree, and there is sometimes a self-pitying tone in her voice; loyalists, however, insist that "she could always tear your heart out"; career at MGM was brief—eight movies between '35 and '38; then took her make-up kit to Broadway, starring in *Behold the Bride, Saint Joan, A Kiss for Cinderella*; in '43 went to Paramount for one, *Hostages*, an anti-Nazi film with William Bendix, then quit the screen; on rare occasions has returned to Hollywood for TV guest-star roles— in '65 for "Combat," in '83 for "The Love Boat"; the daughter of a wealthy importer, she was hailed as a star from her first hour on the stage; was famed throughout Europe for portrayals of the heroines of Shakespeare, Ibsen, Pirandello; never made a movie on the Continent; divorced from playwright Clifford (*Golden Boy*) Odets after a brief (1937–40) marriage, she has been married since '43 to British publisher Robert Knittel, making her home in London; their daughter is an actress using her married name, Patricia Norsa; still giving occasional stage readings, the star insists, "I haven't retired even though I may not work continuously—no one ever retires."

MOVIE HIGHLIGHTS: *Escapade, The Great Ziegfeld, The Emperor's Candlesticks* (all three with William Powell), *The Good Earth, The Big City, The Great Waltz, Toy Wife, Dramatic School, Hostages.*

Claude Rains

(b. William Claude Rains, Nov. 10, 1889, Camberwell, London, England; d. May 30, 1967) A smallish man (aided no little by elevator shoes) but a towering talent, he played many great roles but never romantic ones—except, the record shows, off screen; had six wives; in sequence, they were Isabel Jeans, Marie Hemingway, and Beatrix Thomson, three of the most beautiful women on the London stage; the first two divorced him, he divorced Thomson charging desertion; was next wed (1935–59) to much-younger American stage actress Frances Propper, becoming a first-time father at 49 (daughter Jennifer, now called Jessica, is an actress); in '59 married Hungarian pianist Agi Jambor, who divorced him six months later; wed Rosemary Clark the following year, becoming the stepfather of three; a child of the London slums (son of a failed actor), he made his stage debut at 11 in *Sweet Nell of Old Drury*; was later a call-boy and stage manager before returning to the boards in 1911 in *The Gods of the Mountains*; had to first overcome a Cockney accent and a pronounced lisp; in WW I served first with the London Scottish and then with the Bedford Regiment, rising from private to captain; later, while acting on stage, he also taught at the Royal Academy of Dramatic Arts; students included Charles Laughton and John Gielgud, who has reported that "his vitality and enthusiasm made him a delightful teacher, and most of the girls were in love with him"; was highly active on Broadway in the '20s and '30s, notably in *The Man Who Reclaimed His Head*, which he later filmed; made his screen debut at 43, his haunting voice making him a star in *The Invisible Man*, in which he was never seen; was four times nominated for a Best Supporting Oscar—in *Mr. Smith Goes to Washington*, *Casablanca*, *Mr. Skeffington*, *Notorious*.

MOVIE HIGHLIGHTS: *Crime Without Passion, The Mystery of Edwin Drood, Anthony Adverse, The Prince and the Pauper, They Won't Forget, The Adventures of Robin Hood, White Banners, Four Daughters, The Sea Hawk, Here Comes Mr. Jordan, Kings Row, Now Voyager, The Phantom of the Opera, Passage to Marseilles, Caesar and Cleopatra, Deception, The Unsuspected, Lawrence of Arabia.*

Basil Rathbone

(b. Philip St. John Basil Rathbone, June 13, 1892, Johannesburg, South Africa; d. July 21, 1967) Playing Sherlock Holmes for the first time in

1939's *The Hound of the Baskervilles* made him, after a decade as a character star, a name-above-the-title; was seen as Holmes 14 times before abandoning the role after *Dressed to Kill* ('46); typical of his earlier roles had been that of the stern and heartless Mr. Murdstone in *David Copperfield*; the son of a well-off mining engineer, he was given a classical education in England, his home after age 4; first a solicitor for an insurance firm, he became an actor in 1912 when he joined the Shakespearean company of Sir Frank Benson, his cousin; performances in *Romeo and Juliet* and *The Taming of the Shrew*, in the English provinces and on an American tour, made him a stage matinee idol; at 21 he married young English actress Ethel Marian Forman, his Shakespearean leading lady; after the birth of a son, Rodion, they were divorced; fought at the Front, as a lieutenant, in the Great War, winning a military cross for valor; made his London stage debut at 25 as Constance Collier's leading man in *Peter Ibbetson* and was an immediate hit; was starring on Broadway when he met and married (in '26) screenwriter Ouida (Fitzmaurice) Bergere, with whom he had a daughter, Barbara; through all their years together in Hollywood, the Rathbones were celebrated for hosting the community's grandest galas, and he, who had ever been a social recluse, confessed, "I have changed, and learned to enjoy people and places, because of Ouida, who has a relish for exacting the most from every waking moment"; after making a number of silents, his performance in a talkie, *The Last of Mrs. Cheyney* ('29), set him on the road to fame and two Best Supporting Oscar nominations— in *Romeo and Juliet* (as Tybalt) and *If I Were King*.

MOVIE HIGHLIGHTS: *The Bishop Murder Case, Anna Karenina, A Tale of Two Cities, The Last Days of Pompeii, Captain Blood, Kind Lady, Tovarich, The Dawn Patrol, The Adventures of Robin Hood, Tower of London, The Adventures of Sherlock Holmes, Crossroads, Frenchman's Creek, Bathing Beauty, The Court Jester.*

Gene Raymond

(b. Raymond Guion, Aug. 13, 1908, New York, N.Y.) Blond, blue-eyed, and of French parentage, he had a smile, a pleasant singing voice, and a breezy cheerfulness that made him catnip for femme fans; before his birth, his mother, a native of Alsace from whom he inherited his *joie de vivre*, pronounced, "My first born shall be an actor"; true to the prediction, he was acting at 5 in a stock company production; attended the Professional

Children's School in Manhattan, studying to become an actor as others did to be doctors or engineers; was on Broadway at 15, wearing his first long pants, in *The Potters*, and rapidly becoming a leading juvenile; among his later plays were *Cradle Snatchers*, *Mirrors*, and *Young Sinners* (took the name "Gene" from his character in this two-year hit); made his movie debut at 23, opposite Nancy Carroll, in *Personal Maid*; admitted then and later, "Luck came my way; I never had to starve for my career"; his mother and brother also went to Hollywood and lived with him until June 16, 1937, when, for the first and only time, he was married; his bride was Jeanette MacDonald, and it is said that his mother, after guiding his career so long, only reluctantly gave her blessing to the marriage; rarely given the chance to display his athletic prowess in his roles, he was an expert at tennis, fencing, polo, and horseback riding, winning many blue ribbons on jumpers in shows; was such a romantic idol in his heyday that, on one personal appearance junket in the '30s, feminine furors in nine major cities brought out the police to handle crowds around the theater where he was appearing; outside his hotel in Chicago, more than 1,000 women waited an entire morning to catch a glimpse of him; no egotist, he took little stock in this adoration, insisting, "It isn't really me that they admire, it's the men I portray; I could be the same person and drive a truck for a living and I'd go unnoticed."

MOVIE HIGHLIGHTS: *Stolen Heaven, If I Had a Million, Red Dust, Ex-Lady, Zoo in Budapest, Flying Down to Rio, Transatlantic Merry-Go-Round, Sadie McKee, Behold My Wife, Love on a Bet, The Woman in Red, The Bride Walks Out, The Smartest Girl in Town, There Goes My Girl, Mr. and Mrs. Smith, Smilin' Through, The Locket.*

Bill "Bojangles" Robinson

(b. Luther Robinson, May 25, 1878, Richmond, Va.; d. Nov. 25, 1949) Great black tap dancer who taught Shirley Temple to dance up and down stairs in his Hollywood debut, *The Little Colonel* ('35); had first done the routine in '27, on Broadway, in *Blackbirds*; raised by his grandmother, a former slave, he began dancing on street corners at 6, after being expelled from school; leaving home at 8, he took the name "Bill" from his brother—they fought for it, he won, the brother became "Percy"; worked in a racing stable in Washington, D.C., earning extra money peddling newspapers and dancing in beer gardens; at 30 was working as a waiter at Richmond's Jefferson Hotel when he accidentally, and luckily, spilled soup on a man named Marty Forkins, who happened to be a showman; learning that he was "really" a dancer, Forkins put him in vaudeville (Butler and Robinson was the act) and remained his manager for decades; as a single, he next starred in black musical revues, and then, as the first black dancer to star in white vaudeville shows, he soon was earning $3,500 weekly; known as an "easy touch," he shared the wealth with many individuals and, over the years, gave more than $1 million to charities; the Honorary Mayor of Harlem, whose chauffeur-driven Duesenberg was familiar to all, he had an innate dignity enabling him to move with ease in white and black circles; first feature film, shown in theaters patronized exclusively by blacks, was *Harlem Is Heaven* ('32); performed for the Queen of England, was a personal friend of Eleanor Roosevelt, and a founder of the Negro Actors Guild; once cited his "hobby" as "ice cream" (ate eight pints of vanilla every day); married three times; when he died, one million people lined Broadway as his body was carried from Harlem to Times Square.

MOVIE HIGHLIGHTS: *In Old Kentucky, Hooray for Love, The Big Broadcast of 1936, The Littlest Rebel, One Mile from Heaven* (his only serious role, as a policeman), *Rebecca of Sunnybrook Farm, Road Demon, Just Around the Corner, Up the River, Stormy Weather.*

Edward G. Robinson

(b. Emmanuel Goldenberg, Dec. 12, 1893, Bucharest, Rumania; d. Jan. 26, 1973) *Little Caesar*—one title defines much of the early part of this star's long career; played gangsters or others on the wrong side of the law some 40 times, but the most memorable of all remained Rico; was one of his two favorite roles, the other being in *Dr. Ehrlich's Magic Bullet*; brought to the U.S. at 9, he had early ambitions of being a rabbi, then won his master's degree at Columbia, expecting to become a lawyer, before deciding to act; first appeared in vaudeville in a short drama, *The Bells of Conscience*, which he wrote; stock company jobs around the country led finally to Broadway and more than 40 plays, in only one of which, *The Racket*, did he portray a gangster; took the name "Robinson" from a character in a play he once saw, *The Passerby*; appeared in one silent, *The*

Bright Shawl, starring Richard Barthelmess; debuted in talkies in '29, opposite Claudette Colbert, in *The Hole in the Wall*; breaking out of his typecasting mold, he eventually played doctors and lawyers (which his four brothers became), detectives, fight managers, farmers, even, in *The Ten Commandments*, the Biblical figure Dathan; privately, the gentlest of men, he collected rare books and nineteenth- and twentieth-century French Impressionist works; also a man of linguistic accomplishments, he was in England for many months during WW II, broadcasting to the Continental underground movement in nine languages; from '27 until '56, when they divorced, he was married to former stage actress Gladys Lloyd; had one son, named Emmanuel but called Manny; starred in 101 movies; last was 1972's *Soylent Green*, in which his final moment before the cameras was a death scene; never nominated for an Academy Award, he was accorded a special one just weeks before he died.

MOVIE HIGHLIGHTS: *Outside the Law, East Is West, Five Star Final, The Hatchet Man, Silver Dollar, Little Giant, The Man with Two Faces, Barbary Coast, Bullets or Ballots, Kid Galahad, A Slight Case of Murder, The Amazing Dr. Clitterhouse, Confessions of a Nazi Spy, A Dispatch from Reuter's The Sea Wolf, Manpower, Destroyer, Double Indemnity, Scarlet Street, Woman in the Window, The Stranger, Key Largo.*

Charles "Buddy" Rogers

(b. Charles Rogers, Aug. 13, 1904, Olathe, Kans.) For years at Paramount he was the studio's in-house campus hero; with crisp, black curly hair, dimples, and a gentle, sincere manner, he was the essence of the college senior voted Most Likely to Succeed; a graduate of the University of Kansas, where he was a fraternity man, he was a musical virtuoso; adept at many instruments (trumpet, piano, sax, etc.), he played the trombone in a jazz band at the university and made a trip abroad with it before being groomed at The Paramount Pictures School for movie fame—which came when he starred in *Wings*; college classmates have described him as "straight" and "square"; was the son of a Sunday school teacher and a judge; his father, once urged by a reporter to tell "the good as well as the bad" about his famous son, replied, "Buddy has no faults. He has never given his mother or me one single moment's worry or unhappiness"; falling in love with a married woman (and, by a decade, an older one) was the last thing anyone ever expected of the actor but that is what happened, at 23, when Mary Pickford—then the wife of Douglas Fairbanks—chose him as her leading man in *My Best Girl*; biding his time, he won her exactly 10 years later and, from the time of their June 1937 wedding, was utterly devoted to her; lived throughout the marriage at Pickfair, the fabled house she had built with Fairbanks; aided her in restoring and preserving her great silent movies and, later, when she was physically unable to do so, he journeyed all over the globe to film festivals where the films of America's Sweetheart were honored; phasing out his own screen career in the late '30s, he was a popular band leader for a while and then a successful movie producer, notably of Lupe Velez's "Mexican Spitfire" comedies.

MOVIE HIGHLIGHTS: *Fascinating Youth, Get Your Man, Abie's Irish Rose, Varsity, Close Harmony, Here Comes the Bandwagon, Young Eagles, Along Came Youth, The Reckless Age, Halfway to Heaven, Dance Band, Old Man Rhythm, Take a Chance, Best of Enemies, The Lawyer's Secret, Week-End Millionaire, Let's Make a Night of It.*

Ginger Rogers

(b. Virginia Katherine McMath, July 16, 1911, Independence, Mo.) From the "Show Me" state, this indomitable star's own motto could have been "Show *Them*"; did show that she could convincingly be whatever the role required—the dancer (those 11 immortal Astaire-Rogers musicals), the light comedienne *(Bachelor Mother)*, the wisecracking realist *(Stage Door)*, the sophisticate *(Lady in the Dark)*, the plucky working girl *(Kitty Foyle* won her an Oscar), the historical figure (Dolly Madison in *The Magnificent Doll)*; *Time* magazine once described her well: "Less eccentric than Carole Lombard, less worldly-wise than Myrna Loy, less impudent than Joan Blondell, Ginger Rogers has a careless self-sufficiency they lack"; the child of divorced parents, she was adopted by (and took the name of) her insurance-man stepfather; left school in the sixth grade; with mother Lela as her manager, she began in vaudeville at 14—dancing, singing, and doing the baby-talk routine featured in some of her early movies; was married at 17 to hoofer Jack Pepper, with whom she toured in an act called "Ginger and Pepper," before they divorced; at 19, while singing and dancing on Broadway in *Top Speed*, she made her feature-movie debut, playing a wisecracking flapper ("Cigarette me, big boy," said she, a nonsmoker), in

Young Man of Manhattan; was the first of 73; scored a great hit next on Broadway in *Girl Crazy,* was whisked off to Hollywood where, in *Flying Down to Rio* (her 20th movie), she danced the Carioca with Fred Astaire and screen history was in the making; less successful in private life, she married and divorced four more husbands, all actors: Lew Ayres (1934–41), Jack Briggs (1943–49), Jacques Bergerac (1953–57), William Marshall (1961–73); says she: "I've made thousands of mistakes, but they've all been stepping stones toward a better concept of life."

MOVIE HIGHLIGHTS: *The Sap from Syracuse, 42nd Street, Gold Diggers of 1933, Finishing School, The Gay Divorcee, Roberta, Top Hat, Follow the Fleet, Swing Time, Shall We Dance, Having Wonderful Time, Vivacious Lady, The Primrose Path, Lucky Partners, Roxie Hart, The Major and the Minor, I'll Be Seeing You, Weekend at the Waldorf, The Barkleys of Broadway, Dreamboat, Oh Men! Oh Women!*

Will Rogers

(b. William Penn Adair Rogers, Nov. 4, 1879, Oologah, Indian Territory [Okla.]; d. Aug. 15, 1935) "When I die," he said in that inimitable drawl, "my epitaph is going to read: 'I joked about every prominent man of my time, but I never met a man I didn't like' "; and no one didn't like the folksy, gum-chewing humorist in the double-breasted blue serge suit whose homespun witticisms never missed the target; samples: "The difference between doing a thing for money and doing it for nothing makes it legal" and "Rumor travels faster but it don't stay put as long as truth"; part Cherokee (and Irish), he played up being an uneducated country boy; actually had 10 years of schooling—at an Indian school (Drumgoole), a Presbyterian mission school, Scarrett College (high school), Kemper Military Academy, even for a while a girls' school (Harrell Institute); first job was as a $4-a-day cowpuncher on a ranch in Higgins, Texas; broke into show business as a rider-roper in the Zack Mulhall Wild West Show at the St. Louis Exposition in 1904; went into vaudeville then as a lariat-twirling comedian, which he was later on Broadway as a star of the *Ziegfeld Follies*; made his screen debut in '18 in *Laughing Bill Hyde*; was in three dozen silent comedies (*Cupid the Cowpuncher, Jes' Call Me Jim,* etc.) before becoming, in talkies, the most beloved man of his time and Hollywood's highest-salaried star ("Heck, I ain't a real movie star, I still got the same wife I started with"); she was Betty Blake, to whom he was married from 1908 on; a goodwill ambassador without portfolio, and a friend of every president from Roosevelt (Theodore) to Roosevelt (FDR), he traveled widely and made friends for America the world over; son Will Jr. portrayed him in *The Will Rogers Story* ('52); is buried at the Will Rogers Memorial in Claremore, Okla., where more than 1500 visitors still come daily to pay their respects.

MOVIE HIGHLIGHTS: *They Had to See Paris, So This Is London, Ambassador Bill, A Connecticut Yankee, State Fair, Doctor Bull, Mr. Skitch, David Harum, Handy Andy, Judge Priest, County Chairman, Life Begins at Forty, In Old Kentucky, Steamboat 'Round the Bend.*

Gilbert Roland

(b. Luis Antonio Damaso de Alonso, Dec. 11, 1905, Ciudad Juarez, Mexico) They call him "Hollywood's true aristocrat," for he is a well-traveled, well-read, and, in the best sense of the word, sophisticated man; the Mayor of Los Angeles, a few years back, honored him with a city commendation citing that "in his long and illustrious career he has always portrayed the Latin American as a man of honor, courage, fortitude, and idealism and in his private life has exemplified the true gentleman in the best hidalgo tradition"; the son of a famous matador from Spain, he was 5 when he fled with his family to El Paso to escape the wave of violence during the raids of Pancho Villa (though his father was a Villa admirer); at 13 he hopped a freight to Hollywood, where he became a $3-a-day extra, often going hungry and sleeping on a church bench; lithe, dark, handsome, and born to be a Latin Lover, he was signed at 19 to a Paramount contract; casting him in a Clara Bow movie, *The Plastic Age*, studio topper B. P. Schulberg decided to rename him "George Adams"; rebelling, he chose his own screen monicker from the names of his favorite stars, John Gilbert and Ruth Roland; starred in a dozen silents, including *Camille*, in which he was the passionate Armand Duval of Norma Talmadge, who became his real-life amour; her estranged but irate husband, movie mogul Joseph Schenck, saw to it that the actor was unemployed for a while; became one of the screen's great ladykillers in the '30s; said: "If I had my choice of ways to die, it would be in the bull ring or the arms of a beautiful woman"; was married (1941–46) to Constance Bennett; two daughters:

Lorinda and Gyle; since '54 has been wed to Gia Cantu of Mexico City; lives by this credo: "Make each day count. Be happy. Believe in God. Dream of the past if you will, but don't live in it."

MOVIE HIGHLIGHTS: *Monsieur Le Fox, The Men in Her Life, A Parisian Romance, Call Her Savage, Our Betters, She Done Him Wrong, Mystery Woman, Ladies Love Danger, Last Train from Madrid, Juarez, The Sea Hawk, Captain Kidd, Cisco and the Angel, Malaya, We Were Strangers, The Furies, The Bullfighter and the Lady, The Bad and the Beautiful.*

Shirley Ross

(b. Bernice Gaunt, Jan. 7, 1911, Omaha, Neb.; d. March 9, 1975) Charming Paramount musical star, blonde with gray eyes, who joined forces with Bob Hope to introduce "Thanks for the Memory," which became his theme song; was on screen from '33 (*Bombshell*) to '45 (*A Song for Miss Julie*); grew up in New York and Hollywood, where, graduating from Hollywood High, she went on to UCLA with ambitions of becoming a concert pianist; the chance to become a blues singer with Gus Arnheim's orchestra changed that; while appearing with the band at the Beverly-Wilshire Hotel, she was discovered by an MGM talent scout and signed to a studio contract; in three years and nine movies at Metro, she played minor roles such as that of the girl who lost her saloon job to Jeanette MacDonald in *San Francisco*; made a greatly successful stage debut in '36 in the Los Angeles production of *Anything Goes*; Paramount borrowed her to co-star with Bob Hope in *The Big Broadcast of 1937* and, halfway through the filming, bought up her contract from MGM; long-delayed popularity quickly came her way but fame did not turn her head; a realist, she lived conservatively, saying, "My goal is to make money so that I shall be secure for the rest of my life. When I have made that much, I hope I shall have the courage to leave pictures"; took time out from movies in '40 to star on Broadway in *Higher and Higher*, a huge hit, in which she sang a most memorable song, "It Never Entered My Mind"; returned to Hollywood for just three more pictures then, financially well off, quit the business cold; was married from '38 until his death in '51 to agent Ken Dolan, by whom she had two sons, John and Ross, and then to Edward Blum, becoming the mother of a daughter, Victoria.

MOVIE HIGHLIGHTS: *Manhattan Melodrama, The Girl from Missouri, Hollywood Party, The Merry Widow, Calm Yourself, Devil's Squadron, Age of Indiscretion, Hideaway Girl, Waikiki Wedding, Blossoms on Broadway, Prison Farm, Thanks for the Memory, Paris Honeymoon, Cafe Society, Some Like It Hot, Unexpected Father, Sailors on Leave, Kisses for Breakfast.*

Norma Shearer

(b. Edith Norma Shearer, Aug. 10, 1900, Westmount, Montreal, Canada; d. June 12, 1983) "The First Lady of Hollywood"; pinned on her by the publicity department at MGM, where her "boy genius" husband, Irving G. Thalberg, was production chief, this was no idle claim; she *was* the studio's reigning femme star, one of the greats—stylish, sparkling, warm—with a personality perfectly attuned to the camera and a beautiful speaking voice; and she *was* a lady, of a well-to-do Canadian family that lost its fortune; personal life was scandal-free, though several times she marvelously played shady ladies; was equally adept at high comedy (*Private Lives*), sentimental fare (*The Barretts of Wimpole Street*), heavy drama (*Marie Antoinette*); physically there was a flaw—eyes that were not perfectly aligned, forcing cautious camera work; starting in '20, was popular in many silents (*He Who Gets Slapped, Pretty Ladies*, etc.) before marrying Thalberg in '27; taking charge of her career, he guided her to the cinematic heights; film historian Richard Griffith has noted that "she used her position as his wife to secure the pick of MGM parts . . . but so discreetly that her sister stars never had cause to complain—openly"; six times nominated for Oscars, she won as Best Actress for *The Divorcee*—but was bested by brother Douglas Shearer, brilliant head of MGM's Sound Dept., who snagged 12; two children: Irving Jr. and Katherine; dying at 37, Thalberg left her $4.5 million and a huge bloc of studio stock; in '42, the year she left the screen, she became— and remained—the wife of handsome younger (by 14 years) Martin Arrouge, ex-ski instructor; age and time were unkind—became blind some years before her death.

MOVIE HIGHLIGHTS: *The Trial of Mary Dugan, The Last of Mrs. Cheyney, Their Own Desire, A Free Soul, Smilin' Through, Strange Interlude, Romeo and Juliet, Idiot's Delight, The Women, Escape, Her Cardboard Lover, We Were Dancing.*

Anne Shirley

(b. Dawn Evelyeen Paris, April 17, 1918, New York, N.Y.) Winsome, flame-haired beauty who, known as "Dawn O'Day," was in dozens of silents, starting at the age of 3 in William Farnum's *Moonshine Valley*; her father died when she was an infant and she became the financial support of her mother, first as a commercial artists' model, when only 14 months old; of the support her mother gave her, she said in recent years, "What I eventually became justified my mother's hard work, dedication, and the sacrifices she had to make on my behalf"; acquired her famous screen name at 16, taking it (legally, finally) from the character she played in *Anne of Green Gables*; gave what many considered her finest portrayal when only 19, as Barbara Stanwyck's daughter in *Stella Dallas*; remarking on the "warmth and brilliance" she brought to the part, Stanwyck has said, "Anne played the exquisite Laurel with a sensitivity rare in one so young"; other Shirley admirers plump for her role as Carole Lombard's tragic sister in *Vigil in the Night*; much like Olivia de Havilland in voice, smile, and gentle femininity, she was at one time a contender for Melanie in *Gone With the Wind*; she and John Payne were Hollywood's most-publicized "ideal young marrieds" from '37 until '43, when they divorced; daughter: Julie Anne; second husband (1945–49) was Adrian Scott, writer-producer of *Murder, My Sweet* ('44), the final film in which she starred before quitting the screen for good at 26; gave up her career because "I felt it was time to begin living a full, private life, and I've never regretted that decision"; was finally wed, from '49 until his death in '76, to the brilliant writer Charles Lederer (nephew of Marion Davies), by whom she has a son, Daniel.

MOVIE HIGHLIGHTS: *Steamboat 'Round the Bend, Chasing Yesterday, M'Liss, Make Way for a Lady, Mother Carey's Chickens, Meet the Missus, A Man to Remember, Girls' School, Sorority House, Anne of Windy Poplars, The Devil and Daniel Webster* (a.k.a. *All That Money Can Buy*), *The Powers Girl, The Mayor of 44th Street, Saturday's Children, Bombardier, Government Girl.*

Sylvia Sidney

(b. Sophia Kosow, Aug. 8, 1910, New York, N.Y.) Before becoming Paramount's ace "weeper" in Depression dramas of the early '30s, this fiery, petite, large-eyed charmer already had been hailed as the most popular young actress of the Broadway theater; made her stage debut at 16 as the ingenue lead in *Crime*, with Chester Morris, giving, said Brooks Atkinson of *The New York Times*, "the most ingratiating performance"; other Broadway leads followed in *Mirrors, Nice Women*, etc.; acquired her professional surname when her immigrant parents (Rumanian father, Russian mother) divorced and she was adopted by her mother's second husband, Dr. Sigmund Sidney; was starring on stage in *Slightly Dishonorable* when Hollywood agent Ad Schulberg discovered her and, to this woman's eventual regret, persuaded her husband, Paramount chief B. P. Schulberg, to sign her to a contract; the romance that developed between the actress and the studio boss is detailed, not without rancor, in the autobiography penned by the Schulbergs' son Budd, *Moving Pictures: Memories of a Hollywood Prince*; born with her dukes up, the star soon developed a reputation for being temperamental, which she does not deny; when first in Hollywood, she once said, she did what she was told to do, but "when I learned I didn't have to, I became a bitch on wheels"; specialized in playing unfortunate, unhappy girls in the slums *(City Streets)*, factories *(An American Tragedy)*, and prisons *(Ladies of the Big House)*; career as a screen star continued—sometimes bumpily—from '31 to '47, when, she laughs, "they terminated me"; a three-time divorcee, she was married to publisher Bennett Cerf, actor Luther Adler (father of her son Jacob), agent Carlton Alsop; becoming a character actress, she was nominated for a Best Supporting Oscar in *Summer Wishes, Winter Dreams*.

MOVIE HIGHLIGHTS: *Confessions of a Co-ed, Street Scene, Merrily We Go to Hell, Make Me a Star, The Miracle Man, Madame Butterfly, Jennie Gerhardt, Thirty-Day Princess, Good Dame, Accent on Youth, Mary Burns–Fugitive, Fury, Trail of the Lonesome Pine, You Only Live Once, Dead End, You and Me, One Third of a Nation, Blood on the Sun, The Searching Wind, Mr. Ace.*

Penny Singleton

(b. Mariana Dorothy Agnes Letitia McNulty, Sept. 15, 1908, Philadelphia, Pa.) Moviegoers first knew her (1930–37) as dark-haired Dorothy McNulty, and ever thereafter as delightfully daffy Penny ("Blondie") Singleton; her permanent screen name came via an impermanent (1937–39) marriage to orthodontist Lawrence S. Singleton, father of her daughter Dorothy Grace; "Penny" already was her nickname as she was an avid collector of copper coins; was married from '41 until his death in '63 to Robert Sparks, producer of the first 12 (of the 28) "Blondie" comedies that made her a star; their child: Robin Susan; the daughter of an Irish-American newspaperman, she began on the stage as a child; after winning $5 by singing in an amateur contest, she was hired to sing illustrated songs at a silent movie theater; leaving school after the sixth grade, she sang and danced in a cross-country tour with a vaudeville act, "The Kiddie Kabaret," which featured two other juveniles headed for fame, Gene Raymond and Milton Berle; began on Broadway at 18 with a minor role in *The Great Temptations*, starring Jack Benny; was later in such Main Stem musicals as *Hey, Nonny, Nonny!* and *Walk a Little Faster; Good News*, a 1930 musical, marked her screen debut; a supporting player in a score of movies following it, she alternated between playing song-dance girls and floozies such as the hardboiled night club singer in *After the Thin Man*; became Dagwood's "Blondie" on the rebound; Shirley Deane, of "The Jones Family" comedy series, who was already signed to play the role, became ill and was forced to withdraw before the filming of *Blondie* began in '38; was still a brunette when she did her screen test but that soon changed for all time; had a post-"Blondie" career as president of the American Guild of Variety Artists.

MOVIE HIGHLIGHTS: *Love in the Rough, Vogues of 1938, Sea Racketeers* (as Dorothy McNulty), *Blondie Meets the Boss* (. . . *Takes a Vacation;* . . . *Brings Up Baby;* . . . *Plays Cupid;* . . . *Goes Latin,* etc.), *Go West Young Lady, It's a Great Life, Footlight Glamour, Young Widow, The Best Man.*

Sir C. Aubrey Smith

(b. Charles Aubrey Smith, July 21, 1863, London, England; d. Dec. 20, 1948) For decades to millions of moviegoers, this old party, with the craggy face, bushy brows, and ever-present pipe, was the very map of the British Empire; a favorite with English stage audiences after 1892, he was prominently featured in British movies for 16 years following his debut in 1915's *Builder of Bridges*; was first seen on stage in the U.S. in 1903 in *The Light That Failed*; went to Hollywood in '31 to film his stage success *The Bachelor Father* for MGM and scored such a personal triumph that, but for

154

an occasional movie role, he never went home again; a great storyteller, he relished telling of having read his own "obituary," which appeared in London papers when he was 26; a famous athlete then, he was touring South Africa with a championship cricket team when, developing typhoid, he sank into a coma with no hope given for his recovery; a member of the Wanderers Club, of which he was a member, issued a call for a band to play at his "funeral" and someone jumped the gun, cabling London the news of his "death"; lived, of course, to become the cinema's Grand Old Man, respected and beloved; once said he stayed—"and undoubtedly will end my days"—in Hollywood because he liked the work, the climate, and the cricket competition (with the many resident British actors there), then he added, chuckling, "Also, my wife wouldn't let me live anywhere else"; was married from 1896 on to Isobel Wood, by whom he had a daughter, Honor; for reason, his Hollywood estate was called The Round Corner; in his undergraduate days at Cambridge, where he studied medicine, he was captain of the university cricket team and was known as "Round-the-corner" Smith because of his unique style of bowling; the last of his scores of Hollywood movies, the remake of *Little Women*, was released after his death.

MOVIE HIGHLIGHTS: *Trader Horn, Son of India, Love Me Tonight, Trouble in Paradise, The Scarlet Empress, Bombshell, Queen Christina, Cleopatra, Lives of a Bengal Lancer, Clive of India, China Seas, Little Lord Fauntleroy, Wee Willie Winkie, The Prisoner of Zenda, The Hurricane, Lloyds of London, Rebecca.*

Ann Sothern

(b. Harriette Lake, Jan. 22, 1907, Valley City, N.D.) Charm with humor is what this blonde star has always had, and a career that would rise and set and rise again like the sun; began under her real name in '29 playing bits in *The Show of Shows*, etc.; visiting Hollywood, Florenz Ziegfeld saw her on screen, met her, and urged her to try the stage; starred on Broadway and in national tours, still as Lake, in musicals: *Smiles, America's Sweetheart, Of Thee I Sing*; Columbia signed her in '34 as the lead in *Let's Fall in Love*, and held a contest to find a new screen name for her; many musicals and straight leads followed; too many were B's, her career plummeted and she wound up supporting other stars; was restored to popularity via MGM's

"Maisie" comedies; 10 times between '39 and '47 she played the brassy, wise-cracking Brooklyn blonde with a heart of gold (in *Congo Maisie*, *Swing Shift Maisie*, etc.); between these she did sophisticated comedy *(Dulcy)*, drama *(Cry Havoc)*, more musicals *(Panama Hattie)*; place of birth was an accident—her opera-singer mother, Annette Yde, was in Valley City only between engagements of a concert tour; actually grew up in Minneapolis and Seattle; attended the University of Washington, where she studied music after winning prizes for original piano compositions while at Seattle's Central High; is a descendant of Simon Lake, inventor of the submarine; gained new fame on TV, starring in two long-running series, "Private Secretary" and "The Ann Sothern Show"; after an early marriage ("an adolescent mistake"), was married to bandleader Roger Pryor (1936–42) and actor Robert Sterling (1943–49), father of her only child, actress Tricia Sterling.

MOVIE HIGHLIGHTS: *Folies Bergere, Smartest Girl in Town, Trade Winds, Hotel for Women, Brother Orchid, Lady Be Good, April Showers, Words and Music, A Letter to Three Wives, Nancy Goes to Rio, Blue Gardenia, The Best Man, Lady in a Cage, Crazy Mama.*

Barbara Stanwyck

(b. Ruby Stevens, July 16, 1907, Brooklyn, N.Y.) A Broadway billboard announcing *"Barbara Frietchie* starring Jane Stanwyck" gave her the name the world has long honored; all the rest, the beauty, the glow, the rich, husky voice, the talent to delight you in comedy or tear your heart out in tragedy, was strictly her own; has been four times nominated for the Best Actress Oscar—in *Ball of Fire, Double Indemnity, Sorry, Wrong Number,* and *Stella Dallas,* the '37 film that is her personal favorite; says: "The task was to convince audiences that Stella's instincts were fine and noble even though, on the surface, she was loud, flamboyant, and a bit vulgar"; ever the pro, the actress has been cherished by all her directors, even tough taskmaster Cecil B. De Mille, who said he "never worked with an actress who was more cooperative, less temperamental, and a better workman, to use my term of highest compliment, than Barbara Stanwyck"; the fifth of five children, she was orphaned at 4 and brought up in foster homes; went to work at 13 (telephone operator, pattern-shop receptionist, floor-show chorine); became an overnight star on Broadway at 19 in *The Noose,* a dramatic hit that was followed by an even greater one, *Burlesque*; 1927's *Broadway Nights*, a silent (her only one) made in New York, in which she was heroine Lois Wilson's pal, marked her screen debut; married to actor Frank Fay in '28 (divorced, bitterly, in '35), she went with him to Hollywood; her first film there, *Mexicali Rose*, flopped; then made nine unsuccessful screen tests before director Frank Capra signed her, without a test, for *Ladies of Leisure* ('30), and an enduring favorite was born; married Robert Taylor, her leading man in *This Is My Affair*, in '39 and divorced him in '52.

MOVIE HIGHLIGHTS: *Night Nurse, So Big, The Bitter Tea of General Yen, Shopworn, A Lost Lady, Annie Oakley, A Message to Marcia, Banjo on My Knee, The Plough and the Stars, Always Goodbye, Union Pacific, Golden Boy, Meet John Doe, The Lady Eve, The Great Man's Lady, Lady of Burlesque, Christmas in Connecticut, The Strange Love of Martha Ivers, B. F.'s Daughter, The Furies, Titanic, Executive Suite, Walk on the Wild Side.*

James Stewart

(b. James Maitland Stewart, May 20, 1908, Indiana, Pa.) With his laconic delivery and gangling frame as his trademarks, he has been a reigning star almost from the day he arrived at MGM in '35, and one of Hollywood's most honored luminaries; besides winning the Best Actor Oscar for *The Philadelphia Story*, was also nominated for *Mr. Smith Goes to Washington, It's a Wonderful Life, Harvey,* and *Anatomy of a Murder*; also snagged two New York Film Critics' Awards, a Venice Film Festival citation, and France's Victoire trophy; oddly, only hit his stride at the box office in '50; throughout the following decade, excepting '51, was in the Top Ten each year; in '55 was #1, thanks to *The Glenn Miller Story* and *Rear Window*; the son of a hardware merchant (proudly kept the Oscar on display in his store window), he went to Princeton to study architecture; after graduation in '32 he joined fellow Princetonian Josh Logan's summer stock company at Cape Cod and got sidetracked into acting; made his Broadway debut in *Goodbye Again*, next did summer stock, returned to New York for a major role in *Yellow Jack*; snapped up for movies, he appeared first in *Murder Man*, starring Spencer Tracy; enlisting as a private in the Air Force in '41, he flew 25 missions over enemy territory in

Europe, winning the Distinguished Service Medal, the Air Medal, DFC with Oak Leaf Clusters; holds the rank of Brigadier General in the Air Force Reserve; was long famous as Hollywood's most eligible bachelor; marrying Gloria McLean in '49, he became the stepfather of two: Michael and Ronald (killed in action in Vietnam in '69); father of twins, Judy and Kelly, born May 7, 1951; in '84 received the Gold Medal of the USO, its highest honor.

MOVIE HIGHLIGHTS: *Rose Marie, Navy Blue and Gold, You Can't Take It with You, Destry Rides Again, Shop Around the Corner, The Mortal Storm, Ziegfeld Girl, Call Northside 777, Rope, The Stratton Story, Broken Arrow, The Man Who Knew Too Much, Vertigo, The Man Who Shot Liberty Valance.*

Lewis Stone

(b. Lewis S. Stone, Nov. 15, 1879, Worcester, Mass.; d. Sept. 11, 1953) Gray-haired character star known to and beloved by millions as wise Judge Hardy, father of Andy (Mickey Rooney), in the "Hardy Family" series; did the role 14 times between *You're Only Young Once* ('38) and *Love Laughs at Andy Hardy* ('46); did not create the part—Lionel Barrymore played Judge Hardy earlier, and just once, in the first of the series, 1937's *A Family Affair*; was ever noted for his military bearing, and for good cause; following a brief stint on Broadway after college, he served as a lieutenant in the Spanish-American War; was next recruited with other former officers to go to China to instruct Chinese troops; resigned his colonelcy at the outbreak of the Boxer Rebellion; was back in military uniform in WW I as a cavalry major, and retained his commission in the Army Reserve; just prior to this, had become a matinee idol on Western stages, starring in *The Bird of Paradise, The Girl of the Golden West*, etc., going directly into movies, beginning romantically opposite Bessie Barriscale in 1915's *Honor Altar*; starred, often swashbucklingly, in dozens of silents: *Scaramouche, Don Juan's Three Nights*, etc.; was a Metro stalwart from '28 to the end, acting first alongside Garbo in *A Woman of Affairs* and last in support of Robert Taylor in *All the Brothers Were Valiant* ('53); athletic and passionate about physical fitness, he was an expert rider, fencer, and boxer; after first wife Margaret Langham died, he was married to and divorced from Florence Oakley (two daughters: Virginia, Barbara), then from '30 on, was wed to Hazel Wolf; was nominated for the Best Actor Oscar in *The Patriot.*

MOVIE HIGHLIGHTS: *The Big House, Mata Hari, Grand Hotel, Queen Christina, David Copperfield, China Seas, Shipmates Forever, Suzy, The 13th Chair, Yellow Jack, State of the Union, Stars in My Crown, Key to the City, Angels in the Outfield.*

Gloria Stuart

(b. Gloria von Dietrich Stuart Finch, July 14, 1910, Santa Monica, Calif.) In 1931, before she ever set foot on a sound stage, two studios fought to sign this gorgeous, classy blonde to a contract, each claiming to have discovered her first in a Pasadena Playhouse production of *The Sea Gull*; Paramount lost—the Will Hays Office's arbitration board voting in favor of Universal; elated studio topper Carl Laemmle Jr., professing he had "never seen such poise, such delicate beauty, such depth," said, "We will have to find some truly distinguished stories for her, because nothing else would be quite fitting"; his was an empty promise, as this daughter of a wealthy Texas oilman soon learned; became the studio's Queen of B's—and the dream girl of millions of Saturday matinee males; had given up college (UCLA) to marry a young sculptor, Blair Gordon Newell, whom she divorced in '34; this marriage was once characterized as "a famous experiment of separate abodes, which didn't work"; three weeks after receiving her decree, she became and remained the wife of scriptwriter Arthur Sheekman; they were noted for their ideal marriage and for being Hollywood's perfect hosts; at their bungalow at the Garden of Allah hotel on Sunset Boulevard, they provided the feasts for Dorothy Parker, Robert Benchley, and other visiting intellectuals from the East; columnist Sheilah Graham, their neighbor then, recalls, "The Sheekmans were catalysts. They brought people together at their bountiful table. The beautiful Gloria was a beautiful cook. Arthur has always been the friendliest and most helpful of men"; their daughter, Sylvia, is a well-known author (and the mother of four); after leads in 49 movies, the star left the screen in '46 (*She Wrote the Book* was her last), and had a later career as a professional painter.

MOVIE HIGHLIGHTS: *Street of Women, The All-American, Airmail, The Old Dark House, Back Street, The Invisible Man, Roman Scandals, Secret of the Blue Room, Sweepings, Gift of Gab, Here Comes the Navy, I'll Tell the World, Laddie, Prisoner of Shark Island, 36 Hours to Kill, Poor Little Rich Girl, Rebecca of Sunnybrook Farm, The Girl on the Front Page, Keep Smiling.*

Margaret Sullavan

(b. Margaret Brooke Sullavan, May 16, 1909, Norfolk, Va.; d. Jan. 1, 1960) Brilliant, beautiful, and spirited—and a superb actress—she was a true star of both the stage (which she loved) and Hollywood (which she loathed); "If ever I've known someone who was unique, it was Maggie," said Henry Fonda; married when she was 21, they divorced, almost remarried, then reared their children (by other spouses) on neighboring Connecticut estates as best friends; was a willful personality with only a tentative grasp on her own emotional balance, but it is said that she felt "she *knew* what was best for her children, for her husband [stage producer Leland Hayward], for anyone who came under her spell"; misery and tragedy ensued—her son being in and out of psychiatric institutions, a daughter who died, a possible suicide, at 21, and finally, her own death (also perhaps by her own hand) in a New Haven, Conn., hotel room during the pre-Broadway tryout of a play; the star's story, and that of her family, was superbly, if harrowingly, recounted in the best-seller *Haywire*, penned by surviving daughter Brooke Hayward; of a distinguished Virginia family, she was educated in private schools and at Sullins College before joining Cape Cod's University Players; after playing the lead on tour in *Strictly Dishonorable*, she conquered Broadway in *The Modern Virgin*, *Happy Landings*, *Chrysalis*; went to Hollywood in '33 for the starring role in *Only Yesterday*; strangely, was at her best in weepy movies like *Three Comrades* (her one Oscar nomination) and frothy Broadway comedies (*The Voice of the Turtle*, *Sabrina Fair*, *Janus*).

MOVIE HIGHLIGHTS: *The Good Fairy, So Red the Rose, The Moon's Our Home* (with Fonda), *Next Time We Love, The Shopworn Angel, The Mortal Storm, The Shop Around the Corner, So Ends Our Night, Back Street, Cry Havoc, No Sad Songs for Me.*

Robert Taylor

(b. Spangler Arlington Brugh, Aug. 5, 1911, Filley, Neb.; d. June 8, 1969) "Pretty Boy" image or no (overcome via he-man roles and, finally, a wrinkle or two), this "too handsome" star was as macho as they come—a hunter, fisherman, boxer; was also a licensed pilot, using this experience in WW II as a flying instructor (Lt. j.g.) in the Navy's Air Corps; growing up in Beatrice, Neb., the only child of a grain merchant-turned -physician, he graduated from public schools then attended Doane College at Crete, Neb., for two years; transferred to California's Pomona College, where he was an outstanding scholar, played cello, was a star tennis player; graduating with a liberal arts degree in '33, he took the advice of a talent scout who'd seen him in a college production of *Journey's End* and studied at a Hollywood drama school; after juvenile leads in two movies elsewhere signed a long-term contract ($35 a week) at MGM; his second feature there, 1935's *Society Doctor* (weekly salary now $50), made him a star overnight, his suddenly vast femme following being fully as vocal as that of Presley and The Beatles later; remained at Metro through 1959's *The House of the Seven Hawks* (salary $6,000 a week); forgotten fact: sang ("I've Got a Feeling You're Fooling") and danced on screen only once, in *Broadway Melody of 1936*; co-starred with Barbara Stanwyck in *His Brother's Wife* and *This Is My Affair*, and was married to her on May 14, 1939; divorced in '52, they teamed again on screen in '65 in *The Night Walker*; in '54 he married German actress Ursula Thiess; two children: Terence and Tessa; personal favorite of his 81 movies: *Waterloo Bridge*.

MOVIE HIGHLIGHTS: *Magnificent Obsession, Camille, A Yank at Oxford, Three Comrades, The Crowd Roars, Escape, Billy the Kid, Johnny Eager, Bataan, Undercurrent, Quo Vadis, Ivanhoe, Knights of the Round Table, Above and Beyond, Many Rivers to Cross.*

Shirley Temple

(b. Shirley Jane Temple, April 23, 1928, Santa Monica, Calif.) Many fruitless decades later, Hollywood finally gave up trying to replicate, duplicate, or discover a "new" Shirley Temple, with her dimples, curly top, dancing feet, enchanting smile, and heartbreaking tears (always glycerine, for she was "too happy" to cry); beyond argument, she was the most famous, best-loved moppet in movie history; from '35 through '38 was Number One at the box office, with a weekly salary, at her peak, of $10,000 (equal to $50,000 or more today), which was well invested by her banker dad and housewife–studio guardian mom, who were both of German descent; millions more came from endorsements and "Shirley Temple" dolls (any little American girl who didn't possess one was deprived indeed); President Roosevelt, one of multimillions, doted on her, and gossip columnist Sidney Skolsky became legendary in Hollywood as the only person known to have turned her over his knee and given her a spanking (in a brattish mood, she had tossed his hat across a room—twice); the year she became a star ('34) she was accorded a special Oscar (miniature statuette) "in grateful recognition of her outstanding contribution to screen entertainment"; 20th Century–Fox did what studios often do for stars—lied about her age, making her one year younger; dancing as early as she walked, she appeared first, when 4, in two series of satiric comedy shorts for Educational Pictures: "Baby Burlesks" and "Frolics of Youth"; made her feature debut in '32 in *The Red-Haired Alibi* starring Grant Withers; was next in Randolph Scott's *To the Last Man*, Slim Summerville's *Out All Night*, and Kay Francis' *Mandalay*, before signing with Fox (at $150 a week); *Stand Up and Cheer*, with her show-stealing "Baby Take a Bow" song-and-dance routine, catapulted her to international fame; inevitably growing up, she was married (1945–49) to actor John Agar; their daughter, Linda Susan, made her a first-time grandmother (of Teresa) in '80; has been wed since '50 to business exec Charles A. Black; two children: Charles Jr. and Lori; became the U.S. ambassador to Ghana and—the first woman in 200 years to hold the job— U.S. protocol chief in the Foreign Service; speaks today of her childhood self as "that little girl," humorously adding, "I class myself with Rin Tin Tin; people in the Depression wanted something to cheer them up, and they fell in love with a dog and a little girl."

MOVIE HIGHLIGHTS: *Little Miss Marker, Bright Eyes, Now and Forever, Curly Top, The Littlest Rebel, Our Little Girl, The Little Colonel, Captain January, Dimples, Poor Little Rich Girl, Stowaway, Wee Willie Winkie, Heidi, Rebecca of Sunnybrook Farm, Just Around the Corner, Little Miss Broadway, Susannah of the Mounties, The Little Princess, The Blue Bird.*

The Three Stooges

Moe Howard (b. Moses Horwitz, June 19, 1897, Bensonhurst, N.Y.; d. May 4, 1975), **Curly Howard** (b. Jerome Lester Horwitz, Oct. 22, 1903, Brooklyn, N.Y.; d. Jan. 18, 1952), and **Larry Fine** (b. Louis Feinberg, Oct. 5, 1902, Philadelphia, Pa.; d. Jan. 24, 1975) From '33 to '46, in slapstick two-reelers, they were the original unholy three—bossy ringleader

Moe, with his black chamber-pot haircut and blacker rages; moon-faced Curly (Jerry), with his infantile grunts, squeals, and shaved billiard-ball head; and frizzy-haired, peacemaker Larry, sometimes described as "reality's bridge" between them; for years earlier, while stooging for comedian Ted Healy, on stage and in their first movie (1930's *Soup to Nuts*), the trio was Moe, Larry Fine, and *Shemp* Howard; though Moe, Curly, and Larry started in shorts at MGM, Columbia signed them to a long-term contract in '34; their first two-reeler there: "Woman Haters"; the original three starred together in a total of 97 shorts; their zany pantomime—with someone forever getting "a bop on the casaba"—transcended all language barriers, and they quickly became internationally popular, having fan clubs from Caracas to Calcutta; Moe and Curly were the sons of a clothing cutter father who opposed their show business aspirations; Moe began playing small parts in silent comedies at 12 and then, for a while, was a diving "girl" in Annette Kellerman's aquatic act; ran away from home at 16 and acted in melodramas on a Mississippi river boat before going into vaudeville; was married for almost 50 years to his wife, Helen, and had two children, Joan and Paul. . . . Nicknamed "Babe," and an introvert off screen, Curly was the most popular Stooge; like brother Moe, he never finished high school; broke into show business at 25, doing a comic-conductor routine with a band; became one of the Stooges (with Ted Healy) in '32, when brother Shemp quit the act; had a teenage marriage that was annulled and two later wives who divorced him, before having a happy marriage, from '47 on, with Valerie Newman; had a daughter, Marilyn, by wife #2, and another, Janie, by his last; died in a sanitarium named Baldy View. . . . The son of a jewelry shop owner, Larry had violin lessons as a child that served him well when he went into vaudeville; was one-third of an act called Haney Sisters & Fine, in which he simultaneously played the fiddle and did a wild Russian dance; one of the sisters, Mabel, became his lifelong wife and the mother of son John (died at 24 in an auto accident) and daughter Phyllis; when Curly Howard became ill, brother Shemp replaced him in '47 and, eventually, this third stooge role was also filled by Joe Besser and Joe DeRita; a book covering *all* the Stooges, *The Three Stooges Scrapbook*, was published in '82.

MOVIE HIGHLIGHTS: *Meet the Baron, Turn Back the Clock, Myrt & Marge, Dancing Lady, Fugitive Lovers, Hollywood Party* (features all, with Moe, Curly and Larry); Curly and Moe also appeared in *Broadway to Hollywood*.

Franchot Tone

(b. Stanislas Pascal Franchot Tone, Feb. 27, 1905, Niagara Falls, N.Y.; d. Sept. 18, 1968) Well-born (son of the president of the Carborundum Co. of America) and well-educated (Cornell; Phi Beta Kappa), he was one of the most sophisticated, cultivated stars on the MGM lot; was often seen in white tie and tails playing, he said, "a slick, well-groomed, well-heeled stuffed shirt"; different casting in *Mutiny on the Bounty* rated him an Oscar nomination; entered movies in '31 after five years on the Great White Way, acting alongside Lunt and Fontanne, Katharine Cornell, etc.; first movie: *The Wiser Sex*, made in N.Y.; despised Hollywood, loved the stage (was a founder of the Group Theatre), and between films always returned to the boards; appeared often opposite Joan Crawford, who became his first wife (1935–39); long after their divorce she described him as "an extremely loving, intelligent, considerate man"; also confided to reporter Roy Newquist: "I wasn't as nice to him, as considerate, as I should have been . . . I didn't realize that his insecurities and dissatisfactions ran so deeply. His sex life diminished considerably, which didn't help matters"; parted "after hundreds of running arguments and a few physical rows"; married actress Jean Wallace next (1941–48); two sons: Pascal Franchot and Thomas Jefferson; made tawdry headlines in '51 when he and brawny Tom Neal fought it out over Barbara Payton, the late blonde sexpot; suffering a broken nose and fractured cheekbone, he was able to resume his career only after radical plastic surgery; was then married to Payton for one year till she divorced him and resumed with Neal.

MOVIE HIGHLIGHTS: *Dancing Lady, Bombshell, Sadie McKee, Suzy, The Gorgeous Hussy, Quality Street, The Bride Wore Red, Man Proof, Three Comrades, Three Loves Has Nancy, Five Graves to Cairo, Phantom Lady, Thunder Afloat, His Butler's Sister, Dark Waters, Advise and Consent.*

Spencer Tracy

(b. Spencer Tracy, April 5, 1900, Milwaukee, Wis.; d. June 10, 1967) The first male star to win two Best Actor Oscars in a row, for *Captains Courageous* and *Boys Town* (1937–38); nominated seven other times (a record for actors)—for *San Francisco, Father of the Bride, Bad Day at Black Rock, The*

Old Man and the Sea, Inherit the Wind, Judgment at Nuremberg, Guess Who's Coming to Dinner; starred in 76 features (first: 1930's *Up the River*) and, even in the poorest, was never less than spellbinding; after long stage experience, established his reputation on Broadway as Killer Mears in *The Last Mile*, the same role that, in the West Coast company, served as pal Clark Gable's ticket to stardom; moviegoers cottoned to his image of folksy, easygoing friendliness; many who worked with him viewed him differently; reporter Bill Davidson once noted: "The Tracy *they* know is rebellious and surly and snaps at his fellow actors when their professional standards do not measure up to his own"; friends chalked up such behavior to his being "a perfectionist," insisting he was "a kind, warm, decent human being"; in '55, after 20 years at the studio, was fired by MGM after starting work on *Tribute to a Bad Man*, allegedly for rebellious misbehavior; when in a New York stock company in '23 he married ingenue Louise Treadwell; two children, John and Suzy; son was born totally deaf and Mrs. Tracy devoted years to teaching him to speak, then founded—with the star's support—the John Tracy Clinic at USC; was separated from his wife in the '30s but they never divorced, and he left his entire estate to her, their children, and his brother; from the time of the first movie they did together, *Woman of the Year* ('42), until his death, Katharine Hepburn was his constant companion.

MOVIE HIGHLIGHTS: *20,000 Years in Sing Sing, Power and the Glory, Man's Castle, Riffraff, Fury, Test Pilot, Northwest Passage, Dr. Jekyll and Mr. Hyde, A Guy Named Joe, 30 Seconds Over Tokyo, Edward My Son, The Actress, Broken Lance, The Last Hurrah.*

Claire Trevor

(b. Claire Wemlinger, May 8, 1909, Bensonhurst, N.Y.) Blonde star with a built-in throb in her husky voice who won a Best Supporting Oscar for *Key Largo* and was also nominated for 1937's *Dead End* (a one-scene, two-minute role taking a day and a half to shoot) and *The High and the Mighty*; did floozies and other assorted "bad girls" better than her rivals, having a knack of playing with ironic humor and restraint, making audiences sympathize with her character, no matter how wicked; said, "It's more fun to be bad—to walk down a street in black sateen and a feather boa"; her role preference may have shocked her father, a well-to-do Fifth

Avenue merchant tailor; got her stage training with Warners' St. Louis stock company after studying at the American Academy; first calling herself "Claire St. Claire," she became "Trevor" at the suggestion of an office boy in a New York casting office; made her Broadway debut in '32 in *Whistling in the Dark* with Ernest Truex; wrote one critic: "Miss Claire Trevor, a shiny debutante, plays the pretty heroine casually"; was next starred in *The Party's Over*, which she left to accept a contract offer at Fox, where she first played heroine roles in two George O'Brien Westerns: *Life in the Raw* and *The Last Trail*; broke with the studio five years later, after playing young doves of wide-eyed innocence in 23 films, mostly B's; portraying street-walker Francey in *Dead End* started her on her "life of shame"; was first wed (1938–42) to Clark Andrews, producer of the popular radio show *Big Town*, in which she starred for three years (1937–40) as Edward G. Robinson's Girl Friday "Lorelei"; from '43 to '47 was married to Navy Lt. Cylos Dunsmoore; their son, Charles, perished at 34 in a commercial airliner crash; movie producer Milton Bren, by whom she also has a son, Peter, was her husband from '48 until his death in '79; in '82, 19 years after quitting movies, she returned to play Sally Field's humorous mom in *Kiss Me Goodbye*—filmed at Fox, where she'd started in 1933.

MOVIE HIGHLIGHTS: *The Mad Game, Jimmy and Sally, Baby Take a Bow, Dante's Inferno, Navy Wife, Hold That Girl, To Mary—With Love, Career Woman, Big Town Girl, Second Honeymoon, One Mile from Heaven, The Amazing Dr. Clitterhouse, Stagecoach, Honky Tonk, Texas, Crossroads, Murder, My Sweet.*

Lupe Velez

(b. Guadaloupe Velez de Villalobos, July 18, 1908, San Luis de Potosi, Mexico; d. Dec. 14, 1944) Loud, lovable pepperpot from south of the border and the wrong side of the paprika patch; always insisted she was the daughter of an opera singer and an army colonel, but, said those privileged to know the truth, she was actually the illegitimate child of a prostitute; broke into show business dancing in raunchy burlesque houses in Mexico City, soon landing jobs in musical comedies; producer Hal Roach saw her dancing in Hollywood in the *Music Box Revue* and gave her a role in a Charlie Chase comedy; Douglas Fairbanks next made her his leading lady in *The Gaucho* ('27); played only dramatic roles for five years before switching to comedy, for which her broad accent was best suited; was better known for her stormy love affairs than her movies; Gary Cooper was her first famous flame and, as author Budd Schulberg, who was on the scene, has reported, it was local gossip that she "was so jealous of her prized possession that she would meet him at the door when he came home from the studio, unbutton his fly, and, spirited primitive that she was, sniff suspiciously for the scent of rival perfumes"; fireworks also marked her five-year (1933–38) marriage to Johnny Weissmuller; her dramatics extended even to the decor of the bedroom of her Beverly Hills mansion—everything in it was black, silver, or gold, except the massive polar-bearskin rug on the floor, a perfect dazzling white; born under what astrologers term "the tragic fixed star, Proscyn," which deals with poison, she predicted her own fate; after drawing up a chart for her, astrologer Blanca Holmes hesitated to reveal what she saw there; "If you won't tell me, I'll tell you," said the actress. "The stars say I will commit suicide—with poison"; two years later she did the deed, with sleeping pills.

MOVIE HIGHLIGHTS: *Wolf Song, Lady of the Pavements, Tiger Rose, Resurrection, East Is West, Cuban Love Song, Hot Pepper, Joe Palooka, Laughing Boy, Hollywood Party, Strictly Dynamite, The Girl from Mexico, The Mexican Spitfire, The Redhead from Manhattan, The Mexican Spitfire Out West, The Mexican Spitfire's Blessed Event.*

Virginia Weidler

(b. Virginia Weidler, March 21, 1927, Hollywood, Calif.; d. July 1, 1968) This child star—natural, freckled, pigtailed (and with a genius I.Q.)—often acted her elders right off the screen: Pauline Lord in *Mrs. Wiggs of the Cabbage Patch*, John Barrymore in *The Great Man Votes*, Katharine Hepburn in *The Philadelphia Story*; as typically "American" as any kid on the screen, she was the sixth child of an opera star and a noted architect who came to the U.S. from Berlin; began movie acting at two, in John Barrymore's *Moby Dick*; was already an experienced "actress"; at their San Fernando Valley home, the young Weidlers had their own little theater where they staged and acted in plays they wrote themselves; her sisters and brothers (one of whom, George, grew up to be Doris Day's second husband) also worked in movies but never achieved her prominence; was five when cast in Constance Bennett's *After Tonight*, the role calling for a child able to speak German, French, and English, which she did; made her stage debut at 6 in *Autumn Crocus*; a bit of a tomboy, fond of jeans and playing football on the family team, she was an unhappy eight-year-old when, in Gary Cooper's *Peter Ibbetson*, she was obliged to don fluffy blonde curls and a beribboned dress; far more to her liking was a role she did at 11 in *Out West with the Hardys*, which won her an MGM contract; playing a hard ridin', straight shootin' young terror at a dude ranch, she made teenaged star Mickey Rooney look like a dirty deuce in a wet deck; stole other scenes from him in *Young Tom Edison* and *Babes on Broadway*; left the screen at 16 after *The Youngest Profession*; starred last at 18, on Broadway, in *The Rich Full Life*; married and had two sons.

MOVIE HIGHLIGHTS: *Laddie, Freckles, Maid of Salem, Too Hot to Handle, Mother Carey's Chickens, The Women, Bad Little Angel, All This and Heaven Too, Barnacle Bill, Born to Sing, This Time for Keeps, Best Foot Forward.*

Johnny Weissmuller

(b. Peter John Weissmuller, June 2, 1904, Windbar, Pa.; d. Jan. 20, 1984) Several did the part before him, and many came later, but nobody wore Tarzan's loincloth quite as naturally as this brawny (6'3", 190 lb.) swim champ; set 67 world records, won 39 National championships and five Olympic gold medals (at Paris in '24, in Amsterdam in '28), and never lost a race; was a first-generation American, his father (later a brewmaster) having been a captain and an engineer in the Austrian army; family moved to Chicago when he was young; quit school in the 8th grade when his father died; learned to swim (to combat a sickly constitution as a youth) in the Chicago River; first screen appearance was in a Grantland Rice sports short in '29, demonstrating his swimming form; MGM starred him as Tarzan six times between '32 and '42; only non-Tarzan stint at Metro: a guest star appearance in a '34 musical mishmash, *Hollywood Party*; his most famous "Jane" was Maureen O'Sullivan (in all his MGM pix); had one other in his later series at RKO, blonde Brenda Joyce (*Tarzan and the Amazons* and three more); other leading ladies Frances Gifford (*Tarzan Triumphs*) and Nancy Kelly (*Tarzan's Desert Mystery*) did not play "Jane"; had more "mates" off screen; was divorced five times—from Camille Louier, musical-comedy actress Bobbe Arnst, star Lupe Velez, socialite Beryl Scott (three children: John Scott, Wendy Ann, and Heidi, who died in a car crash at 19 in '62), and golfer Allene Gates; from '63 to the end was married to Maria Brock, a Bavarian divorcee; left off as Tarzan at 44 (Lex Barker took over) and began a new career as Jungle Jim; said of his famous chest-thumping role; "It was like stealing. There was swimming and I didn't have to say much. How can a guy climb trees, say 'Me Tarzan, you Jane,' and make a million?"

MOVIE HIGHLIGHTS: *Tarzan the Ape Man, Tarzan Escapes, Tarzan Finds a Son, Swamp Fire, Captive Girl, Jungle Jim in the Forbidden Land, Killer Ape, Jungle Moon, Voodoo Tiger.*

Mae West

(b. Mae West, Aug. 17, 1892, Brooklyn, N.Y.; d. Nov. 22, 1980) Sex is what she sold on film, Paramount's immortal, well-upholstered blonde goddess, with her undulating stroll, hand on hip, silken nasal drawl, "Come up an' see me sometime" catch-phrase, and bedroomy manner of sweeping a handsome male from head to toe with her mile-long artificial lashes; blonde hair was phony too—always wore wigs; was the first to do movies that were purely and undeniably about sexual affairs, but always with humor, precluding, astonishingly any trace of vulgarity; in light of her legendary status, it is amazing that in 48 years in Hollywood, she starred in just 12 movies; *She Done Him Wrong*, her first starring film, based on her own play, remained her personal favorite, and its leading man was also the one she liked best—Cary Grant; the co-star she heartily disliked: W. C. Fields; the violet-eyed daughter of a featherweight fighter and a French-born mother, she studied dancing as a child and made her stage debut at 7 at Brooklyn's Royal Theater; played juvenile roles (in *Mrs. Wiggs of the Cabbage Patch, Little Nell*, etc.) on the road before going into vaudeville at 15; reviewing her in a 1911 cabaret show in New York, *A La Broadway*, *Variety's* critic noted: "A girl named Mae West, hitherto unknown, pleased by her grotesquerie and a snappy way of singing and dancing"; appeared on Broadway in her own play, *Sex*, which landed her in a New York City jail for 10 days ("A lot of my fans were there," said she. "And I was treated like a society figure—the warden took me driving every night"); played a secondary role (winning all the notices) in her debut movie, *Night*

After Night; film contains a brief scene that introduced a classic West line; to the awed hatcheck girl who gasps, "Goodness, what beautiful diamonds," she purrs, "Goodness had nothing to do with it, dearie"; *Goodness Had Nothing to Do with It* became the title of her autobiography; in another picture she said, "When I'm good, I'm very, very good, but when I'm bad, I'm better"; a self-creation, she knew whereof she spoke.

MOVIE HIGHLIGHTS: *Night After Night, She Done Him Wrong, I'm No Angel, Belle of the Nineties, Goin' to Town, Klondike Annie, Go West Young Man, Every Day's a Holiday, My Little Chickadee, The Heat's On* ('43), *Myra Breckinridge* ('70), *Sextette* ('78).

Michael Whalen

(b. Joseph Kenneth Shovlin, June 30, 1902, Wilkes-Barre, Pa.; d. April 14, 1974) Virile, handsome, and dark, and teamed repeatedly with Gloria Stuart, he was Fox's romantic King of the B's; a popular bachelor and an Irish charmer, squiring Alice Faye, Claire Trevor, and Cecilia Parker about town, he never married; came closest when engaged for a while to Ilona Massey; when new in Hollywood, he lived with his two sisters and mother (her father's name became his professional monicker), and in later years, with a man friend; came from a family of achievers; his ancestors, coming to America in the 1700s, were pioneers in the anthracite coal region of his native state, one grandfather was a hotel owner, the other, a wealthy fire-brick manufacturer, became mayor of Avoca, Pa.; however, his father, a successful contractor and city council member, sank his every cent in a Texas oil well, which came in dry; at 17, when his father died, he dropped out of Penn State and took a job as stock boy at Woolworth's to support the family, and worked his way up to manager; his mother's remarriage finally freed him, when 23, to try the theater; success as an actor in New York came slowly, though he did soon become illustrator James Montgomery Flagg's favorite male model; made his stage debut, playing an elderly man, in 1927 in *The Cradle Song*, and had some minor success as a singer on radio stations WGBS and WABC; after many small parts on stage, he packed up and moved to Hollywood; there, except for supporting roles in a few plays (*The Hairy Ape, Common Flesh*, etc.) at major playhouses, he worked for years in nonpaying little theater productions;

shortly before being signed by 20th Century-Fox, where he started in leads, he was working as a houseboy and gardener in Beverly Hills; made his movie debut, at 33, in *Professional Soldier*; finally became a Broadway star, too, in 1944's *Ten Little Indians*, a massive success.

MOVIE HIGHLIGHTS: *The Country Doctor, Poor Little Rich Girl, My Second Wife, Career Woman, Sing, Baby, Sing, The Man I Marry, Wee Willie Winkie, Walking Down Broadway, Speed to Burn, Time Out for Murder, The Mysterious Miss X, Ellery Queen–Master Detective, While New York Sleeps, Sign of the Wolf, Tahiti Honey.*

Warren William

(b. Warren William Krech, Dec. 2, 1894, Aitkin, Minn.; d. Sept. 24, 1948) When John Barrymore severed ties with Warner Bros. in '31, the studio sent out a frantic SOS to this suave Barrymore look-alike and sound-alike, who was starring on Broadway in *The Vinegar Tree*; 12 hours after making a flying trip to Hollywood, he was deep in the intricacies of a screen love scene with beautiful Dolores Costello—*Mrs.* John Barrymore; the movie, *Expensive Women*, was followed by many others in which, emoting with every top femme star, he was similarly occupied; while it marked his first in talkies, this son of a newspaper publisher had made his debut years earlier, in '22, as the leading man in a Pearl White serial, *Plunder*; abandoning an early interest in marine engineering, he studied for the stage at the American Academy; played a few minor roles with a Brooklyn stock company before enlisting in the infantry during WW I; made sergeant by the time the Armistice was signed and was in southern France when he volunteered to appear in a play the Y.M.C.A. sponsored to entertain the troops; buoyed by his triumph as the lead in this melodrama, *Under Cover*, he returned to New York and waged a successful campaign to win Broadway roles; made his stage debut in '20 in *Mrs. Jimmie Thompson*, a quick flop like many of his later plays; in nearly a dozen years on Broadway, he had only four hits, but one of them—*Twelve Miles Out* in '25—made him a star; before he went to war, actress Helen Nelson had promised to wait for him and did—until '23, when their most successful marriage began; an ace screen law-and-order man, he played Perry Mason often (*The Case of the Velvet Claws*, etc.), was The Lone Wolf more times than any other actor (eight features), and Philo Vance once (in *The Gracie Allen Murder Case*).

MOVIE HIGHLIGHTS: *The Match King, Beauty and the Boss, The Mouthpiece, Gold Diggers of 1933, Lady for a Day, Goodbye Again, The Case of the Howling Dog, Cleopatra, Imitation of Life, Dr. Monica, Don't Bet on Blondes, Satan Met a Lady, Times Square Playboy, The Firefly, Madame X, The Man in the Iron Mask, Lillian Russell, Arizona, The Lone Wolf Strikes, The Lone Wolf Keeps a Date.*

Jane Withers

(b. Jane Withers, April 12, 1926, Atlanta, Ga.) As a brat of 8, a heller on wheels (a tricycle), in *Bright Eyes*, she made Shirley Temple's life miserable—and herself very famous; being a nice kid in *Handle with Care*, two years earlier, didn't do a thing for her; with a readymade (and unexpected) juvenile star on its hands, 20th Century–Fox presented her as a lovable tomboy in a string of comedy features, and by '38 she was among the Box Office Top Ten; the only child of an employee of a rubber-manufacturing firm, she studied singing and dancing from age 2; at 4 was on the vaudeville stage in her home town, doing imitations of Garbo and other stars; next, billed "Dixie's Dainty Dewdrop," had her own radio show, "Aunt Sally's Kiddie Review," on Atlanta station WGST; her mother had given up her own theatrical ambitions when she married, but not without eliciting a promise from her husband that, if they had a daughter, she could be groomed for show business; fortunately, that daughter proved to be a natural; taken to Hollywood by her mom (dad soon followed), she did more radio programs and worked as an extra in movies; after *Bright Eyes*, she and Shirley Temple did not act together again; has said: "Someone close to Shirley became jealous of me and we were never allowed to work together. In fact, I had to shoot my pictures on the Fox Western lot, while she did hers at the main Beverly Hills studio. Shirley and I never had a feud—the adults surrounding us did"; is superstitious—and Friday is her lucky day; made her stage and radio debuts on a Friday, won her star-making role on one Friday and began playing it on another, and signed her Fox contract on Friday, Dec. 7, 1934; was wed first (1947–54) to Texas millionaire William Moss; children: Wendy, William III, and Randy; was then married, from '55 to '68, when he died in a plane crash, to lawyer Kenneth Errair, by whom she has a son, Kenneth, and a daughter, Kendall.

MOVIE HIGHLIGHTS: *Ginger, The Farmer Takes a Wife, This Is the Life, Gentle Julia, Paddy O'Day, Pepper, The Holy Terror, 45 Fathers,*

172

*Wild and Woolly, Checkers, Always in Trouble, Keep Smiling, Arizona
Wildcat, Rascals, Chicken Wagon Family, High School, Shooting High, A
Very Young Lady, Small Town Deb.*

Anna May Wong

(b. Wong Lui Tsong, Jan. 3, 1907, Los Angeles, Calif.; d. Feb. 3, 1961)
Born in Chinatown, the daughter of a laundry man, she was given a name
that translates "Frosted Yellow Willow"; became a photographer's model
while attending Hollywood High; was 13 when an actor cousin, James
Wong, who worked in Westerns, showed a photo of her to director Marshall Neilan, resulting in a bit in *Dinty*; fame came three years later when
cast as the sinuous Mongol slave girl in Douglas Fairbanks' *Thief of Bagdad*; with her trademarked bangs, and often in silken sheaths, she became
and remained the only Oriental woman to make it to major movie stardom;
in public, always dressed to suit her image, wearing Oriental brocades or
delicate fabrics, but privately, she preferred sweaters and slacks; did a few
offbeat roles, such as that of Tiger Lily in Betty Bronson's *Peter Pan*;
otherwise, alternated between heroines and wicked women; the American
censorship code of the time allowed her to have romantic scenes with
Occidental males but never to kiss one; had her first Caucasian screen kiss
in '35 when she co-starred with John Loder in *Java Head*—made in England; a globe-trotting star, she also did films in France and Germany,
went to Vienna in the '30s, where she wrote and acted in a stage musical,
Tschun-Tshi, starred on stage in London (once with Laurence Olivier, in
Circle of Chalk), and, in '36, made her first visit to China, writing for the
New York Herald Tribune a series of articles of her impressions; starred on
Broadway in *On the Spot*; finest performances may have been in *Piccadilly*,
with Charles Laughton, and *Shanghai Express*, as the courageous courte-
san; never married; final role was a small one in *Savage Innocents*, starring
Anthony Quinn who, in '37, played a minor one in *Daughter of Shanghai*,
in which she was the headliner.

MOVIE HIGHLIGHTS: *The Flame of Love, Daughter of the Dragon,
Tiger Bay, A Study in Scarlet, Chu Chin Chow, Limehouse Blues,
Dangerous to Know, Island of Lost Men, When Were You Born?, Ellery
Queen's Penthouse Mystery, King of Chinatown, Lady from Chunking,
Bombs Over Burma.*

Fay Wray

(b. Fay Wray, Sept. 10, 1907, Wrayland, Alberta, Canada) *King Kong*—if she had done nothing more than look lovely and scream lustily while in the ape's hairy paws atop the Empire State Building, she would still have had a permanent place in screen history; "When I go to New York," she says, "I look at the Empire State Building and feel as though it belongs to me—or is it vice-versa?"; her blonde hair in *King Kong* was a wig covering naturally brown tresses; landed her famous role only after the producers tried and failed to borrow Jean Harlow from MGM; saw her first movie at 13, when her family moved from their Canadian farm to Salt Lake City; soon moved again, to California, where she attended Hollywood High, acted on stage in *The Pilgrimage Play* and began working as a screen extra during school vacations; won her first lead in *Gasoline Love*, a slapstick comedy, at 16; played heroines in silent Westerns at Universal for three years before, in 1926, Erich von Stroheim gave her a star-making role in *The Wedding March*; her work in this brought a contract at Paramount, where she remained for five years; one of the most popular actresses of the '30s, she eventually starred in more than 100 films, being cast romantically with top-rank males like Ronald Colman, Joel McCrea, George Raft, and Gary Cooper; the year she did *King Kong* ('33), she also played leads in 11 more; after 1942's *Not a Ladies Man*, was off the screen for 11 years before returning to play (mother roles, usually) in a dozen movies of the '50s; was married to playwright John Monk Saunders from '28 to '39, by whom she has a daughter, now a stage actress billed Susan Riskin; Oscar-winning screenwriter Robert Riskin was her husband for 13 years before his death in '55; two children: Robert Jr. and Vicki; in '72 married Dr. Sanford Rothenberg, a Los Angeles neurosurgeon.

MOVIE HIGHLIGHTS: *Thunderbolt, Four Feathers, Dirigible, The Conquering Horde, Mystery of the Wax Museum, Dr. X, Ann Carver's Profession, One Sunday Afternoon, Shanghai Madness, The Bowery, The Countess of Monte Cristo, Viva Villa!, The Affairs of Cellini, The Richest Girl in the World, Adam Had Four Sons.*

Loretta Young

(b. Gretchen Young, Jan. 6, 1912, Salt Lake City, Utah) Receiving her Academy Award for *The Farmer's Daughter*, she addressed the Oscar and asked, "What took you so long?"; was then 36 and had been playing leading roles for 21 years; screen debut, however, came much earlier—at age 4 in a small part in a silent starring Fanny Ward; her career as a young adult happened by accident; director Mervyn LeRoy phoned to offer a role in *Naughty But Nice* to her sister, Polly Ann Young, who was out of town, and Loretta, volunteering her own services, won the part; became a star the following year when cast opposite Lon Chaney in *Laugh, Clown, Laugh*; her father deserted the family when she was an infant and her destitute mother took her daughters—Polly Ann, Betty Jane (who became Sally Blane), and Loretta —to Hollywood, where the children went to work as movie extras; remarried, the mother had another daughter, Georgiana; all four sisters later worked together on screen, just once, playing sisters in *The Story of Alexander Graham Bell*; made an easy transition from silents to talkies, and for three successive years, the American Institute of Voice Teachers honored her for "possessing the finest feminine voice on the screen"; lists her favorite roles as being the title character in *Ramona* ('36) and the dauntless nun in *Come to the Stable* ('49), for which she was Oscar-nominated; had a brief marriage to actor Grant Withers, which was annulled in '32; in '37, as a single parent, adopted a daughter, Judy; married TV exec Tom Lewis in '40, was separated from him in '56, and divorced him in '69; two sons: Christopher and Peter; published her auto-biography, *The Things I Had to Learn*, in '61, and its co-author, close friend Helen Ferguson, once described her this way: "What she says she will do, she does. What she says, she means. What she learns, she remembers. And, let's face it, what she wants, she gets."

MOVIE HIGHLIGHTS: *The Man from Blankley's, The Hatchet Man, A Man's Castle, The House of Rothschild, The White Parade, Clive of India, Caravan, The Crusades, Call of the Wild, Cafe Metropole, Wife, Doctor and Nurse, Four Men and a Prayer, Suez, Kentucky, The Doctor Takes a Wife, China, Along Came Jones, The Bishop's Wife.*

Robert Young

(b. Robert Young, Feb. 22, 1907, Chicago, Ill.) Though this smooth actor was an MGM star for 13 years (1931–44, from *The Sin of Madelon Claudet* to *The Canterville Ghost*), studio chief Louis B. Mayer decreed he had "no sex appeal," so he most often lost the girl—to Robert Taylor, William Powell, etc.; was a headliner in 87 movies, sometimes making eight a year;

The Enchanted Cottage ('45) remains his favorite; says, "The role symbolized my own life, though I wasn't a veteran who returned from war tragically disfigured. It demonstrated my theory that we are all, somehow, handicapped. Shyness and a fear of people were my invisible scars. These were finally overcome, just as in the movie, because of the love of a woman who saw the 'perfect man' through all the imperfections"; has had one wife, high school sweetheart Betty Henderson, whom he married over studio protests ("Movie idols are bachelors") in '33; call their Rancho Santa Fe, Calif., house "The Enchanted Cottage"; they have four daughters (Carol, Barbara, Elizabeth, Kathleen), five grandchildren; growing up in Los Angeles, he held many jobs—drug clerk, newspaper copy boy, bank teller—before hitting on acting; trained for four years, in 40 plays, at the Pasadena Playhouse; appeared first in a Charlie Chan movie, *The Black Camel*; roster of his leading ladies reads like a Hollywood "Who's Who": Garbo, Crawford, Hepburn, Garson, Shearer, Harlow, etc.; leaving the screen in '54, he enjoyed a great TV career: six seasons starring in "Father Knows Best" (after four years on radio) and another seven in "Marcus Welby, M.D."; won Emmys for both; a self-declared recovered alcoholic, he says, "My wife saved my mind, body, and soul by making me realize I had so much to live for."

MOVIE HIGHLIGHTS: *Lullaby, Carolina, House of Rothschild, Navy Blue and Gold, I Met Him in Paris, Three Comrades, The Mortal Storm, Northwest Passage, H.M. Pulham, Esq., Joe Smith, American, Journey for Margaret, Claudia, The Searching Wind, Crossfire, Sitting Pretty, Goodbye My Fancy.*

INDEX

178

Willis, Si, 44
Winchell, Walter, 83
Wynn, Ed, 5

Young, Collier, 70

Young, Robert, 125

Zanuck, Daryl F., 1, 13
Ziegfeld, Florenz, 26, 100, 155
Ziegfeld Follies, 21, 25, 67, 78, 148